THE HISTORY OF PHILOSOPHY

THE NINETEENTH CENTURY:
PERIOD OF SYSTEMS,
1800–1850

THE HISTORY OF PHILOSOPHY
VOLUME VI

THE NINETEENTH CENTURY: PERIOD OF SYSTEMS, 1800-1850

BY ÉMILE BRÉHIER

TRANSLATED BY WADE BASKIN

THE UNIVERSITY OF CHICAGO PRESS

CHICAGO AND LONDON

Originally published in 1932 as Histoire de la philosophie:
La Philosophie moderne. III: Le XIXe siècle. Période des systèmes (1800–1850)
© *1932, Presses Universitaires de France*

*The present bibliography has been revised and enlarged to
include recent publications. These have been supplied by
the translator and Wesley Piersol.*

*Library of Congress Catalog Card Number: 63–20912
The University of Chicago Press, Chicago 60637
The University of Chicago Press, Ltd., London W.C.1
Translation © 1968 by The University of Chicago
All rights reserved. Published 1968
Printed in the United States of America*

CONTENTS

GENERAL CHARACTERISTICS

THE BOUNDS of three great periods in the history of
philosophy since 1800 are easily discernible. Between 1800 and 1850
there was an extraordinary flowering of vast, constructive doctrines,
which claimed to reveal the secret of nature and of history and to
acquaint man with the law of his destiny, individual and social. The
Catholic doctrines that De Maistre and De Bonald constructed as a
reaction against the eighteenth century, the psychology of Maine de
Biran, which culminated in religious insights, the great German
post-Kantian systems of metaphysics—the systems of Fichte, Schelling, and Hegel, of which Victor Cousin's spiritualism was an imitation—and the social doctrines of the Saint-Simonians, of Comte,
and of Fourier all shared a prophetic or revelatory quality. Between
1850 and 1890, however, a revival of the critical and analytical spirit
again focused attention on the thought of Kant and Condillac. Pure
philology triumphed over the philosophy of history; criticism replaced metaphysics; physics and chemistry ousted the philosophy of
nature; practical, economic, and social policy replaced propheticism.
This was the period of Renan and Max Müller, of Taine, Renouvier,
Cournot, and the neo-Kantians, of Marxist socialism; and the mechanical character of the favorite doctrines of the period, Darwinism
and Spencerian evolutionism, remind us of ideas current in the
eighteenth century. Finally, about 1890, a new period began. Generally speaking, the reality of spiritual values seemed to contradict
the philosophical results which supposedly could be drawn from the

sciences. Analysis of the conditions of scientific knowledge (criticism of the sciences) revealed the limited significance of results and prompted the search for new means of gaining access to those spiritual realities which, during the preceding period, had been considered illusory or inaccessible. To be sure, the search was undertaken, not with the confidence manifested in the vast doctrines of the Romantic generations but with an uneasiness which gave birth to the most diverse and even conflicting trends.

What had changed at the beginning of the nineteenth century was the perspective from which man saw himself. In his *Philosophy of History* Hegel was utterly opposed to the distinction Rousseau made between the state of nature and the social state, as if one could apprehend man's essence, immediate and absolute, and add morals afterward. A human being is seen only against the background of history, and one does not reach humanity by an abstraction that strips off all its attainments but by the very law of this acquisition, which gradually makes humanity what it is. At the beginning of the century this feature of Hegelianism was universal; all knowledge was supposed to be mediate and to reflect the development that had produced it. Such a perspective again raised all sorts of philosophical problems. For Maine de Biran the study of the self was not the authentication of a preexisting reality but the reproduction of the act through which the self was realized. In a more general way, neither nature nor man was realized. For the most part nature and man were studied only in the context of their evolution; both were assumed to be real and substantial only as a result of the states through which they had passed.

It seems that there was, on the whole, a decrease in the popularity and prestige of analysis that had distinguished the eighteenth century. Even before the end of the century, Rousseau and many of the illuminists seemed to tire of analytical procedures and turned to means of investigation that go beyond analysis—to faith, instinct, conscience, sentiment, intellectual intuition, intuition of historical development. To understand the real unity of this vast movement, whose representatives were frequently unaware of one another, one must pay particular attention to the connection between the revival of *religious philosophy* and the *metaphysical significance attributed to history*. Christianity contains an essentially historical view of the universe in the sense that it focuses on certain points in the course of time which radically alter the direction of human destiny—creation, fall, redemption, resurrection. Apocalypses or revelations concerning the last days, constructed around these doctrines during the early stages of Christianity, gave rise during the Middle Ages and the Reformation to many socially oriented heresies concerning the kingdom of the Spirit—profound and intimate history, known only by revelation or faith, and beyond human authentication. Such a historical view of human nature lends itself quite naturally to two interpretations. On one hand, it suggests that the individual and social destiny of man has its mysterious reason in a historical development that transcends his intelligence. This point of view was held by De Maistre and the traditionalists who turned from the *Essay on Morals* to the *Discourse on Universal History*. On the other hand, it calls attention to the profound transformations man has undergone and to the future that awaits him. This was the framework that supported a view of history and of prophecies as absolute laws, reminiscent, with wholly new messianic overtones, of eighteenth-century rationalistic theories of progress, but differing from these by positing, like the Apocalypse, a final state of repose for humanity. This second interpretation of the Christian doctrine was espoused by thinkers with widely varying views, ranging from those who claimed to be most faithful to it, like Ballanche, Schelling, or Hegel, to those who, like Saint-Simon, Fourier, or Auguste Comte, knowingly deviated from it while retaining its general inspiration and the notion of a positive evolution.

Thus, during this period, the sense of history and development, which transformed all philosophical problems, was linked to faith in a mysterious historical force, a force transcending human reflection: De Maistre's laws of reparation, Hegel's Spirit manifesting itself, or Comte's Humanity. Historians such as Michelet and E. Quinet took upon themselves the task of identifying these mysterious, incoercible forces; and the idea of nationality and race as guiding forces behind events—forces that each person rediscovers in himself as constituting his own essence—emerged mainly in this period. History became a faith rather than a science, a source of energy rather than a curiosity. Men like Hegel and Comte lost no time in setting aside as alien to history all events which did not fit into the line of development as they conceived it—for example, prehistory or the empires of the Far East.

Corresponding to doctrines recognizing the existence of historical forces such as "national spirit," nation, race, or humanity was a philosophy of nature which identified nature and natural forces with a stable, permanent reality. Here again unity was contrasted with dispersion, dynamism with mechanism and atomism; but this was a particular kind of dynamism, quite different from that of Leibniz or Newton, who held that forces were calculable; here the term refers to a vast reservoir from which living beings take what they need to maintain their eternal youth—a universal soul or will to live, or in any case a biological entity which makes dynamism a true vitalism, analogous to that of the Renaissance.

Lack of confidence in the reflective combinations of human intelligence, confidence in mysterious realities which transcend it—such were the dominant traits of the period. This confidence was tinged with doubt and genuine sadness inspired by the contrast between human impotence and the heights to be attained. Alongside enthusiasts and messiahs we find the brokenhearted, the "children of the century," the despondent, like Sénancour, Musset, and Vigny, whose thoughts kept crossing into the domain of philosophy and served as a constant reminder of the difficulty of its task. Sénancour found the cause of his perpetual boredom in "the contrast between what is felt, between the barrenness of what usually is present and the fulness of what is envisioned."[1] His difficulty stemmed from his weak will, which was incapable of firm adhesion. "Has belief ever

---

[1] *Rêveries* (3d edition), p. 110.

depended on will?" This was the question he raised as an objection to Pascal's wager, and through nonchalance he allowed himself to be seduced by opposing systems. "There is no contradiction on this point," he wrote in reply to a criticism. "I offer them only as hypotheses; besides, I do not accept both of them, I accept neither of them positively, and I do not pretend to know what man does not know." He reached a kind of stoicism bordering on despair, which, except for its one, was close to the stoicism of Alfred de Vigny.

If the unreasonable goals of the philosophical speculation of the period had as their counterpart despair and renunciation, they also made possible the development of illuminism, charlatanism, and everything associated with false enthusiasm. The period brought forth a host of sellers of social panaceas, unrecognized geniuses, converts who loudly proclaimed their confessions of faith. These shadows should not be passed over in silence. After Obermann, the weak-willed creature, came Julien Sorel, the ambitious hypocrite, the strong-willed plebian whose slightest physical movements were calculated to enable him to play to perfection his role as a believer.

Everything here fitted into a pattern: the messianic pride of inventors of systems, the fervor of traditionalists, the despair of men incapable of believing, the publicity given to new faiths, the desire always to be above or below intelligence in the region of soul and intuition. All these violent, contrasting sentiments, often of dubious sincerity, collectively form what may be called Romanticism, a vast movement, which should not be mistaken for a literary theory. Romanticism was reflected in every trend of thought and sentiment and is indispensable to an explanation of the philosophical movement of the period, with its dark, concentrated ardor, its awareness of its basic social importance, and its heavy systems. The upsurge of Romanticism was not a morbid phenomenon, but a particularly clear example of the law of oscillation in the evolution of thought. In his discussion of the history of English literature M. Cazamian describes the law as follows: when reflection and critical analysis have been the dominant faculties of one era, the next is marked by a predilection for sentiment and immediate intuition, a desire for action and dream, an aspiration toward universal synthesis. Sentiment, dream, action are the springs at which Goethe shows Faust rejuvenating his soul after it has been withered by knowledge; magic, which unleashes the supreme forces of nature—the Mothers —and is able to effect every possible transmutation, takes the place, in the poet's imagination, of dead and superficial knowledge; and in his next two dramas we find every tendency of the period, stylized and stripped of its mediocrity.

New tendencies are accompanied by new literary forms. The fluency of Diderot, the denuded style of Voltaire, the search for conciseness and clearness manifested in many works intended for a wide public—all seemed to mark superficiality of mind. Good writers like Chateaubriand or Goethe were exceptional among philosophers; during this period philosophy lost the informal tone and the disdain for studied technique which it had been acquiring since the sixteenth century, mainly under French influence. Constraint, effort, stiffness, conventionality replaced ease and naturalness. Consider, for example, the perpetual uneasiness of Maine de Biran, whose thought always seemed to him to be on the verge of escape, Victor Cousin's rhetoric molded by the revolutionary declamations taught at the imperial university, and above all else the prophetic and apocalyptic tone used so frequently, from Novalis to August Comte, by all authors of social panaceas, of moral reforms or of philosophies of history. Voltaire, Diderot, and Rousseau created through their works an atmosphere for events which they in no way foresaw, and philosophers of the period confidently foretold events which never happened, and with their massive doctrines, generally exerted only an immediate influence, weak or of little import. The idea of a historical *fatum,* an immanent law which makes sport of efforts to resist it, had replaced faith in the rational, reflective initiative of human wills. De Bonald, De Maistre, Auguste Comte, Saint-Simon, Fourier—each thought that he had discovered it and had only to announce his discovery. In contrast to the philosophers of the eighteenth century, these men were often theorists rather than men of action, scholarly thinkers rather than publicists or pamphleteers.

THE TRADITIONALIST
MOVEMENT

1 *General Traits*

The revolutionary experience, which had fascinated Kant during his old age because it provided an example of a great nation choosing its own constitution, appeared at the beginning of the twentieth century to be a purely destructive act, critical and incapable of creating anything. To Kant the essence of the French Revolution was the Constituent Assembly, in which the people freely fashioned their own laws. To Auguste Comte it was not the Constituent Assembly with its vain attempt to adapt the English constitution even though it failed to meet the needs of France; it was the National Convention, not as Robespierre saw it, with his efforts to restore absurd religious practices, but Danton's—a dictatorship which, fully aware of its provisional role, destroyed every vestige of the political past. This idea of the purely negative character of the revolution, following all the negations of eighteenth-century philosophy, was the common postulate of almost every philosophy until 1848. The self-appointed mission of philosophers was to discover a positive, constructive principle, which could be used to remake a stable society; moreover, and by virtue of the very conditions of the problem, this principle had to be a reality independent of human arbitrariness and reflective wills; consequently their mission was not to create and produce this principle but to discover it and announce it.

They held that all the errors ascribed to eighteenth-century speculation and to the French Revolution had sprung from the same
source—the false belief that principles, whether intellectual or political, are of human institution and can be constructed from elementary facts such as sensations or needs. In their view, these
principles resisted analysis and transcended the puny strength of
human reason.

II *Joseph de Maistre*

The most zealous enemy of the French Revolution was Joseph
de Maistre (1753–1821), who was ambassador from Savoy at St.
Petersburg from 1803 to 1817. Most of his writings were published
after his death. His views took shape in the circle of the illuminists
of Lyon, of whom we have spoken elsewhere, and whose sympathies
for Catholicism are reflected in the theocracy of De Maistre's treatise
On the Pope (1817). His early illuministic fervor never abandoned
him completely, and whereas the two other French representatives
of Christian thought, Chateaubriand and De Bonald, were hostile
to Martinism, De Maistre's doctrine has been defined as a transpor-
tation of occult beliefs into Christian beliefs.[1] "Oh, how dearly the
natural sciences have cost man!" he exclaims in *Evenings in St.
Petersburg* (1821).[2] De Maistre had to pay for them by the denial
of the supernatural and with it the denial of any religious life,
which is nothing other than man's communication with the sphere
above humanity.

Those responsible for the eighteenth-century current of thought
which had done so much harm were Bacon and Locke, and De
Maistre lays the blame squarely on these men, even more than on
Voltaire and Diderot. Like De Bonald, he defends Cartesian innatism against their empiricism, and the way he interprets and re-
introduces the doctrine merits examination.

It may seem paradoxical, but this fiery adversary of the *Phi-*

---

[1] Cf. Viatte, *Les sources occultes du romantisme*, 1928, II, pp. 92, 133, 138.

[2] *Soirées de Saint-Pétersbourg*, in *Œuvres posthumes*, 6th edition, I, 310.

losophes seems to have borrowed his conception of science and the physical universe from Voltaire. This conception has two essential traits: the fixity of species and the inexplicable character of ultimate phenomena, such as elasticity and gravitation. De Maistre adopts them and skillfully uses them for his purposes. Each species retains the place or domain it occupies in the universe: "Each active being exerts its influence within the circle marked off for it and can never emerge from this circle (*Evenings*, I, 40 ff.).

But the fixity of species and the notion of separate domains have many other consequences, related to the consequences of the incomprehensibility of causes. Animals have their own domain and understand nothing about man's domain; instinct is at most the "asymptote of reason." Cannot our reason, in its circle, be the asymptote of a higher mind, which might be to us as we are to animals? Thus one order would be included in another, and the lower one could not penetrate the mystery of the higher one. But the higher one could exert an influence on the lower one, so that phenomena associated with the lower one but inexplicable in terms of its laws might be the result of this influence. Here De Maistre is thinking not only of miracles but of ultimate phenomena whose causes escape us completely—gravitation and elasticity; more exactly, and according to a very old apologetical procedure used by Philo of Alexandria, he likens these forces to miraculous operations, reflecting in one sense the spirit of Malebranchean occasionalism. "There are no causes in matter, and only religious men can and will admit it" (*Evenings*, II, 228). But this is Malebranchism, minus the austere idea of order, which governs God himself. De Maistre's doctrine provides a glimpse of a mysterious operation, wholly arbitrary and impenetrable to human reason, rather than a divine activity based on reason. His whole outlook is colored by this consequence: prayer can be just as effective against lightning as a lightning rod. Thanks to the combination of second causes with a higher operation, the field of the possible is not limited by consideration of natural causes, and this opens the door to all sorts of fantasies: prophetic dreams, mysterious powers of numbers. Illuminism encounters only one obstacle in De Maistre's thinking, and this springs not from logic but from fear that the individual character of inspirations will lead to the discovery of the principle of a sacerdotal hierarchy. Illuminism, useful in Protestant countries, can be dangerous in Catholic countries.

Thus agnosticism, derived from Newton and patently ambiguous, made possible De Maistre's violent reaction against the *Philosophes*. In stressing the rational character of divine operations, Leibniz and Malebranche risked coming within the range of deism and naturalism, which substitute rational laws for the person of God, and it is this whole movement that De Maistre opposes. God's justice has nothing in common with ours, and his providence has nothing in common with human prudence. Man's justice is based on the responsibility of the guilty, whereas God's justice has as its principle the reversibility of the mistakes of the guilty on the innocent. An act typical of divine justice is Christ's sacrifice, in which we see one who is innocent pay for the guilt of mankind. This blood ransom is the mysterious principle of sacrificial rites, common to many religions, but it also explains incessant wars and reveals the real secret of the French Revolution, in which so many innocent victims perished for mistakes not their own. The executioner and the soldier are ministers of the divinity. All the facts that a rational theodicy had so much difficulty in interpreting are the direct expression of a justice which seems to us to be irrational.

The political philosophy of the eighteenth century is wholly a product of human prudence, which sought, through the social contract, to discover a rational construction of society. Experience shows, however, that the most successful constitutions are those in which choice and deliberation count least—those which, from the human point of view, favor arbitrariness and chance (for example, the hereditary monarchy)—whereas democracy, a product of human reason, meets only with failure.[3] The *Philosophes* failed to take into account man's perversion: "Men, of sound intelligence and perverse will, must be governed. . . . Since mankind is united and governed

[3] *Essai sur le principe générateur des constitutions*, Lyon, 1822.

by necessity, its will has no part in the establishment of a government." [4]

III *Louis de Bonald*

Louis de Bonald (1754–1840), a peer after the restoration of the Bourbons, tried to systematize traditionalism. He formed a coherent notion of the revolutionary spirit before attacking it; he showed the inner logic of this heresy before condemning it. He tried to reveal the link between the principle of popular sovereignty and the favorite theses of eighteenth-century philosophy: atheism, eternity of matter, empiricism, theory of language as an arbitrary convention, negation of general ideas. According to him these theses formed a perfectly interconnected doctrinal bundle, which would fall apart if one of its affirmations were withdrawn.

This kind of revolutionary coalition, an idea that strongly influenced nineteenth-century thought, seems to have been De Bonald's invention. The doctrine of popular sovereignty implies atheism, he tells us, since atheism puts supreme power over men in the hands of the very men it is supposed to contain and "tries to make the dike spring from the torrent." Furthermore, both the doctrine of popular sovereignty and that of the eternity of matter arise from the same source: the predominance of imagination over reason, the incapacity of men who see in the universe only images of seas, volcanoes, stars, fire, and in society only images of assemblies and orators, "weak men who can think only in images, who would no longer be able to think if these inner representations were missing." The same men insist that language is only a sign of thought and that the value of this arbitrarily invented sign depends on a convention, for to say that man is the inventor of language is to say that "he has constructed everything—his thought, his law, society—and can destroy everything."

In De Bonald's view, this body of philosophy is tied to the

---

[4] *Du Pape,* (Lyon, 1829), II, i.

Protestant heresy. To say with Luther that "rational men have no need of visible authority to govern their religious belief" amounts to saying with Jurieu that "men of authority have no need of reason to validate their political acts." And underlying what should rightly be termed the revolutionary heresy is the moral corruption that explains it. The idea of popular sovereignty must have arisen "in a century of profiteering, among men driven by cupidity to mercantile speculations. By a play on words, a political society, which is necessary, was compared to a commercial society, which is merely a contingent, voluntary association."

Such is the structure of the heresy: at the base, concupiscence, and at the top, pride, which asserts that nature and man are independent of God. This heresy has demonstrated its strength for it explains the French Revolution and it can be judged by its fruits. "The social cycle was complete, for the experiment with popular sovereignty resulted in a return to authority and religion.[5] From their ordeal, according to his *Analytical Essay on Natural Laws and the Social Order,* men learned that "left to themselves, they would never have consented to put themselves in a state which requires the sacrifice of their personal passions."[6] The social contract, as it was interpreted by Rousseau, is a moral impossibility, and destructive passions can be reformed only by a social power which is outside and superior to individuals. From their ordeal men also learned obedience (*Primitive Legislation,* II, 110). The same school that calls for active resistance to the social power in the name of the people exacts absolute obedience to what it considers to be the sovereign power. The dictatorship of Robespierre is based on the principle of the Protestant Jurieu: the people constitute the sole authority, which does not need to be right to validate its political acts. Bossuet had already answered that God himself needs to have right on his side! No democracy has ever been stable. The elective system ruined Poland, and as for Switzer-

[5] *Législation primitive* (1802); edition of 1829, II, 128.
[6] *Essai analytique sur les lois naturelles de l'ordre social,* 4th edition, 1840, p. 62.

land and Holland, their popular governments "were preserved by the power of France and Germany, and the fall of the latter brought about their own dissolution" (*Analytical Essay,* p. 213).

The social philosophy of De Bonald (on which his whole philosophy depends) is a critical reflection on the experiment with popular sovereignty and in a sense continues the philosophy of the preceding century. Rousseau, having determined a priori the characteristics of sovereignty (indivisibility, unity, fixity) thought he had demonstrated that they were reunited in the people considered as a body. De Bonald recognizes all of these characteristics, and although he does this in order to demonstrate that they cannot reside in the people, he shares with Rousseau the postulate of the necessity of a sovereign. What has been called De Bonald's social realism is simply the belief that society must be governed by a principle that exists outside individuals and survives them. Like Rousseau, he tries to determine where sovereignty resides. For the people, he substitutes God: "The law is the will of God according to some, the will of men according to others (*Analytical Essay,* p. 115). Theocracy replaces democracy because God actually has the characteristics that the people seem to have: a constant, rational, stable will.

Broadly speaking, De Bonald's philosophy consists in realizing as a transcendent power each of the immanent powers generally recognized during the previous century. "Modern philosophy," he writes, "fails to make a distinction between spirit and organs in man, sovereign and subjects in society, God and nature in the universe, and it destroys any general and particular order by eliminating any real power of man over himself, of chiefs of state over people, of God himself over the universe" (*Primitive Legislation,* II, 35). That intelligence is reduced to the conventional signs of language, that sovereignty resides in the people, that ultimate reality can be ascribed to matter—those are the three tenets De Bonald attempts to refute by positing an intelligence superior to language, a sovereign above the people, a God who is the creator of nature. His doctrine puts intellectual ideas as far above thought and the sovereign as far above the people as Christianity puts God above the universe.

But as God created nature by the intermediary of his Word, the transcendence of ideas necessitates an intermediary to express them to the spirit; and in the same way, the transcendence of the sovereign who is God presupposes between him and the people an interpreter in the form of the political power which derives its authority from God, just as language can derive its power of expression only from a divine author. Thus a theory of intermediaries, of which Christianity is the highest form, presents itself as soon as transcendence is substituted for immanence, and this theory unites and provides a basis for the two key tenets of the doctrine—the theory of language and the theory of political power.

Language is the instrument through which God reveals eternal ideas and himself to the human mind; consequently language is of divine origin. To grasp the sense of this famous thesis, we must bear in mind that De Bonald's theory of intelligence goes back by way of Gerdil to Malebranche, his favorite philosopher, whom he often quotes: beings are united by necessary relations, mathematical relations, and relations of perfection, which constitute an immutable order grounded on the nature of God and which find their expression in laws. De Bonald holds fast, on the other hand, to the Condillacian thesis that the mind can know an idea only through its verbal form. He criticizes Condillac for making words only the *sign* of thought; a *sign* is something optional and arbitrary, something that can be the same for contrasting mental states and that consequently will awaken an idea in the mind of another only by means of a convention; a word is not the sign but the *expression* of an idea, and that is why it suggests the same thought to everyone and can express only one thought. Moreover, since Condillac acknowledged only abstract ideas—that is, collective ideas, such as the idea of whiteness, which expresses a collection of white objects viewed from an accidental angle—his sign creates the idea itself; elimination of this sign entails the disappearance of the collection, which existed only in the mind and by virtue of the sign. Condillac was not acquainted with general ideas—for example, the idea of order—which express a simple, unique essence and are to a collection "as the general of an army is to the army." These ideas require not a sign but an expression. Language is to intelligence as light is to objects which are in a dark place and remain unknown to us so long as they are not illuminated. "The word," he writes, recalling the first verses of the Book of Genesis, "brings light into the darkness and calls out, so to speak, to each idea, which answers, like the stars in Job, here I am" (*Primitive Legislation,* III, 163).

Our intelligence is wholly dependent on a social tradition which is expressed through language. From the Malebranchian Gerdil, De Bonald adopts the thesis that instruction merely illuminates ideas already possessed by the mind. Consequently these ideas remain unknown to a human being "until he has received from a society composed of human beings similar to himself the expression preserved in families by tradition or hereditary speech and in nations by imperishable writing" (*Primitive Legislation,* III, 198). This tradition goes back to a primitive revelation of God, for a human inventor could not have understood his own invention. It is therefore necessary for "man to understand his speech before speaking his thought." The human mind goes from words to ideas, from words which are transmitted to him by society to the ideas which he has in himself. Language, supplied by God and preserved by society, is the intermediary between man and ideas, the means through which man may gain access to the intellectual life.

De Bonald's system is a synthesis of Malebranche, who taught him the universality and necessity of ideas, and Condillac, who made language an absolute condition of the act of intelligence. It is a strange synthesis, for its elements are contradictory: the first presupposes direct, intuitive knowledge of ideas; the second excludes such knowledge. This synthesis is characteristic of his doctrine, which consists always in inserting between primary realities and the individual a Word with the indispensable function of guiding the mind to these realities.

As language is the intermediary between ideas and mind, legitimate power is the intermediary between the sovereign, who is God, and the people. The man-God of religion serves as a model of political power, mediator between God and men: in any society which fails to worship a man-God finds legal oppression, slavery, degradation of women, exposition of children (*Analytical Essay,* p. 102). In any country which has no legitimate power, particularly the democracies founded on Protestantism, one finds the dictatorship or absolutism of an authority which has full responsibility for the acts imposed by it and, as Jurieu expressed it, does not have to be right in order to validate its political acts (*Primitive Legislation,* p. 110).

Legitimate social authority is more human. Before the revolution the French monarchy was traditionally considered (notably by Voltaire) to be the people's defense against oppression and arbitrariness. De Bonald accepts this tradition in its entirety and maintains that stabilizing power within a family is the key to constant, invariable progress such as that associated with the monarchy of France, which he contrasts with "the extravagance and weakness of the democracy of Danton and Marat." Furthermore, the family is the "natural society" whose constitution, stable and unalterable, is the model for civil society. It includes essentially three persons: the first of these, the father, corresponds to the cause or power; the second, the mother, to the means or minister; the third, the child, to the effect or subject. This trinity (of which the archetype is to be found in God) is reproduced in the well organized state, in which political administration, originating in God, is hereditary in a family.

In keeping with the Augustinian tradition, which had been revived by the illuminists, De Bonald thus extended trinitarian symbolism to social life as well as to intellectual life. This symbolism accommodated the introduction of the key theories of Rousseau and Condillac—a stable power as the basis of society and language as the condition of thought—but only after they had been transformed by De Bonald's supernaturalism, which made language and power the organ of a transcendent reality.

IV *Benjamin Constant*

Benjamin Constant (1767–1830) was also an enemy of the eighteenth-century philosophers who took pleasure in leaving nothing exempt from ridicule, in heaping scorn on everything, and who "wrote only to encourage egotism and debasement in the generation that was to follow them" (*Diary,* p. 87). He also was scornful of the public responsible for their success: "The French nation is undoubtedly the least suited to receive new ideas; it prefers familiar things, to which it can conveniently give its stamp of approval without examination" (p. 98). That is the judgment of a man who knew, with Mme de Staël, the depths of the German soul. An irreligious attitude is less offensive to his intelligence than to his sensibility. "In irreligion," he writes, "I find something coarse and trite that disgusts me" (p. 103). His acute sensitivity caused him to abandon before its completion his study of the historical development of theism, "which he could not have done without making his book a patently irreligious work."

Constant nevertheless tried to reconcile, without any intention of constructing a system, his intellectual findings and the needs of his soul. The result was his work *On Roman Polytheism* (XVIII, iv), in which he set forth a law of the development of religion. This law, incorporated in its entirety in the doctrine of Auguste Comte, specifies three phases in the development of religion: fetishism, polytheism, theism. But the development of polytheism itself includes three phases: a crude polytheism unrelated to the moral sense; a refined, spiritual polytheism, exemplified in the Greek mysteries; and the polytheism of philosophers—for instance, Stoic polytheism, which contained the seeds of its own destruction and culminated in theism. Thus a doctrine is established, becomes more and more refined, and finally destroys itself. In theism, the next stage, we find a similar and more or less inexorable progression toward a destructive criticism. Theism is never crude, for the doctrine issues from a refinement of Greek thought; but there is a spiritual theism—the theism of the Christian priest. Then philosophy penetrates theism and performs a task similar to that performed by Greek philosophy with respect to polytheism. As a result, God is replaced by nature and natural laws. Priests are powerless to stop the inexorable progression, but the last word has not yet been said about religion. "I have my religion," Constant writes in his *Diary,* "but it consists entirely of sentiments and vague emotions which cannot be translated into a system." But the law he thinks he has discovered applies to systematic religious thought and not to sentiment. "Religion seems again to be destroyed, but even during the struggle religious sentiment is testing diverse forms," among them mystical theism, which clamors for a kind of *independence of sentiment.* That is pushing Rousseau's attitude to the extreme, for it eliminates the rational support that he provided for religious truths.

v *Félicité de Lamennais*

Félicité de Lamennais (1782–1854), born at Saint-Malo in 1782, came from a middle-class Breton family. It was mainly during his retirement to La Chênaie, from 1805 to 1808, in the company of his brother Jean, also a priest, that he formed the ideas he was to elaborate in his *Essay on Indifference in Matters of Religion* (1817–23). A royalist and an ultramontanist, he founded the journal *L'Avenir* in 1830 to support Catholic interests; but he widened the idea of traditionalism to the point of making Christian truths depend on the general beliefs of mankind instead of on a revelation that occurred at a precise moment in history and was reserved to the Church. Condemned by two encyclicals, one in 1832 and another in 1834, he broke with the Church (*Affairs of Rome,* 1836–37), became the democrat of *Words of a Believer* (1834), and served as a deputy in the constituent assembly of 1848. He died in 1854.

In his *Essay* Lamennais considers indifference in matters of religion to be moral and intellectual suicide. He finds that indifference is rooted in confidence in the infallibility of private judgment: the first stage is heresy, which predicates this confidence, then deism, which bases our belief in God on rational and personal arguments; their inadequacy leads to atheism, and the spectacle of the contradictions of reason finally leads to indifference. Faith in reason gave way because too much faith was placed in it initially.

To attack the evil at its source, we must determine whether private judgment is ever capable of providing us with some measure of certainty and, in a more general way, what are the conditions of certainty. Lamennais discusses this purely philosophical problem of the foundation of certainty in the eighth chapter of his *Essay*. His prime target is Cartesian evidence—evidence accessible to an individual isolated from the world and his fellow men. Is not madness an invincible and yet erroneous individual conviction? One of his correspondents raises as an objection the certainty of existence demonstrated by the *Cogito*. His answer makes the same criticism of the *Cogito* that he finds in many Catholic writers: "Descartes demonstrates nothing. To say 'I think' is to say 'I am a thinking creature.' He is positing as certain that which is to be proved" (*Works*, edited by Blaize, I, 403). Certainty must be sought in a common judgment: "I call this common judgment authority." Certainty springs from agreement between facts and common convictions; axioms themselves are recognized as true because they affect the judgment of all men in the same way. The *Essay* applies to knowledge in general the rule by which the Church determines beliefs: *Quod semper, quod ubique, quod ab omnibus traditum est.* "The Catholic faith and human reason rest on the same foundation and are subject to the same rule; thus to avoid the most absurd inconsistencies, one must either be a Catholic or renounce any form of reason" (*Ibid.,* 411).

The *Essay,* together with its *Defense* (1821), created much excitement. Lamennais' thesis, which carried De Bonald's ideas to the extreme, is distinct from the philosophy of common sense as it was interpreted from Buffier to Reid. As Lamennais himself notes (*Ibid.,* 417), Buffier grounds certainty resulting from consent or common sense upon an individual faith which he calls inner certainty. To Lamennais common sense is in itself a criterion and needs no support. The *Essay* was viewed with hostility by the Gallicans, who had his treatise on *Religion Considered in its Relations with the Political and Civil Order* condemned in 1826 because it attacked the famous edict of 1682 establishing Gallican liberties. But he also alarmed the orthodox by comparing popular certainty with the certainty of religion. *Progress of the Revolution and the War against the Church* (1829), in which he maintained that the Church alone is capable of instructing, and denied the civil power any independence, was opposed by many French prelates.

The Revolution of 1830 brought about a change not in Lamennais' philosophy but in his politics. The journal *L'Avenir*, which he founded and edited with Gerbert, Lacordaire, and Montalembert, instituted a kind of liberal Christianity advocating complete freedom of worship. According to Lamennais, freeing the Church from civil domination would bring out the purity of the Christian spirit, identical to the universal spirit. "Set free by extraordinary events, the Church will be regenerated." Its cause is no different from the cause of freedom. This confusion between political enfranchisement and the distinctive goals of religion brought about the condemnation of Rome. "The goal of the innovators," said the encyclical of 1832, "is to lay the foundations of a new human institution and to cause the Church, which is divine, to become completely human." The encyclical rejected freedom of the press and any proposition that might weaken the authority of princes. *Words of a Believer* (1834), which Lamennais published during this period, is written in the prophetic and apocalyptic style used by the poet Mickiewicz in *Polish Pilgrims*. Monarchs conspiring against the people, wickedness and cupidity of men of property perventing the fraternal sharing of the wealth of the earth, warning of a decisive battle good and evil—these are the themes of the impassioned, somber book which the encyclical of 1834 denounced as leading to anarchy.

Lamennais saw that he was being rejected by the people, abandoned by all of his ecclesiastical friends. But he did not become a democrat in the ordinary sense of the word. He expected little of laws and constitutions, everything of "a strong religious faith which will surely emerge, but of which we scarcely perceive the germs" (letter to Cabet, 1838, in *Works,* edited by Blaize, II, 155). That religion constitutes the substructure of society was a familiar idea during his time; it is found in Schelling, who identified the religious conscience with the social conscience, and in *Le Catholique,* a periodical published by Baron Eckstein, beginning in 1826. The people alone can be the instrument of their own liberation, but on condition that they change their false ideas. "The future of humanity depends entirely on its future conception of God," (letter to Mazzini, 1841, *Ibid.,* II, 170-72). The contradiction between power, which is universally despotic, and the "social conscience," which is universally democratic, will bring about a revolution. But Lamennais always remained hostile to communism, in which he saw only an abject materialism that would result in the condemnation of the people to forced labor.

It is in the *Outline of a Philosophy* (1841-46) that Lamennais put forth the conception of God that was to dominate social reform. This work had been planned long before his break with Rome. As early as 1827 he had begun an *Essay on a Catholic System of Philosophy,* which remained unpublished until 1906. Like the illuminists, he recognized adulterated and distorted elements of Christianity in every non-Christian religion. In the first *Essay* of 1827 he saw the essential dogma of Christianity in the theory of the Mediator through whom fallen men are brought back to divine life. In the *Outline* this role is played by the dogma of the divine Trinity. He resolutely opposes the idea of an original sin transmitted to man, of redemption through Christ, of grace, and, in general, any idea of a supernatural intervention in nature or man. All that remains, as a point of departure, is the idea of an infinite God in three persons, but philosophy is wholly dependent on this idea. "If the trinitarian doctrine is false," he wrote to Mazzini, "the entire work [*the Outline*] is equally false, for it is only a deduction from the doctrine."

All creatures whatsoever (here he seems to be generalizing an Augustinian idea) are images or impressions of the divine Trinity, and philosophy consists in revealing these images, after their model has been posited. This is the starting point for his plan. First, theology, which shows us a triune God: God as being, who, through his infinite power, posits himself as force (the Father); God becoming acquainted with himself (the Son); God loving and possessing himself (the Spirit). Then the theory of creation, which is the manifestation of divine nature and not, as Leibniz thought, the result of a choice between possible worlds. The universe manifests everything that infinite being can confer on finite being. Finally, the theory of species of beings, from inorganic bodies to man. From the simplest body, which presupposes a force or power to posit it, a form to shape its contours and define its properties, a life to bind force permanently to form, to man, who is an active, intelligent, loving being—each species offers us a clearer image of the Trinity.

Lamennais' philosophy is essentially that of a theologian, rather technical and at times artificial. The *Outline* cannot be said to justify his ambition to construct a popular philosophy, but it contains some valuable passages, particularly the brilliant pages of the third volume, in which he makes art an essential function of human life rather than a product of the odd fancies of an undisciplined mind.

Although Lacordaire and Montalembert were separated from Lamennais after the condemnation of 1832, the liberalism they introduced into Catholicism can be said to be the fruit of their collaboration on *L'Avenir*. Lacordaire criticized Lamennais in *Considerations on the Philosophical System of M. de Lamennais*, charging him with ignoring the authority of the Church and relying on his own judgment in an attempt to represent the common sense of mankind, and labeling his system "the most comprehensive statement of Protestantism that has yet appeared." Lacordaire returned to the traditional Thomist theory, accepting complete freedom in philosophy within the limits of its conformity with faith. But he sat on the left in the National Assembly and remained an implacable foe of the Empire. During the July Monarchy, Montalembert campaigned against Cousin in favor of liberty of instruction, which was finally voted in 1850 (Falloux' Law).

Bibliography

I

Boas, G. *French Philosophies of the Romantic Period.* Baltimore, 1925.
Lévy-Bruhl, L. *History of Modern Philosophy in France,* trans. G. Coblence. Chicago and London, 1924.
Soltan, Roger. *French Political Thought in the 19th Century.* New Haven, 1931.

II

Texts

de Maistre, J. *Œuvres complètes,* 14 vols. Lyon, 1884–87.
————. *Considérations sur la France.* Neuchâtel, Switzerland, 1796.
————. *Du Pape,* 2 vols. Lyons, 1819.
————. *Soirées de Saint-Pétersbourg,* 2 vols. Paris, 1821.
————. *The Works of Joseph de Maistre,* trans. Jack Lively. New York, 1965. Selections.

Studies

Boas, G. *French Philosophies of the Romantic Period.* Baltimore, 1925. See chap. 3.
Ferraz, M. *Histoire de la philosophie en France au XIXe siècle,* vol. 2, *Traditionalisme et ultramontanisme.* Paris, 1880.
Gianturco, E. *Joseph de Maistre and Giambattista Vico.* Washington, D.C., 1937.
Laski, H. J. *Authority in the Modern State.* New Haven, 1919.
Lecigne, C. *Joseph de Maistre.* Paris, 1914.

III

Texts

de Bonald, L. *Œuvres complètes,* ed. Abbé Migne. Paris, 1859.

Studies

Boas, G. *French Philosophies of the Romantic Period.* Baltimore, 1925. Chap. 3.
Laski, Harold. *Authority in the Modern State.* New Haven, 1919.
Moulinié, H. *De Bonald.* Paris, 1915.
Sainte-Beuve, C. *Causeries du lundi.* Paris, 1851–62, vol. 4, p. 426.

V

Texts

Lamennais, F. de. *De la Tradition de l'église sur l'institution des évêques,* 3 vols. Liège and Paris, 1814.
———. *Essai sur l'indifférence en matière de religion,* 4 vols. Paris, 1817–23.
———. *Défense de l'Essai sur l'indifférence.* Paris, 1821.
———. *Paroles d'un croyant.* Paris, 1834.
———. *Œuvres complètes,* 12 vols. Paris, 1836–37. Not complete.
———. *Œuvres choisies et philosophiques,* 10 vols. Paris, 1837–41.
———. *Esquisse d'une philosophie,* 4 vols. Paris, 1840–46.
———. *Amschaspands et Darvands.* Paris, 1843.

Studies

Duine, F. *Lamennais. Evreux,* 1922.
Gibson, W. *The Abbé de Lamennais and the Liberal Catholic Movement in France.* London and New York, 1896.
Mourre, M. *Lamennais, ou l'hérésie des temps modernes.* Paris, 1955.

IDEOLOGY

IDEOLOGY DESIGNATES the philosophical movement that originated with Condillac and persisted for a long time in France in spite of strong opposition. The golden age of ideology began in 1795 with the creation of the Institute of France, of which the second constituent was the Academy of Moral and Political Sciences. The Academy included the whole group of Condillacians: Volney, Garat, Sieyès, Guinguené, Cabanis, as well as Larominguière, Destutt de Tracy, and Degérando, who were associate members. Many were partisans of Bonaparte and were favorable to the coup d'état of 18 Brumaire (November 9–10, 1799); the consul appointed several of them to the Senate or to the Tribunate. Meetings in Auteuil in Mme Helvétius' salon, mentioned frequently by Maine de Biran, added to the strength of the movement.[1] Everything changed as soon as the ideologists (*idéologues*) sensed that Bonaparte was not the liberal continuator of the revolution they had though him to be. He found them hostile to his draft bill on crimes against the security of the state; he excluded the "sullen men of Auteuil" from the Tribunate, and in 1803 suppressed the Academy of Moral and Political Sciences. The decrees establishing the imperial university were drawn up by the enemies of the ideologists: Fontanes, a friend of Chateaubriand, Cardinal de Bausset, and De Bonald. The ideologists were united in their opposition. They met in sur-

---

[1] On all these points, see the excellent book by P. Alfaric, *Larominguière et son école*, 1929.

27

roundings where the spirit of the eighteenth century was still preserved against the encroaching *Genius of Christianity*—in the salons of Mme de Condorcet or Mme Lebreton. They supported Moreau's conspiracy in 1804 and were charged by Napoleon, in an attack delivered before the Council of State in 1912, with responsibility for Mallet's plot. "All the misfortunes suffered by our beloved France," he said, "must be attributed to ideology, to this dark metaphysics, which cunningly investigates first causes and seeks to establish the legislation of nations on these foundations instead of adapting laws to knowledge of the human heart and to the lessons of history." It was rational analysis against Romantic intuition, the spirit of Stendhal—who in a recently published fragment assigned roles to anti-Voltairians and enemies of philosophy[2]—against the spirit of Chateaubriand.

The ideologists were particularly hostile to the restoration of religion. "Theology is the philosophy of the world's childhood," wrote Destutt de Tracy in his *analyse* of Dupuis' *L'Origine de tous les cultes,* "and must now give way to that of the world's age of reason. It is the creation of imagination, like bad physics and bad metaphysics, which originated with it in times of ignorance and which serve as its basis, whereas the other philosophy is grounded on observation and experience."[3] Ideology provides the link between the philosophy of the eighteenth century and positivism.

1 Destutt de Tracy

During their period of triumph the ideologists felt the need, following the anguish of the revolution, of reorganizing the national system of education. They were concerned with the creation of central schools. It was for this reason that Antoine Louis Claude Destutt de Tracy (1754–1836) wrote his *Elements of Ideology,* composed of an *Ideology* (1801), a *General Grammar* (1803), a *Logic* (1805), and a *Treatise on the Will* (1815). In his *Commentary on*

[2] *Mercure de France,* August 1, 1931.
[3] Quoted by Chinard, *Jefferson et les idéologues,* 1925, p. 239.

the Spirit of Laws, which, though written in 1806, could not be published in France until 1819, after its publication in America (1811), he speaks out against a system of education which has the sole purpose of securing the political power of a sovereign by availing itself of religion, by paying writers and professors, by restricting the most advanced training to erudition and the exact sciences, and by excluding philosophical studies. Destutt de Tracy is not at all impressed by the presumed educative value of religion and mathematics. "It seems futile to me," he says, writing of Montesquieu, "to try to discover what the author of a religion should do to make it palatable and popular. I venture to believe that no new ones will be devised, at least in civilized nations."[4] As for mathematics, it is no more suitable than any other subject for sharpening the mind; it provides no more opportunities than any other discipline for learning to guard against error and must even be said to provide fewer, inasmuch as it involves reasoning with ideas that are more abstract and less subject to error. Destutt de Tracy considers the physical and natural sciences, especially chemistry, to be the key to the shaping of a sound mind.[5]

The primary evil of the system of education that he is criticizing is its lack of unity. The different branches of the sciences "seem alien to each other; each seems to have its own cause of certainty; . . . all have several unknown causes behind their first principles." The function of ideology in the broad sense is to rediscover unity. It is identical, in his view, to first philosophy, which applies to reality in general and not to a particular object; to true logic, which is not the practical art of reasoning but the speculative study of means of knowing; to Condillacian analysis, which is identical to the scientific part of logic. It is quite distinct, however, from metaphysics, "this art of the imagination intended to satisfy us, not to instruct us." If it seeks unity, this is the unity of the human point of view, the common sources of the three operations of judging, speaking, willing; the practical rules are already given by the arts of logic,

---

[4] Quoted by Picavet, *Les idéologues,* p. 382, note 3.
[5] *Principes logiques,* in *Œuvres* (edition of 1825), IV, 252.

grammar, and ethics, which leave out no human activity (*Works*, edition of 1825, III, 338–48).

Hence the five parts of the *Elements of Ideology*: ideology in the strict sense, which studies the human faculties and their division; grammar or the study of signs, which deals with discourse; logic, which is concerned with means of arriving at certainty in judgments; the treatise on the will and its effects, which contains ethics and political economy; finally, the part that studies the elements of all the physical and abstract sciences (*Works*, III, 350 ff.).

Ideology is an analysis of the human faculties, similar in content but quite dissimilar in inspiration to the analysis of Condillac, who must not be confused with the ideologists, no matter how often they claim his support. Destutt de Tracy was not a "genealogist" in search of the genesis of the faculties, and his writings exhibit none of the reductive analysis of the *Treatise on Sensations*. He charges that Condillac was guilty on two counts, the opposite to one another: making distinctions when unity was necessary, uniting when it was unnecessary. Condillac abused the division of the faculties, separating attention from will, though attention is only one of the effects of will, and judgment from comparison, though they amount to the same thing. Furthermore, imagination or reflection are only uses of our faculties and not, as Condillac thought, special faculties. Condillac was equally wrong in uniting, under the name of understanding, sensibility, memory, and judgment, which he opposes, collectively, to will (*Works*, I, 146).

Finally, and most important, Condillac saw a series of faculties engendering one another, where one should properly speak of primitive and independent faculties (*Works*, I, 97). For example, in his view, sensation comes before judgment, and judgment conditions desire, for he believed that the only point of departure was sensation pure and simple, which teaches us nothing except our own state and contains no relations; hence the necessity of constructing these relations which are called judgments. But he was badly mistaken: first, sensations can be simultaneous but still distinct, and simultaneity is an immediately perceived relation; next, the immediate feeling of agreeableness or disagreeableness contains the feeling of a relation between sensation and our sentient faculty, and it can provoke a desire prior to judgment; consequently sensation, judgment, and desire are equally primitive.

There is in these views a tendency to contrast immediate, concrete observation with the more or less arbitrary results of reductive analysis. It is significant that Destutt de Tracy himself compares this tendency with that of his friend Cabanis, who, demonstrating the immediate influence of physical phenomena on our judgments and inclinations, must have been somewhat dissatisfied with the purely ideal, external genesis offered by Condillacian analysis. Destutt de Tracy's attitude is particularly clear in the problems which posed the gravest difficulties for Condillac. For example, instinct, of which the Condillacian analysis had seemed absurd to Rousseau, is treated by Cabanis and Destutt de Tracy as being only an immediate result of organization, like the motions involved in the process of digestion. Moreover, Destutt de Tracy impressed Maine de Biran by solving the problem of external perception, extremely complicated with Condillac, in terms of the feeling of resistance that our voluntary movements encounter when matter is involved. "Our will," he writes, "causes our muscles to contract, . . . and we are warned by a certain feeling. . . . Soon numerous experiences teach us that the existence of this feeling is due to the resistance of what is called matter; we realize with certainty that our will is being resisted by something other than our sentient faculty of willing, and that, consequently, something else exists besides this sentient faculty which constitutes our self. . . . If our will had never acted directly and immediately on any body, we would never have suspected the existence of bodies" (*Works,* IV, 212–20).

Here we see clearly the other side of his criticism of Condillac and the deep-seated reason for it: the investigation of primary facts which defy analysis and which have somewhat the same role in philosophy as simple bodies in chemistry. Examples of the same spirit can be seen later in English psychology. But in the writings of contemporary ideologists, such as Daube (*Essay on Ideology Serving as a Introduction to General Grammar,* 1803), we find refutations of the Condillacian theory of transformed sensation. Daube also uses the original character of the faculties to refute the theory: for example, attention, which is activity and preference, cannot be reduced to sensation, which is passive; memory, with the particular sentiment of the past which accompanies it, cannot be a form of sensation, which is always present; finally, the external world cannot be constructed with properties such as extension and stability if they have the contradictory character of being both sensations and properties of bodies. Analysis always comes to a halt in the face of differences.

For these reasons Destutt de Tracy singled out four irreducible modes of sensibility: willing, judging, feeling, remembering.

Grammar and logic relate to the second mode—judgment. In the ideological sense, grammar is the study of signs and their meaning. In the seventeenth and eighteenth centuries words had been considered to be the signs of ideas, and subsequently a judgment had been defined (by Locke, for example) as a relation between ideas because it is expressed in a proposition, which is a synthesis of words. One of Destutt de Tracy's great discoveries was that a word is primarily a discourse: the first sign is an interjection, which already expresses a judgment; later the attribute is separated from its subject and the interjection becomes a verb; the essential elements of language are still (as in the Stoic theory of propositions) nouns and verbs.

The scaffolding of Aristotelian logic, according to Destutt de Tracy, rests on illusory distinctions. The numerous figures and modes of syllogism, with their complicated rules, are traceable to the distinction between affirmative and negative propositions, universals and particulars. Yet negative propositions do not exist, he reasons, since every proposition expresses a relation, and a negation is an absence of relation. The same applies to particulars, for the extension of an attribute is always equal to the extension of its subject: for example, the proposition "Man is an animal" implies that "an animal" is restricted to an animal of the human species.

By these considerations Destutt de Tracy excludes, along with the mechanism of the syllogism, any conclusion *vi formae* other than the one drawn from reasoning based on identical propositions. But he does this in order to demonstrate that true reasoning involves, not relations of extension, which can be classed in a small number of types prepared beforehand, but relations of ideational content, relations which can be discovered in each case only by direct examination of the ideas employed. Any argument states that one idea contains a second, which contains a third, which contains a fourth, and so on. The only means of making certain that an argument is sound is not to have recourse to rules but to examine each idea. But an almost insuperable difficulty arises if we grant that the *idea* discussed by Destutt de Tracy is not an arbitrary construction of the mind but derives its certainty from both its connection with other ideas and the primary fact on which the chain depends. "Then we realize that our examination or exposition can never be completed. To complete our undertaking, we would probably have to choose a single idea and examine all the ideas that we have already formed, since they are all so closely interlinked." Destutt de Tracy's logic rests on a favorite idea of the eighteenth century—the idea of a natural series and a natural classification. It attributes any error to "the perpetual and imperceptible variety of our ideas," to individual variations in different directions, which introduce the artificial and arbitrary into a series of ideas intended to reproduce the articulations of reality. In logic Destutt de Tracy relies, not, like Condillac, on algebraic transformations, but on chemical or natural classifications.

The fourth section of *Elements of Ideology* consists of a treatise on the will and its effects. Destutt de Tracy outlined the first part and completed the second. In the first part, the treatise on the will, he studies ethics—not rules governing our actions but the origin of our desires and their conformity or lack of conformity with the true conditions of our being, "without permitting the imposition of any law" (*Works*, III, 372). Of particular significance in this part is the chapter on love written by Destutt de Tracy, who was not indifferent to Stendhal and his writings on the same subject. The second part, concerning the effects of will, is economics—that is, an examination of the consequences of our actions considered from the viewpoint of their appropriateness in providing for all our needs. Here he shows how the individual and society are affected not only by work but also by circumstances relating to associations, corporations, or families. Destutt de Tracy thinks that in this way the merits or demerits of each can be measured more accurately. In reality, he did not carry out his vast program but limited himself to considerations, borrowed mainly from the economist Say, relating to exchange, production, value, industry, money, and the distribution and consumption of goods.

The fifth part of the *Elements* was to have dealt with the fundamental notions of all the physical and abstract sciences.

II   *Pierre Cabanis*

Closely associated with Destutt de Tracy was the physician Pierre Cabanis (1757-1808). The first six treatises of the twelve comprised in his *Relations of the Physical and the Moral in Man* (1802) were read at the Institute in 1795 and 1796. They reflect a fervent hope of the period, the hope of establishing moral sciences which would rival the physical sciences in certainty and provide a sufficient basis for a morality independent of philosophy and connected with the rational investigation of individual happiness, which was then considered to be firmly linked to the happiness of all. According to Cabanis, however, the eighteenth-century practice of separating the study of the human faculties from the study of the living body to which they are linked (especially in the case of Helvétius and Condillac, both insufficiently acquainted with physiology) ruled out any hope of attaining certainty in the matter. "The wave of hypotheses put forward to explain certain phenomena which seem at first glance to be alien to the physical order could not fail to put the stamp of uncertainty on these sciences; and it is not surprising that their very existence as substantive doctrines has been called in question even by judicious minds." Thus Cabanis assumes that the linking of analysis to physiology confers on analysis the certainty it lacks. It is in no way a materialistic solution of the metaphysical problem. "Some men," he says in the Preface, "seemed to fear that this work would have as its aim or effect the reversal of certain doctrines and the establishment of others relating to the nature of first causes. . . . The reader will often see, in the course of the work, that we consider these causes to be outside the sphere of our inquiries, forever hidden from the means of investigation which man received with life" (edition of 1830, p. 18). This agnosticism, still bearing the imprint of the eighteenth century, was transmitted by the ideologists to Comte, who also devoted one chapter of his physiology to the analysis of the human faculties.

One positive part of Cabanis' work is very important: the six treatises (from the fourth to the tenth) on the intellectual and moral influence of age, sex, temperament, disease, and climate. If we disregard the part which owes its value mainly to wealth of detail, one essential idea stands out. This is the importance of the role played, in the functioning of our faculties, by inner impressions. Cabanis (like Maine de Biran) was an invalid who experienced the cruel invasion, in his thoughts, of organic sensations of which Condillac was totally unaware. To this oversight is related the inadequacy of the Condillacian theory of instinct, which treats it as a reflective judgment. To Cabanis, instinct, which designates all inner impulses, independent of external impressions—for example, the movement of suction in the newborn and especially spontaneous acts relating to the reproduction of the species—is the crucial fact behind the existence of organic sensibility. Instinct is the result of impressions received by internal organs, just as moral ideas and determinations, according to the analysts, are the result of external impressions.

This distinction transforms the notion of sensibility (*Treatise* x, 2d section, part 4, note). The practice then was to separate irritability (the unconscious property exhibited by a muscular tissue when it responds to a stimulus by contracting) from sensibility, which was linked to consciousness; but if irritability can account for movement itself, it cannot explain the organization of movements, such as occurs in instinct or any organic function—for example, in digestion. These movements, comparable by virtue of their systematization to the movements of a deliberate act, are occasioned by a felt internal impression, like the external impression which precedes acts.

But this parallelism (the only proof of his theory offered by Cabanis) in turn implies that consciousness, contrary to a common belief, is not the exclusive and distinctive character of sensibility. Consciousness can arise only if an impression is perceived by the self, yet sensibility determines a number of important, regular functions even when the self receives no warning. Cabanis has in mind experiences which show that stimulation of a muscle produces a habitual movement even after the nerve that innervates the muscle has been severed. He also has in mind the unnoticed influence exerted on our consciousness by organic changes in circulation or digestion. He is ready, according to Van Helmont, to acknowledge several centers of sensibility, each with a kind of partial self.

The duality introduced by Cabanis between consciousness of self and unconscious, private sensibility of self was one of the points of departure of Maine de Biran, and his manner of presenting the opposition between the continuity of the activity of the internal organs and the discontinuity of external impressions (*Treatise* iii, part 4) recalls the duality of two lives in Bichat. The only difference is that for Maine de Biran, as for Bichat, this duality is an irreducible datum; but in Cabanis we find a kind of monism which makes him consider thought to be a function of the brain, just as digestion is a function of the stomach. "If thought differs essentially from animal heat, as animal heat differs from chyle and semen, must unknown and particular forces be introduced to activate organs of thought and explain their influence on other parts of the animal system?" (*Treatise* xi, part 1). His postulate, implied if not stated, is that of the unity of nature: different bodies, inorganic or living, are composed of the same substance, and their diverse physical, vital, or conscious manifestations are due to the different way in which their elements are combined; the physical and the moral are therefore completely homogeneous, and the influence of the first on the second is a particular instance of reciprocal influences among organs. That is why the eleventh treatise, titled *The Influence of the Moral on the Physical* and devoted to the influence of the functioning of the brain on the rest of the organism, stays, like all the rest of the work, within the confines of pure physiology. Cabanis was not only a monist; he shared the naturalistic optimism of the eighteenth century. In his view, nature contains the necessary and sufficient conditions of its progress; contrary to the belief of the Cartesians, the "physical" is not a cause of confusion, which, ideally, should be eliminated, but contains the principles without which our inclinations and intelligence would lack direction. The great mistake of the analysts was in having isolated the moral by an artificial abstraction. If Condillac was right in making every mental operation a transformed sensation, he failed to see that it was impossible to consider sensation an isolated datum which could be conferred at will on a statue (*Treatise* x, 2d section, part II). Sensations can be conceived only as being dependent on each other and tied to all the other organic functions.

III   *The Influence of Ideology*

There were no great thinkers among the ideologists. They were mediocre writers who used a dull and, at times, affected style, which had not been influenced by the Romantic fervor and which preserved the worst traditions of the last years of the eighteenth century. But ideology is a spirit rather than a doctrine, and this spirit animates all of Stendhal's work. It consists in a vision of men in which no universal principle separates the observer from reality. To appreciate its indifference to things, we need only recall illuminism and the rise of Romanticism, which, in history, drama, fiction, and philosophy, made individuals and events the moments and signs of a universal reality manifested and realized through them, as if each were a little Messiah. Stendhalian "egotism" steers clear of these more or less sincere manifestations of enthusiasm, just as ideological analysis rejects, in logic or ethics, all-inclusive principles which fail to come to grips with reality. Religion, which elsewhere is the substrate of a universal doctrine presumed to bring about the transfiguration of the individual, is a means to power in the true individual typified by Julien Sorel; and if Fabrice in *The Charterhouse of Parma,* having made it serve his pleasure and his interests, finally looks to it for consolation, he is even then being served by it more than he is serving it. Stendhal does not believe in an entity called religion any more than Fabrice believes in the battle of Waterloo; for although Fabrice was there, as he tramped back and forth, galloped after his generals, or experienced thirst and hunger, he did not discover what historians refer to as a battle. Similarly, Julien Sorel never discovered religion as a thing in itself in the mediocre ambitions of seminarists or the brilliant schemes of Parisian politicians; and as Condillac tried to discover in sensation a kind of differential the integration of which produces every human faculty, the Stendhalian novel tries to discover in the passions and feelings of the individual everything that is real in the great ensemble represented by a society or a religion.

French ideology, badly received in France, had some success abroad, particularly in liberal countries or parties. Jefferson, then President of the United States, was a friend of many ideologists, and especially of Destutt de Tracy, with whom he corresponded for almost twenty years (1806–26). His correspondence was published by Chinard (1925), and he himself translated and published Tracy's *Commentary on the Spirit of Laws.* In 1818 Jefferson wrote to him (Chinard, p. 184): "I hope that this book [*Elements of Ideology*] will become the handbook of our students and statesmen, and bring about progress here in a science concerning which we have made many mistakes."

In Italy Condillac had found a disciple in Soave (1743–1806), who met him in Parma. His *Institutions of Logic, Metaphysics, and Ethics* (1791) modifies certain points in the teachings of Condillac.

He acknowledged reflection as a source of knowledge distinct from sensation and, before Destutt de Tracy, noted that the sensation of resistance, and not touch, is the source of belief in the existence of the external world. M. Gioia (1767–1835), an economist who was exiled or imprisoned several times on account of his liberal ideas, introduced into his *Elements of Philosophy* (1818) Destutt de Tracy's and Cabanis' theories about instinct; and he abandoned the simplism of the Condillacian doctrine, showing the place of judgment and reflection as faculties distinct from sensation in the formation of ideas. In 1827 Romagnosi (1761–1835), a jurist, published *What Is a Sound Mind?* In this book, which deviates slightly from the teachings of the ideologists, he posits, alongside sensation strictly so called, a logical sense or sense of relations, which is distinct from judgment or reflection. Anticipating pragmatism, he defines the truth of an idea not by its resemblance to its object but by a law of necessary correspondence between idea and object. Delfico (1744–1835), a liberal who welcomed the French invasion of 1796 as a liberation, wrote *Studies of Imitative Sensibility* (1813) and two treatises on organic perfectability (1814–18), in which he defines man as an "imitative animal" and shows that imitation is the key to moral and intellectual progress. P. Borrelli (1782–1849) published his *Introduction to the Natural Philosophy of Thought* in 1824 and his *Principles of the Genealogy of Thought* in 1825. He defends, against Condillac, the irreducibility of three faculties: sensation, a simple occasional cause of thought; judgment, the perception of a difference; and will, an efficient cause distinct from judgment which is its stimulus.

The spiritual kinship of the pessimistic poet Leopardi with the ideologists casts light on the curious affinity of ideology to pessimism. It is in *Miscellany* that Leopardi expresses his admiration for the ideologists, and he offers a spirited satire of "new believers"—that is, traditionalists—in *I nuovi credenti* and in *Palinode*. The Italian ideologists—particularly Verri (*Treatise on the Nature of Pleasure and Pain,* 1773) and Gioia—maintain that pleasure is man's only good and that it consists only in the cessation of pain. This accounts for Leopardi's pessimistic themes: the rarity of pleasures and their illusory character; the dangers of philosophical analysis, which, by revealing truth to man, makes him egotistical, inactive, and unenthusiastic; and the necessity of a return to the illusions of a spontaneous, instinctive life.

Bibliography

Cailliet, Emile. *La tradition littéraire des Idéologues.* Philadelphia, 1943.
Damiron, P. L. *La philosophie en France au XIXe siècle.* 1828. pp. 1–104.
Joyau, E. *La philosophie en France pendant la Révolution.* 1893.
Picaret, F. *Les idéologues.* 1891.
Van Duzer, Charles H. *The Contribution of the Idéologues to French Revolutionary Thought,* Baltimore, 1935.

I

Destutt de Tracy. *Œuvres complètes,* 1824–25.
Boas, George. *French Philosophies of the Romantic Period.* Baltimore, 1925.
    Chap. 2.
Chabot, C. *Destutt de Tracy.* Moulins, 1895.
Chinard, J. *Jefferson et les idéologues.* Baltimore, 1925.
Picaret, F. *Les idéologues,* Paris, 1891. Chaps. 5 and 6.
Van Duzen, C. *The Contributions of the Idéologues to French Revolutionary Thought.* Baltimore, 1935.

II

Cabanis, Pierre. *Œuvres complètes,* ed. P. J. G. Thurot. Paris, 1823–25.
Cailliet, Emile. *La tradition littéraire des idéologues.* Philadelphia, 1943.

III

Braga, G. C. *La filosofia francese e italiana del settecento,* vol. 2. Arezzo, 1920.
Chinard, G. *Jefferson et les idéologues.* Paris, 1923.

THE PHILOSOPHY OF
MAINE DE BIRAN AND
THE DECLINE OF IDEOLOGY

I *Xavier Bichat*

In his *Physiological Investigations Concerning Life and Death*
(1800) the physiologist Xavier Bichat (1771–1802) introduced a
duality into vital phenomena which broke completely with the
monistic spirit animating ideology. He made a distinction between
organic life (functions of digestion, circulation, and the like) and
animal life (sensorial and motor functions). The first, carried on
continuously by asymmetrical organs, is exempt from the influence
of habit and is the source of passions, such as anger or fear; the
second, which has its seat in symmetrically placed organs, is inter-
mittent and interrupted by periods of sleep, and is the source of
understanding and will. This important distinction, contemplated
by Maine de Biran, Auguste Comte, and Ravaisson, had a much
greater influence than eclectic spiritualism on the fate of psychology,
which it freed from the monism of the ideologists.

II *Maine de Biran: The Man*

The doctrine of Maine de Biran (1766–1824) offers one of the
clearest examples of what might be termed the inversion of eight-

eenth-century thought during the nineteenth century. Condillacian ideology apprehended human thought only as it was totally externalized in sensations and their signs; Maine de Biran returns to the unique conscience of man. The ideologists used a single method, analysis, to solve many problems; Maine de Biran uses many methods—internal observation, physiology, pathology—to solve a single problem, the problem of the nature of the human conscience. This inversion was consonant, no doubt, with a general tendency of the period. It could have been given such a palpable form, however, only by a man with the temperament of Maine de Biran, who was called back again and again, by a kind of uneasiness and organic weakness, to the inner life of man. He was in no sense a professional philosopher, and his outward life was that of a political figure and public official. Born at Bergerac in 1766, he was an administrator in the Dordogne (1795–97), a member of the Council of Five Hundred (1797–98), subprefect of Bergerac (1806–12), treasurer to the Chamber of Deputies (1815), councilor of state (1816), and deputy from Bergerac (1818–24).

A contest sponsored by the Academies of Paris, Berlin, and Copenhagen prompted him to write some technical works. Through these works he became acquainted with the ideologists, particularly Destutt de Tracy and Cabanis. He frequented the salon of Mme Helvétius at Auteuil, particularly from 1802 to 1809, and was also the friend and correspondent of Ampère. But it was by a kind of inner necessity that he was drawn to philosophy. His diary is devoted entirely to complaints about his distractions and "natural weak-mindedness" which prevented him from pursuing anything at length, his instability and the ceaseless agitation of organic impresions, which kept interfering with his life. All these troubles were intensified by his social life. "I have clear proof," he writes, "that I am not made for wordly affairs; they disturb me and upset me to no avail. I am worthless unless engaged in solitary reflection; would that I could recapture my worth!" (*Diary,* November 1815; ed. La Valette-Monbrun, p. 193). Yet he knows that his state of agitation is due to nothing external. "When one achieves inner calm, one can meditate and accomplish reflective experiments, even in agitated surroundings, without being disturbed; but when one suffers from inner agitations, everything is distracting, and the deepest solitude will not bring calm." Hence his definition of a philosopher: "To *philosophize* is to reflect, to make use of one's reason, in everything and everywhere, in the tumult of the world as in one's solitude or study" (*Diary*, June 1816, p. 233).

III *Formation of the Doctrine: Habit*

Buffon and Rousseau were his first masters. In *Reflections on Nature* (1745, ed. Tisserand, I, 31–43) he borrows his image of nature from Buffon. In this generalized Newtonian system attraction is considered to be a primary force of matter—one that explains not only phenomena relating to celestial mechanics but also all physical or chemical phenomena, and even impetus.

Along with Buffon, the Rousseau of *Reveries of a Solitary* was at first Maine de Biran's true master. All his descriptions of his troubled instability, his lack of self-control, his shyness in the presence of others, bear the strong imprint of Rousseau (I, 37). He is skeptical of moralists and their flowery prescriptions. "Before seeking to direct our affections, we should of course know the limits of our control over them. I have not seen this question dealt with anywhere. Moralists assume that man can always develop affections, change his inclinations, change the direction of his passions; they claim that the soul is sovereign, exerting absolute control over the senses. But is that true? Or to what extent is that true? (I, 60). He resolves to let himself be born along by the tide. "My will exerts no control over my moral state. . . . What, then, is this so-called activity of the soul? Always at the mercy of impressions originating outside it, the soul is depressed or uplifted, sad or joyous, calm or agitated, according to the temperature of the air or the state of the digestive system. . . . If at times I am afforded peace of mind by the absence of passions and by a pure conscience, I shall no longer try to enchain this contentment. . . . I shall enjoy it when it comes, always keep myself in a position to enjoy it, never set it aside through any fault of my own; but since my activity is powerless to induce it or restrain it, I shall not exhaust myself, as I did some time ago, by vain efforts to induce passions or emotions and to shake off this dead calm" (I, 59, 61). The alternation of confidence and discouragement is irremediable, and the illusion that our activity is under our control soon disappears: "The pleasure that I feel when the fibers of my brain yield to the impetus of my will, the discouragement that possesses me when I sense that these fibers are paralyzed, and my soul—like a musician who, wishing to play his instrument, feels the strings grow slack under his fingers and does not have the strength to tighten them—is powerless to act upon them, the temptation, in my good moments, to persuade myself that I am responsible for them, although comparison shows clearly that this state depends on the current disposition of my organs, over which I am powerless."

Sometimes consciousness of this necessity leads him to a state of quiet composure which is entirely Stoical. If our state depends on the assemblage of our machine, "the source of the evils of our condition is in ourselves much more so than in the external things to which we attribute them. If we were thoroughly convinced of this truth, we would grumble much less about fate, we would not try so hard to free ourselves from these states of anxiety, and we would show more resignation" (I, 84). Thus introspection, to which Maine de Biran was predisposed by the fluctuations of his organic state, enabled him nevertheless to avoid a morbid predeliction for analysis that culminates in finding self-satisfaction in the variable interplay of inner feelings. Instead of a physical state of happiness beyond our control, he urges us to "repudiate noisy pleasures, especially to show benevolence and charity in dealing with the misfortunes of others—in a word, to seek the pleasures attached to a pure conscience and sound health, which alone can lead us to a state of happiness."

Nevertheless the Stoic ideal of harmony with oneself and conformity to nature—the ideal he meditated upon as a result of his studies of Cicero and Seneca—seemed to him hard to attain. Happy is the man who, having gained knowledge of his own tastes and faculties through intensive study of himself, has succeeded in harmonizing his life and conduct with them; but "what seems worse to me in the ordinary condition of men, is that they are, almost without exception, condemned to know nothing of themselves. Potential faculties can remain hidden, unknown to their possessors, until fortuitous circumstancès give rise to their employment." Also "the characteristic sign of wisdom," harmony with oneself, "is easier to envision than to attain; it is to the greatest practical philosopher what a hyperbole is to its asymptotes" (I, 91). Furthermore, our nature is not a sufficiently stable reality to serve as a standard; for example, when Rousseau advises us, in order to achieve happiness, to diminish the excess of our desires over our faculties and to bring power and will into perfect balance, he is forgetting the lesson learned by Helvétius—that the death of our desires would be the death of our faculties, and that it is impossible to diminish one without diminishing the others as well. Finally, we must not condemn an active life, as Seneca did, and preach inner withdrawal. "The whole art of happiness consists only in procuring for ourselves the best possible sentiment of existence; for that we need the help of the objects around us. Wisdom consists not in breaking the bonds that unite us to these objects but in choosing those most appropriate to the goal we must set up for ourselves" (I, 104).

The final proof that the Stoics were wrong is that between ourselves and objects, there is feeling: its influence cannot be eliminated. Montesquieu, at the beginning of his *Spirit of Laws,* speaks of natural, fixed laws resulting from the relations which men maintain among themselves, but he forgets that these relations are unstable. "A strong man does not sense these relations in the same way as a weak man, and a change of temperament is certain to bring about a change in the way a man considers himself with respect to the beings around him. . . . Such is the principle that prevents us from arriving at fixed ideas about our wretched human nature" (I, 112). The Stoic boasts of his independence and his liberty with respect to things, without realizing that his confidence in himself undoubtably depends on the state of his sensory apparatus. Knowledge of causes is supposed to protect us from fear, but "the man who is best informed about the usefulness of temperance will be very intemperate if his gastric juices are overly active" (I, 118). Nevertheless, Maine de Biran was constantly tempted by the Stoic ideal. He comments sympathetically on the *Tusculan Disputations* and supports Epictetus against both Montaigne and Pascal (I, 130–36; 139). While reading Bonnet, he meditated at length on the problem of freedom, and afterward he seems to have gained new insights. He decided to abandon completely the metaphysical question of freedom. The question is insoluble, he concluded, "because it is immediately linked to knowledge of the motive principle of will, to knowledge of the union of the two substances of which man is composed and their reciprocal influence. These mysteries are impenetrable, and the greatest philosophers . . . are no closer to their solution than an ignorant man" (I, 142). The question is also inane, for it has no bearing on ethics. The inner sense, on the contrary, acquaints us directly with our power to arrest our attention and fix it on an object; it shows us the difference between states in which we let our souls drift aimlessly and states in which, after comparing and calculating, we arrange our ideas and try to determine their relations. "Is there not a true activity of the soul? Do I not sense, through the exertion it requires of me, an ensuing lassitude?" (I, 145). The reality of this activity is a datum of the inner sense, independent of any metaphysical speculation; and it makes possible the vigilance that enables me to preserve, against the confusion introduced by sentiment, "this order which I delighted in imposing on my ideas, this order on which I make my happiness depend."

From this moment, in 1795, in the midst of all these oscillations, Maine de Biran's method and doctrine began to assert themselves: a method that consists in identifying the data of the inner sense; a doctrine that isolates in the mind two series of phenomena, always combined—those in which the mind is active and those in which it is passive. But we also see the moral preoccupations and even the vital need to which this doctrine was related.

These considerations account for Maine de Biran's critical attitude toward eighteenth-century philosophy, to which he links, as its sequel, the dogma of popular sovereignty and the revolutionary commotion which issued from it. This dogma is closely related to Helvétius' principle concerning the equality of minds and to his rational philosophy, which stipulates that reason alone should guide the people (I, 166; 303). Rational philosophy, however, is itself indissolubly linked to Condillac's doctrine of the origin and development of the faculties of the human mind. Having made every idea depend on the institution of signs, and having affirmed that analysis in its highest form is a return to analysis as we practice it spontaneously, Condillac should have concluded that no idea is beyond the reach of any mind whatsoever. But, in the first place, to assume that the capacity for thinking does not exist apart from the use of signs is false. How could signs have been created without a mental operation? (I, 283; 289). And since the mind apprehends resemblances and differences between objects, we can conceive of a thought without a sign. "There would then be less subtlety but more reality, less surface but more depth and solidity in our knowledge, which would be wholly affective and would no longer influence our conduct." Next, it is wrong to assume that simple knowledge of the origin of our ideas teaches us to conduct and control the mind, whose functioning depends also on many unforeseeable and unexpected physical conditions (I, 214).

The general mistake of eighteenth-century philosophy was confusing the two domains, already clearly separated, of reflective activity and spontaneity. Condillac saw reflective activity everywhere, even in animal instinct, which, according to him, is intelligently acquired, and he deliberately ignored any dependence on the body (I, 219). Inversely, Rousseau, in the *Savoyard Vicar,* left to instinct, to sentiment, to innateness whatever is under the jurisdiction of reflection; for "if the inner sense cast light on our duties, all books on ethics would be useless; but inasmuch as ways of sensing are quite different, . . . one can establish no certainty on such a variable basis" (I, 191).

Here we find the first statement of the theme that was to dominate the thinking of Maine de Biran: unstable or wavering sentiment in contrast to stable reflection, passivity in contrast to activity. His studies of habit, in his treatise on *The Influence of Habit on the Faculty of Thinking,* have the sole aim of demonstrating and detailing this opposition. Since it affects our passive faculties and our active faculties quite differently, habit is a reagent that will enable us to separate them with certainty. Some faculties, like sensations and sentiments, change and become debased under the influence of habit; whereas others, like perception, improve and acquire greater precision, speed, and ease. "The influence of habit is a positive test which we can apply to these faculties to determine the identity or diversity of their origin; all those modified in the same way in passing through this crucible should be placed in the same class, and vice versa" (II, 301). What interests Maine de Biran is not habit itself but its role in his impassioned investigation of a center of activity surrounded by fluctuating states. We need only consider the definitive plan of his treatise, as it was printed in 1802. The introduction is intended to show the presence of an active faculty in every form of knowledge: beginning with the lowliest perceptions, we receive impressions from the outside passively and add to them something of our own, for we have at our disposal movements by which we can arbitrarily modify the conditions of receptivity. We do not see, we look; and if the perceptions of sight and hearing are clearer than the perceptions of smell and taste, this is because of the more complicated motor systems to which they are linked—the muscles of the eye in one instance and, in the other, the vocal system of emission of sounds. Nor can memory be reduced to the simple repetition of previously experienced passive impressions. How could we succeed in separating them and identifying them when they occur again? "To suppose that the self is identical to all its modifications, yet compares them and separates them, is to make a contradictory supposition" (II, 49). Thus the whole introduction strongly supports, against the Condillacian theory of faculties as transformed sensations, the primitive duality of knowledge. But toward the end of the introduction Maine de Biran adds that "this whole treatise will be only the continuation of previous analyses; it should at the same time serve to confirm them, if they are exact" (II, 66).

In the first section, "On Passive Habits," Maine de Biran aims especially to show that habit gradually obscures our active role in knowledge, with the result that we are finally persuaded by it to confuse sensation and perception, passivity and activity. Investigations of the formation of habit will free us from this illusion, showing us how it is produced; they will enable us to see "how the individual is completely blind concerning his own role in perception, . . . how the composite function of perceiving—by virtue of its speed, ease, and *apparent passivity*—tends always to approximate sensation strictly so called. . . . Habit erases the line of demarcation between voluntary and involuntary acts" (II, 103). The role of the investigator is to retrace this line, reflecting on habit and eliminating what it has done. By deadening sensation, by facilitating and making more precise, movements relating to the organs of the senses, and by forging a stronger link between impressions and adaptive or facilitating movements, habit has gradually put an end to all effort and to awareness of the active part we take in acquiring our knowledge. One of its most singular effects occurs in tactile perception. Here "muscular effort disappears or is no longer sensed, except in its product. . . . The individual, misjudging his own strength, transfers it entirely to an object or resisting term, to which he attributes the absolute qualities of inertia, solidity, and weight" (II, 106). Consequently, in spite of his active movements, which are the conditions of knowledge, when "his perceptive faculty reaches [through habit] the degree of perfection on one hand or blindness on the other, . . . the individual remains passively exposed to the impetus of external causes, which often stimulate him even when he is unaware of them, or to organic influences" (II, 120).

The study of active habits, in the second section, is intended to show us how we regain control and mastery over these movements —how, to use the expression constantly repeated by Maine de Biran, we again have disposition of ourselves." To grasp the significance of his words, we must pay particular attention to his use of the concept *sign*. In the Condillacian tradition, the exercise of thought was considered to be inseparable from language, the indispensable instrument for analysis. Here Maine de Biran is absolutely faithful to this tradition, but he stresses what he considers a primordial characteristic of the sign: it is a movement, and one which, to fulfil its role as a sign, should remain at our disposition. We have at our disposition the power to evoke an idea, and thus, indirectly, we are masters of our ideas. In this sense, movements connected with our impressions in perception are the natural signs of these impressions, insofar as they are available, and they cease to be their natural signs when habit removes them from the will. Then "their natural functions as signs are absolutely forgotten or slighted; there is no longer any available recall" (II, 305). It is then that "the secondary signs of language happily come to check the mobility of habit, to reveal to the individual the kind of control that he can exercise over several of its modifications, to create for him a second memory."

Institutional signs carry on the work, beginning at the point where the results have been checked by habit. But habit lies in wait for these as well as for the preceding signs, and the history of human thought is the history of its various failures to maintain the "availability" of these signs (and, with it, self-mastery), and the description of its efforts to overcome routine.

IV *The Doctrine of the Self: The Primitive Fact*

The test question put out in 1805 by the Academy of Moral and Political Sciences, "How can the faculty of thinking be analyzed, and what are the elementary functions that must be identified in it?" was framed, in the context of Condillac's doctrine, by the ideologists who made up the Academy. To analyze thought was, in this sense, as Maine de Biran knew, to enumerate the diverse forms and characteristics manifested by sensation in the process of its transformation and expressed by the generic term *thought*. Maine de Biran arbitrarily gave it a completely different sense, in keeping with his fundamental preoccupation—the distinction between passivity and activity in ourselves, between what we experience and what we do. What he introduced in this way represented a great innovation, not only in the results of analysis but also in the form of analysis. It was not a new classification but a new plan of cleavage, as if mechanical analysis by division were replaced by chemical analysis, which reveals the presence of heterogeneous elements in seemingly uniform realities.

The inner life of Maine de Biran consisted in the alternation of domination by the body and self-mastery, of states in which we feel that happiness or unhappiness springs from involuntary organic dispositions, and those rare moments when we feel full control over ourselves. His doctrine is a kind of generalization of this awareness of duality, which he discovers in what seem to be the simplest phenomena of consciousness. From the description of the inner life, in which he was anxiously pursuing a procession of affective states whose direction he could not determine, he passes on to psychological analysis, which rediscovers what might be termed the differential of the life of the soul or, to use his own expression, the primitive fact, in which activity unites with passivity the first source of any consciousness.

The joining of these two theses—that the primitive fact is the source of consciousness and that it is at the same time the object of an immediate inner experience—is the nucleus of the whole doctrine of Maine de Biran. "What matters most is to begin . . . with the simplest knowledge, the most certain of all that which our mind can acquire—knowledge without which no other knowledge is possible and with which all other knowledge becomes possible" (Naville's edition, III, 341). The task is therefore twofold: an analytical procedure to identify and isolate the primitive fact; an integral procedure, beginning with the primitive fact, to discover the development of consciousness.

The primitive fact is the muscular effort in which the self or ego perceives itself immediately as a hyperorganic force producing the movement of a muscle. The ego perceives itself only as a cause acting on resistant matter. There is no act of self-intuition, no consciousness outside this act. There is in any consciousness of the self (and any consciousness is consciousness of the self) the intimate union of these two heterogeneous elements—material force and material resistance. The ego apprehends itself as a cause in effort, inseparable from the effect which it produces.

All the errors of philosophers on this point stem from their failure to apprehend the inner experience of effort in its irreducible originality. They substitute for the act of the self, inseparable from the affirmation of an external existence, a thinking substance, which is presented from without as a permanent thing—as a material thing capable of receiving modifications. As Hobbes clearly saw, in contrast to Descartes, the idea of substance is inseparable from the image of an extended substrate; it follows, and Malebranche drew out this consequence, that any modification of the soul—sensation, desire, volition—is uniformly apprehended as a passive mode of the soul, which can have no cause other than God, the universal cause. Even if, like Leibniz, we attribute the series of modifications of the soul to an inner cause, we are still denying any relation of cause to effect between body and soul, and to explain their correspondence we are obliged to have recourse to the forced hypotheses of occasionalism or to preestablished harmony. But that is not all, for in Descartes' substantialism Maine de Biran sees the principle of eighteenth-century materialism: spiritual substance as it was conceived by Descartes differed too little from material substance not to have been assimilated to it.

All these consequences issue from the initial step taken by Descartes: *Cogito ergo sum.* He believed he had found in thought a reflection of self on self completely independent of a causal action on the body, and this led him to isolate thinking substance, as a thing, from extended substance. But these ideas were also confirmed by Bacon's method, which consists essentially in substituting the classification of facts for the impossible and deceptive investigation of productive causes. Applying this method to facts about the soul, the ideologists sought to limit themselves to observing these facts and reducing them, by means of analogies, to general facts, as Newton had reduced all facts about celestial mechanics to gravitation.

Modern philosophy in its entirety, according to Maine de Biran, has neglected inner experience and its immediate data in favor of a representation of its object based on our perception of external things, but without understanding that this second perception is impossible without the first. For, contrary to Descartes, inner observation tells us *certissima scientia et clamante conscientia* that any consciousness is action concerning the external world, an attempt to overcome resistance. Inner experience therefore provides us with no substance but only an active, individual force bound up with the passive term on which it acts. That there is no subject without an object, no object without a subject, is not a universal proposition, such as we find among the Germans, but the expression of an individual, incommunicable experience; an object is resistance, inseparable from power. On the other hand, contrary to Malebranche, Hume, and the ideologists, Maine de Biran interprets this primitive fact as the direct verification of an efficient causal action. "I appeal to the inner sense of each man in the state of wakefulness and consciousness, or *compos sui,* to determine whether he is or is not aware of his effort, which is the actual cause of a particular movement that he initiates, suspends, arrests, or continues as he wishes and because he wishes; and whether he makes a clear distinction between this movement and another which he senses or perceives in certain cases as being effected effortlessly or against his will—for example, the convulsive movements of habit" (Naville's edition, III, 464). According to Maine de Biran, Malebranche's most general objection against the efficacity of voluntary effort is our ignorance of the complicated mechanism of the production of a muscular movement (III, 508-9). How could we be the cause of a movement when we have no clear and distinct idea of the conditions of its existence? This amounts to asking how one could impart the desired movement to the hands on the face of a watch, without knowing how to construct a watch. The force of the objection derives from the fact that an attempt has been made to represent, in the imagination, the relation between the self and the body as identical to the relation between the watchmaker and the watch; but here the relation is one that cannot be translated by the imagination—the relation between the self, which feels free in its effort, and the movement it produces. Malebranche's objection simply signifies that the will did not create its own body and means of action. Maine de Biran therefore thinks he is justified also in responding to the challenge thrown down by Hume, who defied anyone to show him an efficacious action in a single experiential fact.[1] We see it immediately, he reasons, without any dialectical proof or induction, in voluntary effort; in such matters, however, the point is not to offer proof but to prepare the mind, to suppress prejudices which prevent us from adopting the right point of view for observing the mind.

The Biranian notion of effort is nevertheless somewhat unusual, for the term effort naturally suggests an exceptional, discontinuous psychological state, which interrupts the flow of consciousness for a brief interval, whereas the so-called primitive fact is present throughout the interval of the existence of consciousness—that is, during the entire period of wakefulness—and is a relatively constant, uniform fact. Maine de Biran was one of the first to emphasize the multiplicity of voluntary movements, which condition all knowledge and particularly sensory knowledge. For example, thanks to the muscular system of the eye, our visual perceptions can remain distinct; and because a complicated system can produce vocal sounds at will, hearing can play a leading role in our knowledge of the external world and particularly of our fellow men. The direct function of the sign, according to Maine de Biran, is not to repre-

[1] For the critique of Hume, cf. especially *Réponses aux arguments contre l'aperception immédiate d'une liaison causale entre le vouloir primitif et la motion et contre la dérivation d'un principe universel et nécessaire de causalité de cette source,* edited by Cousin, vol. IV.

sent the qualities of an object in their entirety but, because it is voluntary movement, to serve as a stable fulcrum, always available as a verification of prior work. Consequently, during the entire state of wakefulness a perpetual but variable tension is maintained by the will in all of part of our muscular systems. Effort, in the Biranian sense, designates only this voluntary activity.

Biran's constant appeal to inner experience does not prevent his doctrine of effort from leaving several questions unanswered. The idea of a hyperorganic force, which is transformed into nervous energy, or at least produces the nervous energy necessary for muscular contraction, is far from clear. He seems to have in mind a limited force which is always the same in quantity for each subject. Progress is always inherent, not in this force but in its effects; for through habit, the first movement produced by it can become progressively easier and more automatic, leaving it available for another movement; consequently new acts are superimposed on established automatisms. But it seems that in the simplest initial act—in smelling, for example, or in the first stammering of a child—there is no less force than in the most complex act, which simply profits by already established automatisms. Equally obscure are the conditions under which the feeling of effort is produced, for muscular resistance is felt at the very moment of its occurrence, as if feeling followed the course of a neural fluid. Ampère insisted on making a distinction between awareness of the force that is exerted and the muscular sensation itself, which, as such, is afferent and indistinguishable from the sensation produced by an involuntary muscular contradiction. Maine de Biran refuses to concur: "The initial contraction is experienced as a direct effect of my effort, in a manner quite distinct from involuntary contradiction."

Many such enigmas issue from the fact that identical physiological phenomena (for example, the production of movement by an influx originating in the nervous system) are interpreted differently, depending on whether the influx is attributed to an organic or a hyperorganic source. It is still very difficult to unite inner experience and physiological description.

We gain a clearer understanding of the significance of these difficulties if we remember that the aim of Maine de Biran's doctrine was one suggested to him by his inner life: to overcome or at least to thwart physiological fatality. He was openly hostile to De Bonald's famous definition of man as an intelligence served by organs. In reality, during a great part of his life man is, rather, the slave of an organism which determines his happiness or unhappiness, independent of his will. His task is to determine whether, at what point, and to what extent his own acts can influence his organism. Contrary to the favorite hypotheses of the eighteenth century, this goal cannot be reached through a kind of inner progression in complexity, which would gradually change animal life into rational life, but only through the kind of unpredictable revolution in which we see "the center of the sensitive soul [the motor center] come under the control of the free force which is the essence of the human soul, and subordinate itself to this force in such a way as to execute, under its influence, every organic operation of the animal" (Naville's edition, III, 477). This force *sui juris* is provoked by nothing external or antecedent (just as Rousseau's social state was in no way germinal in the natural state but due to the absolute initiative of the social contract). Man has a dual nature: *simplex in vitalitate, duplex in humanitate.* He is not an intelligence served by organs but a rational animal.

Belief in continuous progress, beginning with sensation, was occasioned by the fact that so-called simple states, from which Condillac proceeded, were in reality mixed modes that already contained the term to be explained. Whereas Condillacian sensation means sensation accompanied by consciousness of the self, Biranian analysis makes a distinction between consciousness and purely organic sensibility, which exists only in animals or in a very young child, before the first manifestation of willpower. Maine de Biran had much difficulty in convincing others, notably Ampère, of the existence of these unconscious, unnoticed sensations, in which the self is not involved, and which he calls obscure perceptions in his treatise on Bergerac (Tisserand's edition, vol. V). The reason is that animal sensibility, like effort, is a "primitive fact, complete in its own class" (Naville's edition, III, 400); moreover, the two primitive facts are so closely interconnected in the slightest perception that it becomes very difficult for us to conceive them separately. "That is why the word sensation always includes, implicitly and indivisibly, consciousness of the sensing subject, so that the sensation seems to vanish when the subject is removed." To put his meaning across, he often quotes Condillac's famous dictum: "The statue *becomes* the smell of a rose." The primitive fact of organic sensibility is the absolute passivity causing the soul to identify itself successively with every state that comes to it from the body, giving rise to a disconnected multiplicity. This organic sensibility includes—along with sensation and affections of pleasure and grief, instinct, desire, and passion—every state in which there is no domination by the self and, consequently, no consciousness. In this inferior life the affections are simultaneous and present a series of disappearing pictures (Tisserand's edition, IV, 202, note); in active life, however, facts are successive and present a kind of spatialization and dissemination, which contrasts with constant, lasting activity. A similar contrast is seen in the vitalism of Bordeu and Barthez, which Maine de Biran seems at times to approximate. Against Stahl, who, in keeping with Cartesian dualism, saw the principle of organic phenomena in the rational soul itself, Bordeu considered life to be autonomous activity, peculiar to the organism and consubstantial with it. The driving force of organic phenomena is sensibility, the vital property par excellence. "All elements of a living body," he says, "are sensible by their essence; life depends on the faculty that animal fibers possess for feeling and moving." [2] Precisely the same view is held by Maine de Biran, who considers "sensibility" to be diffused so perfectly through organic matter that it does not need to be concentrated in a nervous system in order to be productive. That is why he condemned the division Bichat was then establishing between organic life (like the phenomenon of digestion) and animal life (like the contraction of so-called

[2] As quoted by Papillon, *Histoire de la philosophie moderne*, II, 327.

voluntary muscles). Since the contraction of these muscles is not due to the will but "as in habit and passions or emotions, to organic connections or sympathies, there is no reason for putting it in a separate class. In this way the demarcation between the two lives—animal life and human life—is definitively established."

The active self and its effort against the body, which resists it, according to Maine de Biran, contains the germ of man's whole intellectual and moral life. Is this primitive fact of inner experience, in its nakedness and with its individual and personal character, sufficient to engender all theoretical and practical reason, with its universal principles? To be sure, during this same period the feeling that the self is isolated in an alien nature led Sénancour to his apology for suicide and Alfred de Vigny to the sad, stoic calm of *The Death of the Wolf.* But Maine de Biran is influenced by the feeling that the self has absolute control over itself in its own domain, which is quite limited, of course; it is the certainty of being a cause which contains the seed of all rationality. "Since I think that there is no intellectual idea," he wrote to Ampère, "no distinct perception or no perception in the strict sense that is not linked originally to an *action* of the will, I cannot refrain from considering the intellectual or cognitive system to be grounded absolutely on the system of the will, so to speak, and to differ from it only by expression" (Tisserand's edition, VII, 400). The demonstration of this thesis is one of the great difficulties of Biranism. We have already noted the importance he attached to the motor elements of perception and, more generally, to the signs, natural or institutional, in intellectual ideas. But does not this voluntary part of the phenomenon concern the personal use we make of our intelligence, rather than its universal content? When it comes to grounding a universal affirmation, such as the principle of causality on knowledge of our own causality in voluntary acts, Maine de Biran's argument is defective. How can we deduce, from the activity in which we are consciously engaged, the permanence of the self during moments when it is inactive? And how valid is the analogy that leads us to believe, because we ourselves are causes, that modifications we experience but do not produce are the effects of a cause outside ourselves? For his argument to be correct, the principle of causality would first have to be accepted, and this principle is precisely what is to be demonstrated. The same applies to moral principles, which we cannot reach by starting from the absolute freedom of the self. Here again, a moral conscience originates because we see, in others, persons similar to ourselves; thus "the individual sphere limits itself spontaneously" (Naville's edition, III, 35). But why this analogy? Perhaps it was hard for Maine de Biran to be consistent on this point without coming face to face with an individualism he wished to avoid. In his writings we find an anthropology out of harmony with his psychology. "By virtue of the anthropological relation," he writes, "no agent can be reduced to its individuality; whatever it knows or feels is shared with another agent or known through another agent. The anthropological relation enters as a necessary element into the conscience of the human self" (III, 36).

v The Later Philosophy of Maine de Biran

This appeal to a kind of immediate communication between persons seeks support in moral life rather than in universal principles. It seeks support in a relation of a new kind—one that transcends the life of the individual and is like a new kind of primitive fact. To reach the universal, Maine de Biran moves, not toward rationalism but toward mysticism. Beginning with the treatise on The Analysis of Thought, he joins Gassendi and Descartes, who claimed that he had stripped thought bare in the self-reflection of the Cogito, by saying that nothing acts on itself and that any action must involve an external term (Tisserand's edition, IV, 194–96). At any rate, he continues, this is true of ordinary states of wakefulness, for in mystical states there is no longer anything but inferiority. Thus the mystical state emerges as a primitive and irreducible fact, which occupies the exact place of the Cogito, in which Descartes is supposed to have made the mistake of mixing together the two lives—the rational human life, which can only be action on something external, and the life of the spirit. Then comes absorption in God, and the soul has no more personality than it had in animal life; it follows that human life is the intermediary between animal life, in which man falls when he surrenders to passions, and the life of the spirit, which is at once absolute autonomy and fusion in God, since "nothing happens in the senses and the imagination that is not willed by the self, or suggested or inspired by the supreme force in which this self is finally absorbed" (Naville's edition, III, 419). Thus the life of the spirit alone puts an end to the feeling of powerlessness which overwhelms Maine de Biran, and frees him from enslavement to the body—something that Stoicism, relying solely on the strength of the will, could not accomplish. Marcus Aurelius applied to the second life that which is true only of the third. The spirit is essentially love in the sense associated with Christian mysticism, that is, "life communicated to the soul, and as an addition of its own life, which comes to it from the outside and from above" (II, 541). Love creates between spirits an immediate relation, independent of signs. The life of the spirit is not continuous with human effort; it can be called into existence only by God, who is to our souls what our souls are to our bodies. Along with its own activity, the soul has "faculties and operations which depend on a higher principle, and these operations are carried out in its depths and without its knowledge; . . . intellectual intuitions, inspirations, supernatural movements, in which the soul is released from possession of itself and placed wholly under the influence of God" (III, 549). The work of Maine de Biran is crowned by a theory of grace.

The three lives—animal, human, and spiritual—are independent. "There is no logical or metaphysical passage from one to the other," wrote P. Tisserand. "One can merely verify their existence, not explain it."[3] In contrast, there is perfect continuity in Maine de

---

[3] L'Anthropologie de M. de Biran, p. 297. Cf. Viatte, Les sources occultes du romantisme, II, 226.

Biran's attitude for he discovered in the life of the spirit the victory over physiological fatality which he had sought in vain to wrest from the will.

vi *André Marie Ampère*

The simplistic conception of the ideologists was also rejected by André Marie Ampère (1775–1836), who proposed a much more complex theory of intelligence. Ampère was the physicist who discovered the law of electromagnetism in 1820, the president of the Christian Society, a mystical group founded in Lyon in 1804, and the correspondent who, between 1805 and 1812, addressed to Maine de Biran veritable dissertations on the classification of psychological phenomena. He was one of the most wide-ranging thinkers of his time and one of those least enslaved to politics and the transient philosophical fashions which made many of his contemporaries seem like fanatics. By his own effort and independent of any direct influence, he rediscovered the philosophical tradition that ties analysis of the mind to analysis of the progress of positive science. Finally, the enthusiasm which stirred his soul frightened his Lyonese friends. "His ardent soul will not allow him to be moderate," wrote Ballanche, when Ampère, having returned to the Christian faith in 1815 after eleven years of unbelief, declared: "Everything augurs a great religious era, but I grieve when I think that I shall not live long enough to see it express itself sufficiently for me to judge what it will be like." [4]

Then the procedure of classification was assigned a preponderant role in the sciences, particularly chemistry and the natural sciences. Everyone believed, contrary to certain tendencies of the eighteenth century, that the question of the genesis of beings should come only after the question of their classification, or should even be postponed definitively. Cuvier's fixed species in natural history corresponded to the simple bodies of chemistry and the irreducible faculties of the Scots. This is the spirit Ampère introduced into the philosophical

[4] Cf. Viatte, *Les sources occultes du romantisme,* II, 226.

sciences. He is known especially for two classifications, the classification of psychological phenomena, elaborated and revised constantly
in his correspondence with Maine de Biran, and a classification of
the sciences, which he expounded in his *Essay on the Philosophy of
the Sciences or Analytical Exposition of a Natural Classification
of All Human Knowledge* (1834). He indicates the significance of
the first when he states that "a good classification of these phenomena is the only means of raising psychology to the level of the other
sciences and uniting the divergent opinions, resulting from mis-
understandings, of those concerned with this science, offering them
both the means of stating their ideas more precisely and the means
of succeeding one day in speaking the same language." [5]

But the classification of psychological facts itself is based on a
wholly new thesis, completely independent of Maine de Biran, to
whom Ampère is much less indebted than he is generally said to
be. This thesis, for which he claimed credit on three different
occasions,[6] dominates his classification. His point of departure is
the Platonico-Cartesian opposition between the "sensible" sun and
the "intelligible" sun. "We know only through our impressions the
phenomenal world in which colors are on objects, the sun is one
foot in diameter, the planets retrograde, etc. . . . Physicists and
astronomers conceive a hypothetical noumenal world in which
colors are sensations aroused in the sentient being by certain rays
and existing only in this being; in which the sun is 507,000 leagues
in diameter and the world is a flattened spheroid which revolves
around it; in which planets always move in the same direction,
etc. . . ." (Tisserand's edition, VII, 368). What is the probable
origin of this rational construction? In keeping with his philosophical orientation, Ampère rejected the Condillacian thesis of transformed sensation which, through a series of identities, reduced
every idea to the sensible. His reasons for rejecting it, however, are
completely different from those of his friends, who reasoned that
sensation was passive and therefore could not account for active

[5] *Œuvres de M. de Biran,* ed. Tisserand, VII, 406; letter of September 27, 1807.
[6] *Ibid.,* pp. 501, 506, 550–51.

facts involving the soul. But whereas they would readily accept—and Maine de Biran first of all—the theory of reasoning which reduces this operation to a series of identities, Ampère sees it as Condillac's weak point. Instead of this "ridiculous theory," "the most deceitful and ridiculous ever devised by men," instead of "Condillac's nonsense" and his "ridiculous identity" (Tisserand's edition, VII, 506, 500, 520, 521), Ampère proposes progressive reasoning which makes new discoveries—the kind of reasoning Descartes and Locke had described. While other philosophers linked Locke with Condillac, Ampère disregards the theory of the origin of ideas which separated them from Descartes and reminds us that Locke and Descartes have the same conception of reasoning: both hold that each link in the chain of reasoning is bound to the preceding link by a connection or relation that is grasped intuitively; that the whole chain of reasoning consists of a successive series of immediate apprehensions of relations, each representing a progression; and that there is judgment "when a new element [connection or relation] enlarges the group by joining it" (*Ibid.*, 518).

What is the nature of this immediate apprehension? Here again, Ampère opposes a scholar's view to the ideological theory predicated on analysis of common opinion. To Condillac a judgment is a group of similar ideas; consequently it is based on a comparison of two terms and depends on the nature of the things compared; it changes when things change. Alternatively, a mathematician works with relations of a wholly different kind—relations that do not change even when the terms that are brought together change completely. "For example, I conceived a relation of resemblance between two leaves from an orange tree. If I substitute a flower for one of these two leaves, the relation between the color of the leaf and the color of the flower will no longer be the same as the relation between the two leaves previously compared. This is not true of relations of position and number. If I first note that a branch is situated between two other branches, I can replace all three branches, or one of them, or two of them, substituting leaves or fruits; when I consider these new sensations I shall see a relation of number,

position, or form, independent of their nature" (*Ibid.*, 477). Thus
he reveals modes of union or coordination that are wholly independent of the sensible impressions with which they are united in
ordinary perception: extension, duration, causality, movement, number, divisibility, and still other relations that give rise to axioms
or primary propositions.

If now we recall the "noumenal world" discovered by astronomers
and physicists, we shall see that it consists of immediate apprehension of these connections or relations, independent of impressions.
The distinction between these impressions and relations is the
same as that made by Cartesians and Locke between second qualities,
which pertain only to the self, and first qualities, which pertain to
reality in itself. But Descartes, who was right in making this
distinction, could not justify it. Ampère thinks he can justify the
distinction once he has proved that these qualities designate modes
of union independent of the things which are united; when this is
done, he has a perfect right to replace the phenomena involved in
these relations by noumena, which will have the same relations;
the laws of coordination are the same for both noumena and
phenomena. Descartes' a priori physics has no part, however, in
the physical theories formulated by Ampère. Although he acknowledges two kinds of laws of coordination, which he himself
compares to the a priori synthetic principles of Kant, he sees in
these laws only the materials for the theories of physicists; but these
theories are similar on every point to the astronomical hypotheses
of Ptolemy or Copernicus, which we can represent only as being
extremely probable, by comparing what the results should be and
what we actually observe.

The thesis of Ampère's thought is also opposed to Kant's. In
keeping with the interpretation of his period, Ampère considered
Kant to have been a subjectivist, who claimed that laws of coordination or categories existed only in and for the self and were valid only
for phenomena; but he believed that any psychologist who made
these relations of coordination depend on sensible impressions and
even (as Maine de Biran did for the law of causality) on inner

experience could not avoid the reef of Kantism. There are many relations that depend on the nature of the terms compared and that disappear with these relations of resemblance; but relations that are independent of the nature and their terms are different, for they are in no way linked to the phenomena in which they first appear.

Here we have a theory of scientific knowledge which can be isolated from the rest of his ideas—the theory which, as we shall see, occupies the leading place in psychological classification. Maine de Biran had accepted a distinction between passive phenomena, which were not perceived by an ego, and active phenomena originating in muscular effort, to which he linked not only will but reason. Ampère accepts these two divisions, which he calls sensitive system and autopsy or *emesthesis,* but he gives them a different interpretation. He assumes that the sensitive system is true knowledge of actual modifications, which are coordinated by juxtaposition; emesthesis is added to this knowledge as new knowledge, that of the ego's causality as it is apprehended in muscular effort (he seeks also to avoid confusing muscular sensation proper, localized in a muscle, with the feeling of effort); at this point, force is for the first time attributed to the self, and the resistance it encounters is attributed to external things. But to these two systems he adds two others which are made possible by autopsy but remain distinct from it: the comparative or logical system, which consists in the formation of general ideas and classes on the basis of resemblance; and, higher up, *synthetopsy* or intuition of relations that are independent of their terms. Synthetopsy discovers the relations that it grasps intuitively in the three prior systems, but they are mixed with phenomena and must be isolated: in the first system, extension; in the second, causality; and in the third, relations of classification. The first system involves axioms which are given by intuition—for example, the mathematical axiom that space has three dimensions. But the same is true of the other two systems. In the second system, an assertion such as "effort is the cause of movement produced in the arm" is, like the preceding, an intuitive datum and an axiom. In the third, the principles of Aristotelian logic—for example, that what is true of a genus is always true of a species, but not the opposite—are also axioms. But the determination of noumena becomes possible whenever the mind has an intuition of modes of coordination independent of things. We have seen this exemplified in physical theories, and we can formulate an equally valid theory with respect to the noumenal self and its relation to the phenomenal self. The phenomenal self is the momentary self, apprehended in the transitory acts of effort; but the relation of causality, isolated from the phenomena in which it manifests itself, brings us to a permanent self which survives the particular conditions of its actual manifestation.

It is apparent that the last term in this classification, synthetopsy, governs everything else. In his correspondence with Maine de Biran, he shows how the first three classes, analyzed independently in the beginning, are defined gradually in terms of their relation to synthetopsy. This is particularly clear with respect to the first class, for here Maine de Biran thought that only affective phenomena, unnoticed by the ego, should be included, whereas Ampère sees knowledge involving a coordination of terms. This is because Ampère regards it as the point of departure of knowledge, like noumena in physics; by the same token, he assumes that effort does not penetrate to the heart of the ego's reality, as Maine de Biran had thought, but has only the value of a phenomenon, leaving the field open to the metaphysical theory of a permanent ego or self. The two men had difficulty in understanding each other, for Maine de Biran was always concerned with internal analysis, and Ampère with the conditions of scientific knowledge.

We should not be surprised, therefore, to find a close relation between this psychological classification of the faculties of the soul, through which the sciences are acquired, and the classification of the sciences in the *Essay*. Convinced that the laws of classification are independent of the objects classified, Ampère applies the methods of Cuvier and Jussieu to this problem. Unlike his predecessors, he tries not simply to draw up a hierarchical table of genera embracing species but to introduce, above genera, families, orders, branches, and kingdoms. Cosmological sciences, which study external nature and noological sciences, which study intellectual man—these are the two kingdoms. The cosmological sciences include two subkingdoms, cosmological sciences proper and physiological sciences. The first are divided into two branches, mathematical and physical, and the second into natural sciences and medical sciences. The noological sciences are divided into noological sciences proper—philosophical sciences (psychology, ontology, ethics) and nootechnical sciences (including technaesthetics, or the study of the arts, and glossology, or the study of literature)—and social sciences, which are divided into ethnological sciences (ethnology, archeology, history), and political sciences.

Ampère claims that this classification should serve as a basis for "a truly methodical encyolpedia, in which all branches of our knowledge would be linked together rather than scattered in alphabetical order" (*Essay*), and for a rational pedagogy in which the elementary part of the sciences would be separated from the higher part.

VII *The Diffusion of Kantianism in France*

We have already seen, in Maine de Biran and Ampère, some indications of the impression made in France by Kant's philosophical revolution. Knowledge of Kantianism spread gradually. In 1801 Charles Villers published *The Philosophy of Kant or Fundamental Principles of Transcendental Philosophy* and, during the same year, wrote a report on the subject for Napoleon. He stressed Kant's triumph over empiricism and his theory of knowledge, which had placed freedom and morality above attack.[7] To him Kant was destined to reform French morals and French philosophy. The same year also witnessed publication of a French translation of a Dutch work by Kinker (*A Succinct Exposition of the Critique*

[7] Cf. M. Vallois, *La formation de l'influence kantiènne en France*, 1924, p. 63.

of Pure Reason), which was discussed the next year by Destutt de Tracy in a communication to the Academy of Moral and Political Sciences, and which was annotated by Daunou. It was from Villers, incidentally, that Mme de Staël borrowed the information for the chapter on Kant in her work *On Germany.*

In 1809, in an article *On Existence and the Last Systems of Metaphysics Which Have Appeared in Germany,* Frédéric Ancillon, a member of the Berlin Academy, spoke of the difficulty of explaining these systems "in a language which will not tolerate the slightest violation and which does not lend itself to the conversion of qualities, states, or actions into substances or beings—a very easy and very common metamorphosis in the writings of the German metaphysicists. By putting the article in front of an infinitive, they change what is most indeterminate into a determinate being, and one would not believe at first glance that this faculty, sometimes useful and sometimes disastrous, has had such a decisive influence on philosophy." During the same period Schelling was complaining of the isolation imposed on German philosophers by their language. Thus it is important for us to consider briefly the way in which such a difficult transmission was accomplished. In general, it was by a comprehensive view of the history of philosophy aimed at integrating the German systems into a universal tradition.

Ancillon himself sees the point of departure of the philosophical problem in a dualism which is expressed in several pairs of correlative terms: subject-object, thought-nature, freedom-necessity, mind-matter, psychology-physics. This dualism is not a constructed notion but a primitive fact, or rather the primitive fact recognized by Descartes in the *Cogito,* for "self-consciousness at the same time brings awareness of something which is not my self." Since the two worlds are separated in this way by reflection, the problem is to reestablish unity within duality. Descartes and Locke tried to do this by denying one of the two terms: Descartes' innatism made consciousness of the real world a product of principles inside the subject, and therefore missed reality; Locke's empiricism missed the universality of principles by reducing knowledge to the outer world. Then came Kant, who preserved the link between the two terms. In his view, "the forms of sensation, the notions of the understanding, the ideas of reason are linked to intuitions by a secret, mysterious, incomprehensible bond, and produce the truth of experience." Here he is not solving the problem, according to Ancillon, but positing as fact that which is in question. Why does the particular, the contingent, the changeable pertain to the object, and the necessary or universal to the subject? Kant says nothing on this point and leaves us in a circle. "If you seek reality, you turn to the object, which refers you to the subject; you question the subject and are referred to the object. We are reminded of two insolvent debtors conspiring to mock their creditor, finally giving him a note signed by a third debtor, whose credit depends on theirs—the reality of experience."

The post-Kantian philosophies were attempts to eliminate the problem by going beyond the first fact. Fichte tried to discover a wholly independent subject, an absolute ego. Schelling set out to find, by intellectual intuition, an absolute which would be neither subject nor object—an impossible solution, since "beyond the primitive duality there is nothing but uncertainty, or, rather, one finds the perfect void."

German philosophy was presented, then, as having exhausted every possible solution to the philosophical problem, but without success. That is how Degérando presented Kantianism in his *Comparative History of Systems of Philosophy* (1804), and that is how Mme de Staël interpreted it in her work *On Germany* (Part 3, chap. vi).

Ampère, one of the few who knew Kant through Kant's Lyonese friends, had a very low opinion of the expositions of Kantianism then accessible to the French public. "The *History of Systems of Philosophy* and the work of Villers," he wrote to Maine de Biran," were intended only to distort, for opposite reasons, any idea you may have of Kant. . . . You rely blindly on what MM. de Destutt de

Tracy and Degérando have said about him, and they have treated him the way Condillac treated Descartes and often Locke: they have twisted his expressions to make him say exactly the opposite of what he meant" (Maine de Biran's *Works,* ed. Tisserand, VII, 520).

Bibliography

I

F. Colonna d'Istria. "Bichat et la biologie contemporaine," *Revue de Métaphysique*, 1908.
——. *La psychologie de Bichat. Ibid.*, 1926.

II to V

Texts

Maine de Biran. *Œuvres philosophiques de Maine de Biran,* ed. Pierre Tisserand and Henri Gouhier, 14 vols. Paris, 1920–42.
——. *Œuvres philosophiques de Maine de Biran,* ed. Victor Cousin, 4 vols. Paris, 1841.
——. *Journal intime,* ed. Henri Gouhier. Neuchâtel, 1954–57.
——. *The Influence of Habit on the Faculty of Thinking,* trans. Margaret Boehm. Baltimore, 1929.

Studies

Bertrand, Al. *La psychologie de l'effort.* 1887.
Boas, George. *French Philosophers of the Romantic Period.* Baltimore, 1925.
Delacroix, H. *M. de Biran et l'école médicopsychologique.* Bulletin de la société française de philosophie, 1924.
Delbos, V. "Maine de Biran," in *Figures et doctrines de philosophes.* 1918.
——. *Vue et conclusion d'ensemble sur la philosophie de M. de Biran.* Bulletin de la Société fr. de philosophie, 1924.
——. *Maine de Biran et son œuvre philosophique.* Paris: Vrin, 1931.
——. *Les deux mémoires de M. de Biran sur l'habitude.* Année philosophique, 1911.
Gouhier, Henri. *Les conversions de Maine de Biran.* Paris, 1947.
——. "Maine de Biran et Bergson," in *Les Études Bergsoniennes,* vol. I. Paris, 1948.
Hallie, Philip. *Maine de Biran, Reformer of Empiricism.* Cambridge, Mass., 1959.
Le Roy, George. *L'expérience de l'effort et de la grace chez Maine de Biran.* Paris, 1934.
Paliard, Jacques. *Le raisonnement selon Maine de Biran.* Paris, 1925.

72

Robef, Euthyme. *Leibniz et Maine de Biran*. Paris, 1927.

Rostan, E. *La religion de Maine de Biran*. 1890.

Sainte-Beuve. (Biography of M. de Biran) in *Causeries du lundi*, vol. 8. Paris.

Tisserand, P. *Essai sur l'anthropologie de M. de Biran*. Paris, 1909.

de la Valette-Monbrun, A. *Maine de Biran, Essai de biographie*. Paris, 1914.

——. *Maine de Biran, critique et disciple de Pascal*. Paris, 1914.

VI

Texts

Ampère, A. M. *Théorie mathématique des phénomènes électrodynamique uniquement déduite de l'expérience*. Paris, 1827.

——. *Essai sur la philosophie des sciences*, 2 vols. Paris, 1834–43.

——. *La philosophie des deux Ampère*, ed. J. Barthélemy-Saint-Hilaire, Paris, 1866, 2d ed., 1870.

Studies

Broglie, Louis de. *Continu et discontinu en physique moderne*. Paris, 1941.

Cantor, Georg. "Über verschiedene Theoreme aus der Theorie der Punktmengen." *Acta Mathematica*, vol. 7, 1885, pp. 105–24.

Lorenta, Borislav. *Die Philosophie André-Marie Ampère*. Berlin, 1908.

ECLECTIC SPIRITUALISM
IN FRANCE

AFTER THE Restoration there developed in France—
as a reaction against ideology and under the combined influence of
Maine de Biran, the Scottish school, and the German philosophers—
a spiritualistic metaphysics, which used introspection as a point of
departure in the search for the universal spiritual realities, God and
the soul. Its precursors were Laromiguière and Royer-Collard.

1 Pierre Laromiguière

Pierre Laromiguière (1756–1837) is known principally for his
Lessons in Philosophy (1815–18), which reproduced a course of
lectures at the Faculty of Letters in Paris. For his inaugural address,
delivered on April 26, 1811, he wrote: "Among the great number
of ideas which make up the subject matter of the metaphysical and
moral sciences, there are a few that seem to belong to unknown
faculties and to conceal themselves in the depths of our being.
Food for bold minds, for ardent imaginations, and for insatiable
curiosity, they have always refused and will forever refuse to yield
to any philosophy that does not know how to observe them at their
source and at the moment of their birth" (3d edition, I, 36).
Philosophy is here defined by an analytical method which explains
all ideas in terms of established, familiar faculties and their interplay,
thus depriving certain ideas—such as the ideas of virtue, God, and

beauty—of their mystery, which, before analysis, seems to come from unknown faculties. In this it represents a protest of the ideologists against an encroaching Romanticism.

But the method of analysis embraces two possibilities: one may describe—that is, separate, by juxtaposing them, traits which are heterogeneous among themselves even though they belong to the same thing; or one may reason—that is, state a series of identical propositions in each of which the same idea, by virtue of the different expressions it assumes, can be followed to its source and in its developments. Condillac's master thesis is easily identifiable in this second definition.

Laromiguière may have borrowed his philosophical method from Condillac, whom he credits with its discovery, but he nevertheless modified it profoundly, taking as his starting point, in addition to the passive faculty of sensation, the active faculty of attention. From attention he moved on to comparison, which discloses every possible relation between things and serves as the starting point of judgment and reason. This renewed emphasis on the free activity of the soul, original and irreducible, may have left Condillac's genetic method intact, but it introduced into the doctrine a completely new tendency, which conforms to Biranism.

Laromiguière, whose only course of lectures—the one offered in 1811—was published in 1815, exerted but a short-lived influence. Paradoxically, it was not revived until the Restoration, when one of the most reactionary ministers of the regime, Frayssinous, suspended Cousin's lectures, closed the École Normale (1822), and summoned Laromiguière and his pupil Thurot. Frayssinous feared the ideologists, enemies of Kant and of the Scottish school, less than he feared the new spiritualists. But Laromiguière's influence subsided once again with the fall of Frayssinous, at the end of 1827.

11 Paul Royer-Collard

Paul Royer-Collard (1763–1845) was professor at the Sorbonne from 1811 to 1814. His spiritualism had been given the stamp of an

official philosophy by a judge who can hardly be challenged—
Napoleon, who, after the first lecture of the course in which
Royer-Collard took issue with Condillac (December 4, 1811), remarked to Talleyrand: "I tell you, Grand Chamberlain, that a
very serious new doctrine is being developed in my university—one
which may bring us great honor and rid us completely of the
ideologists by using reason to kill them on the spot." [1] This doctrine,
expounded for two years and a half at the Faculty of Letters and
known through publication of the inaugural lectures of 1813 as well
as through the *Fragments* published by Jouffroy in 1828, censures
"the philosophy of sensation" by enumerating those of its consequences which are contrary to the common beliefs of men, then
focusing attention, under the name of "philosophy of perception,"
on the obviousness of these beliefs; the parallelism, in which each
error is contrasted with each truth, is perfect. The essence of the
philosophy of sensation is "idealism," which uses the fleeting impressions made on us by objects to construct any reality. It follows
that the self is a collection of sensations, without substance or
identity across time; nature is a collection of sensible qualities, a
series of images which are linked by no substance and contain no
active force; God is a collection of effects without substance. Consequently idealism, which Descartes initiated when he used the
Cogito to shut himself up in his own ego, leads to skepticism and
nihilism, and to egotism in ethics, since other persons, like other
objects in the universe, are only our impressions. The philosophy of
perception begins with evident realities because they are given to
consciousness immediately, and it refuses to formulate any hypothesis concerning their genesis: first, the self exists and knows
immediately that it exists as substance (Descartes was wrong
in thinking that substance must be inferred from existence) and
as thinking substance (Fichte was wrong in positing the self before
consciousness); next, the self is permanent and knows its identity
through the memory, for "we remember only ourselves"; finally,
it knows itself as a cause in voluntary acts and in attention. These

[1] As quoted by Alfaric, *Laromiguière et son école*, 1929.

three characteristics—substantiality, permanence, and causality—are found again in the external world, where we apprehend them not by an immediate intuition but by a kind of induction, badly defined moreover, since ordinary induction leads only to the probable. The induction of Royer-Collard leads us irresistibly to attribute the characteristics of the self to the outer world: solidity causes us to infer a substantial existence; then comes belief in a permanent existence, independent of ourselves, in an unbounded space and time; finally, by consciously suppressing the voluntary, reflective elements in our own causality, we imagine that we see productive causes in space and time. It is the first characteristic—the causality of material beings—that leads us to God, for these partial, separate causes can be harmonized only by a unique cause, an omnipotent will, which is the will of God. Thus philosophy restores the common realities: self, nature, God. In all the great philosophers, from Plato to Condillac, we find only errors, for they substituted their hypotheses for observation of facts.

Royer-Collard's doctrine manifests a profound tendency of the period, but it manifests this tendency in a summary and superficial way. Repelled by the problems of genesis, which, when subject to analysis, make all reality vanish, philosophers tried to demonstrate what was artificial and what was human, using an analysis that began by destroying the originality of its object, which, subsequently, it was forever incapable of rediscovering. Royer-Collard heaps criticism on these doctrines, calling them "psychogony," which he contrasts with his psychology, as a Newtonian might contrast the hypothetical cosmogony of Descartes with the new cosmology. Are these analyzable realities apprehended by immediate intuition or by natural belief? On this essential point, which was an important theme in French philosophy after 1850, Royer-Collard remains vague. We must not forget, moreover, that he was born in 1763 and was forty-eight years old when named to a professorship which lasted only two years and a half; he was a statesman before he was a philosopher. A member of the Commune of Paris in 1792 and a member of the Council of the Five Hundred in

1797, he was an informer for Louis XVIII from 1797 to 1803, for at the time he favored a monarchy which used fundamental laws to limit its own power. Thus in 1816, after the interlude of his teaching at the Sorbonne, he became one of the stanchest defenders of the *Charte* in the Chamber of Deputies and the moving spirit of the "Doctrinaires," who considered the political system of France to be the product of reason itself.

From its birth, then, spiritualism resembled a very limited kind of liberalism and was dependent on the success of liberalism. Thus the influence of spiritualism diminished during the period of frenzied reaction (1821–28) which witnessed the suspension of Cousin's lectures and the suppression of the École Normale; it revived in 1828, after the fall of Frayssinous, when Royer-Collard presented to Charles X the address of the 221; and under Louis-Philippe it became the doctrine of the University. It was always opposed not only by the clergy, who favored absolutist doctrines, but also by liberal democrats, many of them originally ideologists, who were not satisfied with the liberties accepted by Royer-Collard, with his restricted suffrage and his hereditary peerage. This constant collusion for political reasons caused Edgar Quinet to say: "When I hear a spiritualist, reality disappears and makes room for banality."[2]

III *Théodore Jouffroy*

Théodore Jouffroy (1796–1842) taught at the École Normale and the Sorbonne, and then served, beginning in 1833, as a member of the Chamber of Deputies. Several of his philosophical themes, which he does not even seem to have had the will to unite, remain isolated. The entirely lyrical and personal theme of destiny, which troubled him throughout his lifetime, is hardly related to the subject discussed in his lectures—the independence and scientific character of psychology, natural law, aesthetics. But his manner of disseminating his ideas reflects a basic trait of his character: hesitation and aristocratic disdain for ponderous, doctrinal affirmations.

[2] *L'Esprit nouveau*, 1875, p. 340.

"Vulgar minds, for whom there is no preface," he wrote, "can enter without hesitation, for to them everything is a beginning; that is their privilege." This man, who was tormented by the problem of destiny, was far from rigorous in spiritual matters. He arrived at the conviction that the problem of destiny is a personal one, which each must resolve by his own effort and for himself, and he discovered in the peasants of his village the multifarious solutions offered by philosophies. "Some of them are spiritualists," he told Doudan, "others true mystics, others stoics, some tending toward utter disbelief, all confusedly and in keeping with the natural inclination of their character."[3] In purely philosophical matters, on the other hand, he had firm opinions, but never went beyond prolegomena and never reached precise, concrete doctrines.

In 1822 Jouffroy wrote his famous article on "How Dogmas End," which was published in 1825 in the *Globe,* the liberal journal of the Restoration. In it he explained how philosophy, in a still distant future, was to replace the Christian religion, which was near extinction. Jouffroy himself seems to have been deeply aware of this situation. In 1832, in the second part of his essay *On the Organization of the Philosophical Sciences,* he relates the moral crisis during which, nineteen years earlier on a night in December, 1813, he discovered that he had lost his faith. Such accounts were not rare at a time when the *enfant du siécle* was cultivating his anxiety, and this student, then seventeen, was probably influenced by the Romantic epidemic. He is nevertheless sure that the feeling of emptiness which he experienced at that time dominates his intellectual life. In his lectures on *The Problem of Human Destiny,* with which he opened his course in December of 1830, he is obviously seeking to fill the void left by faith when he defends the principle of finality. To say that no being in nature was created in vain is to say that each being has a destiny, a vocation, a mission; but the principle, interpreted in this way, raises a question instead of providing us with an answer. No one can ignore his destiny, no

[3] Letter of March 5, 1842, as quoted by Charles Adam, *La philosophie en France,* 1894, p. 252.

one can refrain from asking himself what it is, no one can doubt that it will be realized, whatever it may be; consequently, if destiny is not realized in this life, one is forced to believe in a future life. On the other hand, no one can know what this destiny is; the Christian solution is insufficient, and philosophy is not about to be substituted for religion. According to Jouffroy, this ignorance, once it has been demonstrated, brings calm and a kind of negative certainty; there is no longer any reason for being disturbed about problems which are surely insoluble. Still, in the absence of absolute truth, which will perhaps be revealed to us one day, Jouffroy recognizes relative human truths—different religions or metaphysical systems, which correspond to the state of progress of mankind. At this point he is remote from Royer-Collard, who refuses to recognize the role of skepticism, and from Cousin with his "impersonal reason." He is on the path leading to Renan on one hand and to William James on the other. Man creates his own reasons for living. Practical problems, according to Jouffroy, revolve around the insoluble problem of destiny; the question of natural law, for example, which subsumes the question of political law and the question of international law, can be resolved only if man's nature—that is, his destiny—is known; consequently the law of an era ought to vary with its beliefs. In this way he introduced, somewhat timidly and imprecisely, to be sure, the kind of individualistic relativism which later flowered in Renan and Barrès, and which differs sharply from Comte's social and historical relativism.

Jouffroy's speculations on psychology are not closely related to these preoccupations. He does not claim, like Cousin, that an ontology can be found through psychology, but he defends a psychology which is independent of both physiology and metaphysics, and which has the same method and certainly as the physical sciences. Thus in the Preface to his translation of Dugald Stewart's *Outlines of Moral Philosophy* (1826), he insists that one should study psychology as a scientist and an observer, and not worry about difficulties of method or ulterior questions of metaphysics concerning the nature of the soul. This assimilation of psychology and the physical sciences does not prevent him from stating, in his article on "The Legitimacy of the Distinction between Psychology and Physiology" (1838), that, unlike physical facts, the cause of which—gravitation, affinity, and the like—is not given with the facts observed, the facts provided by inner observation are accompanied by their cause, which is the self; but nothing indicates that the self is a substantial metaphysical reality. Jouffroy seems to remain faithful on this point to Cousin's teaching which denied any direct intuition of a substantial reality.

In certain respects, however, his *Course in Natural Law* (1834–35) shows the union of these two preoccupations. The basis of natural law (third lecture) is a moral psychology of man, and it treats the faculties in the order of their appearance. Man's conduct is governed by primitive tendencies, which make demands on the faculties of sensation, intelligence, and will; consequently the child's conduct is unstable and variable, depending on the interplay of these tendencies. But at this stage freedom appears, which is above all a power of concentration—not so much a new force as a disposition to unite our scattered forces against whatever resists us. This freedom is at first irrational; with the awakening of reason, which provides it with motives, it ceases to be impulsive and becomes reflective. But reason itself has two stages: a lower stage, when it is governed by tendencies and offers self-interest as a motive for conduct; and a higher stage, when it attains to the idea of law, which is outside and above the person, an order which is the expression of divine thought. Moral psychology depends entirely, therefore, on the existence of one faculty—reason—which, in its higher form, can cope with the problem of destiny.

Jouffroy's *Course in Aesthetics* (1843) is also crowned by this same idea of order. Jouffroy pointedly disagrees with Cousin, who defined beauty in terms of unity and variety, and notes that no reality fails to present these two characteristics. To define the idea of beauty, he proposes a method quite different from the comparative method, which consists in bringing several beautiful objects together and determining their common quality. Here again, we must attack the question through consciousness and determine first which phenomena beauty produces in us. Although Jouffroy's expression is at times obscure, no doubt because this book consists merely of notes taken during his lectures by a member of the audience, we can discover in his definition of beauty and attempt to pass from our inner states to a certain external order revealing a true reality. "If the state in which we find ourselves is accompanied by a judgment that this state conforms to an order in an external being, the feeling we experience is the feeling of beauty, and the external object is called beautiful." Yet this order is defined no more precisely than the moral order was defined earlier; here again, we are in the mysterious region which touches human destiny.

IV *Victor Cousin*

Victor Cousin (1792–1867) was the founder of spiritualistic eclecticism, which, after a brief eclipse of its influence during the Restoration, served throughout the July Monarchy as the official doctrine of the University, which then was monopolizing instruction. Professor of philosophy at the École Normale after 1814 and then, under Louis-Philippe, peer of France, councilor of state, director of the École Normale, rector of the University, and finally minister of public instruction, Cousin had every possible means of imposing his doctrine. The doctrine of spiritualistic eclecticism was formulated under the influence of Royer-Collard and the Scottish school as well as that of Hegel and Schelling, whom Cousin had occasion to meet during his three visits to Germany, in 1817, 1818, and 1824. What are the essentials of this doctrine?

Cousin claims that his doctrine provides a "scientific statement of the pure belief of mankind, nothing less than this belief nor more than this belief; this belief alone, in its entirety. Its singular character is to base ontology on psychology and to pass from one to the other with the help of a psychological and ontological faculty, at once subjective and objective, which appears in us without belonging exclusively to us, enlightens the herdsman as well as the philosopher, is withheld from no one, and is sufficient for everyone—reason, which extends from the depths of consciousness to infinity and reaches the very being of beings." [4] With its blending of form and content, this sentence, like countless others, is a good illustration of a philosophical style which has long been influential in France. Cousin is an orator rather than a philosopher, and his thought is the natural fruit of the purely formal and humanistic education, almost totally alien to scientific training, provided in the imperial lycées. He himself relates the origin of his vocation. "It has remained and will always remain in my memory, with a feeling of gratitude," he wrote, "that day in 1810, when for the first time, as a student of the École Normale preparing to teach literature, I heard M. Laromiguière. That day determined my whole life; it diverted me from my first studies . . ." (*Fragments,* p. 70). Oratorical themes nevertheless continued to play an important part in his thought, and many of its developments sprang from the desire to outwit or convince an adversary. "The mania for prefaces," which A. Marrast detected in Cousin's school as early as 1828, [5] is characteristic of the need he constantly felt for making his meaning clear to others.

The doctrine of spiritualistic eclecticism finds its clearest expression in the three successive prefaces of *Fragments of Contemporary Philosophy* (1826, 1833, 1838). It has the same basis and the same general traits as the political doctrine of the Restoration and the July Monarchy in France. Under the name of eclecticism it proposes a reconciliation of all systems and the retention of their valuable elements; eclecticism is like a representative government which reconciles all the diverse elements in society. The comparison is from Cousin himself. "Just as the human soul, in its natural development, includes several elements of which true philosophy is the harmonious expression, any civilized society has several wholly distinct elements, which the government should recognize and represent. . . . The July revolution is no different from the English revolution of 1688,

[4] *Fragments de philosophie moderne,* Preface to the 2d edition (1833), edition of 1855, p. 63.
[5] *Examen critique du cours de M. Cousin* (Paris, Corréard, 1828), p. 187 (Preface by Jouffroy to the works of Reid, and Preface by Cousin to the works of Proclus).

but in France, which has much less aristocracy and a little more democracy and monarchy . . . these three elements are necessary. . . . The man who fought against any exclusive principle in science had also to reject any exclusive principle in the state" (*Ibid.*, p. 93). The ambiguity of this position, in philosophy as in politics, is obvious. For either eclecticism possesses from the outset a principle capable of enabling us to choose between the different existing doctrines—and such a principle is itself a doctrine that exists in its entirety before any attempt has been made to use it to judge other doctrines—or there is no such principle, and we can effect a reconciliation only by identifying, in all systems, the elements that can be fitted together without contradiction. Despite his precise formulations, Cousin always hesitated between the two views. When criticized by others, such as Marrast, for collecting ideas without reflecting on them and reaching definite conclusions, and when eclecticism was compared to syncretism,[6] Cousin chose the first view and championed independent philosophical analysis, which subsequently justifies its historical judgments. "We must be able to separate truths from the errors that surround them, . . . and we can do this only if we have a standard of appreciation, a principle of criticism, only if we know what is true and what is false in ourselves; and we can know this only if we have made an adequate study of philosophical problems, human nature, its faculties and their laws. . . . Only then does historical analysis have its turn" (*Ibid.*, p. 228). Furthermore, "eclecticism," far from being the absence of a system, "is the application of a system; it assumes a system, starts from a system. . . . There must be a system to judge all systems" (*Ibid.*, p. 91). But he does not go far in this direction. He is too certain that every possible philosophical system has been constructed and that we can only renounce philosophy completely, "thresh around in the circle of worn-out systems, which are destroying each other," or "identify the true elements in each of these systems and use them to construct a philosophy superior to all systems—one which governs all systems by dominating them all." The difficulty of taking a

[6] *Ibid.*, p. 338

stand, passed off as impartiality, leads him into a vicious circle, which he describes explicitly. "I shall try to carry out the reform of philosophical studies in France," he writes, "as I illuminate the history of philosophy by a system and demonstrate this system by the whole history of philosophy" (*Ibid.*, p. 42).

Nevertheless, in the development of his own thought he certainly searched for a system, in 1817 and 1818, before using the eclectic method in the history of philosophy, in 1819 and 1820.

This system contains two themes which Cousin tried, not without artifice, to connect securely: first, the necessity of employing in philosophy the method of observation and experiment—the very spirit of the century, to which no one could be unfaithful—which assured the success of physics; next, the necessity of discovering, by this method, the common-sense beliefs which exist in every man before any reflection, and which philosophy is committed to rediscover by reason—the reality of the person, nature, and God. But between this method and this necessity Cousin sees a contradiction. The method of observation, used by Locke and Condillac in philosophy, leads only to sensualism and thence to materialism. It has yielded only a "poor philosophy," with which it seems to have been closely associated. That is why German philosophy, relinquishing this method, has tried to rediscover common-sense beliefs by a kind of direct intuition of the absolute; but by constructing the universe on the basis of this absolute, it can enunciate only completely arbitrary hypotheses. To find a method of observation that will lead, by way of irreproachable inductions, to metaphysical affirmations, which thus assume a character as "scientific" as physical laws—such is Cousin's aim.

The method of observation which meets his requirements is psychology, as it is understood by Cousin. Observation, until now, has brought ruinous consequences because it is incomplete and fails to probe deeply enough. Bacon, the father of the experimental method, made the initial mistake of limiting it to physical things, and he was followed by Condillac, who limited the whole content of mind to sensation, to the passive impressions of things on us.

Laromiguière corrected Condillac by calling attention to the existence of irreducible active phenomena such as attention, and Maine de Biran in particular brought to light the inner activity to which consciousness of the self is linked. Thus they developed the idea of two faculties, the passive faculty of sensation and the active faculty of will; but each one of them made the mistake of confusing the active faculty with reason or the faculty of principles. This confusion is exemplified in Maine de Biran's unsuccessful attempt to deduce from apperception as cause the universal principle of causality. Universal, necessary principles of this kind are the object of a third faculty, reason, which goes beyond the contingent data of sensation and identifies objects independent of the active self. Such considerations bring Cousin to his famous theory of the three faculties—sensibility, will, intelligence. According to him, the theory is the result of self-observation, which provides a basis for classifying these faculties but—contrary to what others had thought—does not account for their genesis. To him the necessity and universality of principles are facts, like sense impressions. Moreover, Cousin does not hesitate to have recourse to a kind of dialectical argument to prove the triplicity of the faculties, a so-called datum of observation. This triplicity is, he says, the condition of consciousness, inasmuch as the self perceives itself only by distinguishing itself from sensation, and perceives only by the intervention of reason, which alone is capable of truth.

In any case, the principal attainment of this psychological analysis was the discovery of reason as the immediate datum of consciousness, for this discovery brought about passage from psychology to ontology, which was supposed to provide metaphysics with its certainty. Indeed, the application of rational principles, which are facts of consciousness, to the other facts of consciousness leads to affirmations concerning beings outside consciousness. Thanks to reason—the bridge between consciousness and being—the limitation of our point of departure to inner data, which are the only accessible data, does not confine us to subjective idealism. These principles are reduced to two, causality and substance; they yield the substance self when applied to the inner phenomena of will, and external substance or nature when applied to the phenomena of sensation; finally, since they do not have their reason in themselves, these substances refer us to an absolute substance, which is God. This is Cousin's whole system of metaphysics.

In Cousin's doctrine, therefore, real beings are attained only by a rational induction which begins with the facts of consciousness, the only ones given. The possibility of any such induction has been attacked from all sides, for it is based on reason, itself a fact of consciousness, purely subjective and personal, and cannot be used to transcend consciousness. The objection took two forms. The Kantian school (as interpreted by Cousin, who makes Kant a psychologist) inferred the subjectivity of principles from their necessity; the irresistibility of the belief that we have in them indicates a bond of dependence and relativity with respect to the self. Lamennais and the theological school, on the other hand, contrasted reason with tradition and common sense, and regarded it as a purely individual activity, incapable of arriving at truth by itself. Cousin answers both schools by resorting to a theory of an "impersonal" reason, which is not altogether clear. He rejects completely the Germanic idea of an intellectual intuition which grasps the absolute directly, particularly since such a faculty would make his famous psychological method worthless. Still, if reason is to play its assigned role, its principles must be perceived as having an absolute value, independent of their relation to the self; consequently, in one way or another it must be assumed to have a direct contact with reality. This is what he indicates in the somewhat mysterious words: "In the inner recesses of consciousness and at a stage to which Kant had not penetrated, under the relativity and apparent subjectivity of necessary principles, by observation I discovered and untangled the instantaneous but real fact of apperception of truth, apperception which does not reflect upon itself and therefore passes unnoticed in the depths of consciousness, where it is the basis of what later, under a logical form and in the hands of reflection, becomes a necessary conception. All subjectivity and all reflectivity expire in the spontaneity of apperception." [7] It would be possible, then, under exceptional conditions (Cousin's description of them recalls the style of Maine de Biran, along with totally different aims), for us to apprehend immediately realities which would not be facts of consciousness; at this price we do indeed have an impersonal reason, but then we no longer have need of a psychological scaffolding, and ontology can begin directly.

The radical incoherence of Cousin's system brings us to a trait which Marrast rightly considers essential and which connects his system with all the Romanticism of his era. This is the distinction he draws everywhere between spontaneity and reflection or, in popular terms, between religion and philosophy, and his assertion that reflection, empty and sterile by itself, has no role but that of expressing in clear consciousness what spontaneity first grasped. This distinction reappears in the three faculties; unclear in sensations, it is quite obvious in the active faculty, where spontaneous freedom—that of "immediate inspiration, superior to reflection and often better than reflection"—necessarily precedes freedom accompanied by reflection, which we call will; irreflective and therefore less clear than will, "spontaneity is obscure, and this obscurity which surrounds everything is primitive and instantaneous." We have just seen one form of this distinction in reason, and it points to the conclusion that, before any reflection, truth has already been attained; "philosophy is not to be sought after, it is already formed."

This brings us back to the second stipulation of Cousin's system of philosophy, the necessity of rediscovering the beliefs of mankind. "In my view," he writes, probably under Herder's inspiration, "the mass of humanity is spontaneous and not reflective; humanity is inspired. The divine breath which is in it reveals to it, always and everywhere, all truths in one form or another. . . . The soul of humanity is a poetic soul, which discovers in itself the secrets of beings and expresses them in prophetic songs that reverberate from age to age. Alongside humanity is philosophy, which listens attentively, taking down its words; . . . and when the moment of

[7] *Fragments de philosophie moderne,* p. 20.

reflection has passed, it presents them respectfully to the admirable artist who was not aware of his genius and who often does not recognize his own work." This last remark is an allusion to one of the great difficulties involved in this style of philosophy. For in these conditions we see the full significance of the criticism directed against the new spiritualism—the charge that it did not respect popular beliefs, of which the most perfect expression was generally acknowledged to be the Christian religion. The accusation of pantheism and fatalism, brought up repeatedly against Cousin and his school, generated loud polemics. We should note in passing that they were exacerbated by the respective positions of the clergy and the University under Louis Philippe. To combat the monopoly of instruction attributed to the University, the clergy adopted the stratagem of censuring the irreligious character of its philosophy— an obvious move in view of Cousin's pretensions. Leaving aside the details of these polemics, even though a comprehensive history of them would be of great interest, we shall restrict ourselves to the main point of the argument, which is similar in many respects to the argument that had pitted Jacobi against the rationalists in Germany. According to Jacobi, any form of rationalism leads to pantheism; should not the same be true of Cousin's rationalism with its procedure of investigation? Cousin often contrasts the "abstract God of Scholasticism"—incomprehensible, unknowable, "absolute unity, as superior and anterior to the world as it is alien to the world"—with the God of consciousness, universally present in nature and humanity. We have just seen that in his view God is reached only by induction; but from induction properly so called, which links God to the world as a cause to its effect, Cousin shifts effortlessly to the idea of a symbolic relation in which God is to the world as a model to its image: "Incomprehensible as an abstraction in Scholasticism, God is clear in the world which manifests him and for the soul which possesses him and feels his presence. Universally present, he somehow returns to himself in the consciousness of man, who expresses his most sublime attributes, as the finite expresses the infinite." Cousin's adversaries were not wrong in seeing the influence of Germanic thought in statements of this kind. Cousin freely acknowledges this influence, especially when he makes God the union of contraries—true and real, one and many, eternity and time, infinite and finite all in one. He adds that "there is no more a God without a world than a world without a God" and that the principle of creation is necessary. Certainly the two themes the theme that makes God the creative cause to which one proceeds by induction beginning with the world, following the old proof *a contingentia mundi,* and the theme that makes the world and man episodes of the divine life—are not closely related. The only issue then raised was doubtlessly the purely verbal and somewhat trifling matter of determining whether the second of these themes merited the name pantheism. Cousin takes the negative side, defining pantheism as the "divinization of the Whole and the Universe-God of Saint-Simon," which does not seem to draw a clear distinction between it and his own doctrine.

But the worst part is that this theme introduces into his doctrine an incoherence analogous to the one noted earlier, for along with the concepts of finite and infinite, it contains a dialectic independent of any psychological introduction. Even when Cousin resorts to a dialectical ruse in an attempt to show that the elementary fact of consciousness implies, along with the affirmation of the self, that of the world and God, and consequently that "atheism is an empty formulation," he offers us nothing akin to introspection. Daunou was right, therefore, in observing that analysis is by no means the whole of Cousin's method; on the contrary, Cousin— who makes the ideas apprehended by intelligence as it probes its inner recesses the model of reality, putting the true above the real in the belief that inspiration will illuminate archetypal ideas— practices the very synthesis that he seems in his statements to condemn.[8] He is brought inevitably to this point by the theory of impersonal reason, which places us outside the field of the self. "Reason has no part in our mistakes," Saphary noted, "since it is not ours. . . . On one hand you discredit thought, on the other you deify

[8] In a lecture delivered in 1830, *Cours d'études,* 1849, XX, 399, 410.

it. . . . Such a method, such a language is an exhaust pump applied to philosophy; through it one achieves the most perfect void."[9] German dialectics is added in such an artificial way to the principle of eclecticism that Saphary suspects this doctrine of being "a cloak under which the first attempt was made to import German philosophy."

It is obvious that Cousin fell far short of founding ontology on psychology even though this inconsistent doctrine was supposed to help him to identify valid elements in any system (for any system is partially true), and to use them to reconstruct an integral philosophy. It is not clear that he ever succeeded in identifying such elements, for he imitated his German models and saw systems as necessary products of the human mind, connected in accordance with a law. Enslaved by the senses, the mind first adopts sensualism, which leads it to materialism; then its defiance of the senses leads it to idealism, and its doubts concerning reality lead it to skepticism; but its need for certainty, which can be satisfied only by reason, leads it to mysticism. The four phases of the cycle are repeated endlessly. It is very difficult for us to detect any progress toward a stable state in this circular movement and especially, in the successive phases, which are mutually exclusive, any characteristics which can be used to construct a whole.

Victor Cousin was by inclination a pacifier and an arbitrator. As the statesman of philosophy he tried, in the words of Sainte-Beuve, to found a great school of philosophy "which would not give offense to religion but exist alongside it, be independent of it, often its subsidiary in appearance but still more protective and at times domineering, perhaps expecting to become its heir."[10] It was this political design that motivated all the polemics surrounding the development of his system and, doubtless, all the vigorous attacks which often changed its direction.

[9] *L'école éclectique et l'école française,* 1844, pp. 10, 15.
[10] *Causeries du Lundi,* 3d edition, VI, 151.

BIBLIOGRAPHY

I

Texts

Laromiguière, Pierre. *Projet d'éléments de métaphysique.* Toulouse, 1793.
———. *Sur les paradoxes de Condillac.* Paris, 1805.
———. *Leçons de philosophie sur les principes de l'intelligence.* Paris, 1815–18.

Studies

Boas, George. *French Philosophies of the Romantic Period.* Baltimore, 1925. Pp. 33–42.
Janet, Paul. "Laromiguière, la liberté de penser." *Revue philosophique et littéraire,* vol. 1, 1848, pp. 253–63, 358–68.
Picavet, François. *Les Idéologues.* Paris, 1891. Pp. 520–48, 552–67. Second section referred to deals with Laromiguière's influence.
Taine, Hippolyte. *Les Philosophes classiques du XIXe siècle en France.* Paris, 1868. See chap. 1.

II

Texts

Royer-Collard, Paul. *Les Fragments philosophiques de Royer-Collard,* ed. André Schimberg. Paris, 1913.
———. *Discours prononcé à l'ouverture du cours de l'histoire de la philosophie.* Paris, 1813.

Studies

Boas, George. *French Philosophies of the Romantic Period.* Baltimore, 1925. Pp. 157–64.
Garnier, Adolphe. "Royer-Collard," in *Dictionnaire des sciences philosophiques,* ed. Adolphe Franck. Paris, 1875.
Spuller, Eugène. *Royer-Collard.* Paris, 1895.
Taine, Hippolyte. *Les Philosophes classiques de XIXe siècle en France.* Paris, 1857.

III

Texts

Jouffroy, Théodore. *Mélanges philosophiques*. Paris, 1833.
———. *Cours de droit naturel*. 1st ed., 2 vols., Paris, 1834–42; 2d ed., with additional notes by Philibert Damiron, ed., 3 vols., Paris, 1843.
———. *Nouveaux Mélanges philosophiques*. Paris, 1842.
———. *Cours d'esthétique*. Paris, 1843.

Studies

Boas, George. *French Philosophies of the Romantic Period*. Baltimore, 1925. Pp. 239–50.
Mignet, F. A. "Notes sur Jouffroy." *Mémoires de l'Académie des Sciences Morales et Politiques,* vol. 25, 1853, p. 197.
Ollé-Laprune, Léon. *Théodore Jouffroy*. Paris, 1899.
Pommier, J. *Deux études sur Jouffroy et son temps.* 1930.
Taine, Hippolyte. *Les Philosophes classiques du XIXe siècle en France*. Paris, 1868.

IV

Texts

Cousin, Victor. *Cours de l'histoire de la philosophie moderne de 1815 à 1820,* 5 vols.
———. *de 1828 à 1830,* 3 vols.
———. *Fragments philosophiques,* 4 vols. 4th ed. Paris, 1847.
———. *Fragments de philosophie cartésienne*. Paris, 1852.
———. *Du Vrai, du Beau, du Bien*. Paris, 1837.
———. *Études sur Pascal*. Paris, 1842.

Studies

Barthélemy-Saint-Hilaire. *V. Cousin, sa vie sa correspondance,* 3 vols. 1885.
Bersot, E. *V. Cousin et la philosophie de notre temps.* 1880.
Damiron, Ph. *Souvenirs de vingt ans d'enseignement.* 1859.
Doudan, X. *Lettres,* 4 vols. 1879.
Janet, Paul. *Cousin et son œuvre.* 1885.

Lévy-Bruhl, Lucien. *History of Modern Philosophy in France,* trans. G. Co-
     blence. Chicago and London, 1924. Chap. 12.
Simon, J. *V. Cousin,* 1877.
Veitch, John. "Cousin, Victor," in *Encyclopaedia Britannica,* 11th ed. Chicago,
     1910.

THE SCOTTISH SCHOOL AND ENGLISH UTILITARIANISM FROM 1800 TO 1850

UNTIL ABOUT 1830, English philosophy was almost completely untouched by continental illuminism, which was essentially a revival of metaphysics. The common sense of the Scottish philosophers and the rational designs of the utilitarians were far removed from the Romantic fervor which shook the continent. This situation remained unchanged until the time of Coleridge and Carlyle.

1 Dugald Stewart

Dugald Stewart (1753–1828), professor of moral philosophy at the University of Edinburgh, maintained the tradition of Reid at a time when almost all of Britain, under the influence of Bentham, accepted utilitarianism. His *Elements of the Philosophy of the Human Mind* (3 vols., 1792, 1814, 1827), although it announces no new doctrine, contains many engaging and penetrating pages. Generally, he is less receptive than Reid to the appeal to common sense, and he makes principles indispensable conditions of reasoning rather than of different kinds of knowledge. Thus he returns to Locke and with him affirms the sterility of axioms, which are conditions of reasoning or *vincula* but not objects or *data*. Like axioms, belief in the existence and identity of the self, belief in the outer world and the evidence of memory do not provide us with any knowledge, strictly speaking, but are conditions associated with any exercise of reason. He also distrusts a "false intuition," a conclusion believed to be known immediately because the chain of reasoning through which it was established has been forgotten. Dugald Stewart applies this line of reasoning to the doctrine of abstract ideas, siding with Berkeley against Reid. In a geometrical demonstration, for example, there are two steps: a demonstration which applies to the particular figure before us, and a chain of reasoning by which we extend the demonstration to other figures. But we forget the chain of reasoning, which is always the same, as quickly as we complete it, and we think that we apprehend intuitively triangles in general.

II *Thomas Brown*

Thomas Brown, professor at Edinburgh from 1810 to 1820, had the distinction of defending the unique character of psychological analysis against the attacks of men like Reid as well as against the reductive analyses of Hume and Condillac. We can speak of the analysis of a material object, he says in his *Lectures on the Philosophy of the Human Mind* (1820), because matter is composed of parts, but we cannot speak of the analysis of mental phenomena, since each thought, each feeling is as simple and indivisible as the mind itself, being in truth only the mind as it exists at a certain moment and in a certain state.[1] Many elements are involved in a mental fact, but these elements do not explain the whole; we can say that a judgment involves two terms, A and B, but this does not explain the simple act of judgment. As in a chemical synthesis, the properties of the constituent elements cannot be rediscovered in the compound. One of the best illustrations of this thesis is the theory of space perception. This subject had been under study since Berkeley, who had shown that sight provided extension only by association with touch; Erasmus Darwin had objected that touch

---

[1] Cf. E. Halévy, *Radicalisme philosophique,* III, p. 266.

yielded only discontinuous sensations, and he had been one of the first to introduce the muscle sense as the sense of continuity; Brown adopts the thesis but separates the muscle sense proper (linked to muscular contraction), which is the sense of extension, from the sense of pressure. But this discovery of the diverse elements in extension does not explain the simple originality of our intuition of extension.

As an effect of this conception of analysis Reid's intuitionism and Hume's analysis are brought closer together. According to Brown, they both say the same thing. Hume says aloud, "We cannot prove that bodies exist," and he whispers, "We must believe that they do." Reid says aloud, "We must believe that bodies exist," and he whispers, "We cannot prove that they do."

III *William Hamilton*

Sir William Hamilton (1788–1856), professor at Edinburgh University after 1836, was a Scottish philosopher who had read Kant. He brought an end to the insular isolation of Britain and introduced a kind of metaphysical speculation which previously had been almost ignored. His three articles in *The Edinburgh Review*—"The Philosophy of the Unconditioned," "The Philosophy of Perception," and "Logic" (1829–33)—contain the essentials of his teachings. How can a Scottish metaphysicist be a Kantian? How can the theory of immediate knowledge of things be reconciled with the theory of the relativity of phenomena to our modes of knowing?

His theory of the realism of perception depends on the evidence of consciousness, which the philosopher must treat with religious humility. According to Hamilton, consciousness is to the philosopher what the Bible is to the theologian. Moreover, in the simplest act of perception I am conscious of myself as the perceiving subject and of an external reality as the object perceived.[2] Consequently I have immediate knowledge of things. But to him immediate knowledge means something quite different from what it meant to Kant

[2] *Lectures on Metaphysics and Logic* (4 vols., 1858–60), edition of 1865, I, 82.

and the critical philosophers, namely the necessary relativity of the subject to the object and of the object to the subject. Hamilton realistically imagines things outside the body, endowed with first qualities and powers, which cause second qualities in us. It is absurd for me to think that I perceive objects there where I am not—for example, that I perceive the real sun, which is thousands of miles away. What I perceive is what is present to me, that is, the light rays which reach my eye and are in my organism; it is by inference that I know the sun. The existence of the external world is apprehended, generally speaking, by virtue of the resistance it offers to our muscular energy. Thus immediate perception does exist; it is perception, however, of something in contact with an organism, and that is far from Reid's philosophy. But what we say of space should be said of time; an object from the past is imagined as being at a certain distance in time. Memory cannot know the past directly; it knows only the present image, from which it infers the past.

If the philosophy of the unconditioned, on which Hamilton's fame chiefly rests, can be reconciled with his theory of the realism of perception, it is because he twisted Reid's doctrine and changed the signification of Kantianism. Whereas Kantianism deals with the validity of knowledge, Hamilton deals only with its limits, and these two problems can be radically different. Our knowledge can be such that we arrive at only a portion of reality; determining whether this portion has only the validity of a phenomenon is another question. The Hamiltonian theory of relativity answers only the first of these questions. When he states that thinking is conditioning, he seems to mean only that an object does not exist for us unless we have a faculty for perceiving it. Any knowledge, he says, is possible only under the conditions to which our faculties are amenable, and the mind is the universal, concurrent, and principle cause in any act of knowing. What must be subjected to our faculties is not an object, as in Kant, but our knowledge, and the role of the mind is not to constitute the object but to be ready to receive it. The unconditioned is the part of reality which does not reach our faculties. The conditioned is that which alone is conceivable or thinkable; the unconditioned is that which is inconceivable or unthinkable. (*Lectures,* II, 376; II, 526). The distinction made by Kant between understanding and reason proves to be useless; there is no need for a special faculty—Reason—to construct something unconditioned, determined by a pure negative synthesis.

Hamilton's speculations might have led to a simple agnosticism if he had not, somewhat inconsistently, attributed to the word "conditioned" a second sense, relating to objects. An object is conditioned insofar as it is partial and therefore relates to an unconditioned. This relation removes us from the conditions of our knowledge, for either we conceive the totality, of which the known reality is a part, as being infinite, or we conceive it as being finite and absolute. Between this thesis and this antithesis, the Infinite and the Absolute, the mind has gone beyond its limits and has neither the possibility nor the right to decide. I can conceive space as being neither infinite nor finite; my knowledge is between these extremes, which are contradictory to each other and of which (here Hamilton abandons Kant) one or the other must be true.

This weakness of our faculties, this learned ignorance is the end of philosophy, but it is the beginning of theology. Hamilton's primary aim was, perhaps, to show that philosophy does not force us to abandon our religious beliefs.

Hamilton introduced into logic a thesis that seems quite alien to the rest of his doctrine—"quantification of the predicate." In Aristotelian logic the predicate is considered to be a quality that is affirmed or denied of all or part of the class expressed by the subject; the subject alone is quantified. But in the predicate, the word that expresses a quality also expresses the class of objects to which this quality pertains, and should, if given this interpretation, be quantified; for sometimes the whole class of objects expressed by the predicate, sometimes only a part coincides with the subject. For example, once the predicate of each has been quantified, the propositions "All triangles are trilateral" and "All triangles are figures" become "All triangles are all trilateral" and "All triangles are all figures." In this case the copula always signifies ═, which modifies considerably the classification of propositions and logic as a whole. But these consequences, later studied by Morgan and Boole, the inventors of symbolic logic, were not elaborated by Hamilton.

H. L. Mansel (1820–71), an Oxford professor who, toward the end of his life, was appointed dean of St. Paul's Cathedral, enlists Hamiltonian agnosticism in the service of religion in *The Limits of Religious Thought* (1858). The contradictions that engulf human reason when it tries to reach the unconditioned prove, in effect, that a thing can be real without being comprehensible; consequently rationalists are not justified in attempting to refute certain dogmas—for example, the dogma of the union of three persons in God or of divine and human nature in Christ—by arguing that they are incomprehensible. Here Mansel allies himself closely with Spencer.

IV *Jeremy Bentham*

Like Bacon and Locke, English philosophers have sometimes exerted a strong influence, but they have rarely founded schools. A prime exception is Jeremy Bentham (1748–1832), whose doctrine of utilitarianism or philosophical radicalism formed the core of a real party—one that had an important role in English politics from 1824 to 1832. In 1824 he founded the *Westminster Review,* which advocated the necessity of the constitutional reform that was accomplished in 1832, the year of his death. The reform group was led first by Bentham, the son of an attorney and a jurist in his own right, then, after 1808, by James Mill (1773–1836). A Scot, who accompanied Sir John Stuart, a member of Parliament, to London, Mill was also an economist, a pupil of Ricardo, and an employee of the East India Company after 1919. Bentham gained fame initially as the author of a scheme for a model prison or "Panopticon" (*An Introduction to the Principles of Morals and Legislation,* 1789; 2d edition, 1823), which attempted to apply the utilitarian principle directly to legislation and ethics. His ethics of duty, *Deontology,* appeared posthumously in 1834. Most of his books were published through the efforts of his friends; for example, the treatises titled *The Rationale of Punishment* (1830) and *The Rationale of Reward* (1825) were published in English only after they had been retranslated from the French version prepared from the author's manuscripts by his French friend, Étienne Dumont.

The reality of the principle of utility—which later became the principle of the "greatest happiness of the greatest number," adopted as the principle of government—contrasts sharply with the fiction of a primitive social contract, a fiction offered as such in Blackstone's *Commentaries* (1765-69). To prove a fiction, according to Bentham, one must resort to fiction, yet truth by its very nature requires no proof except truth. Hume in the third volume of his *Treatise of Human Nature,* Helvétius in *Essays on the Mind* (II, xxiv) and Beccaria in *Crimes and Punishment* (translated into English in 1767) had already applied the principle of utility to social justice, in keeping with a tradition which might be traced all the way back to Epicureanism. With Bentham it serves mainly to establish a link between a primary fact of human nature—namely, that pleasure and pain alone motivate actions—and precepts of good and evil. He aims to demonstrate by reason that obedience to moral rules will produce the greatest amount of pleasure, or, if this is not the case (for he is a reformer), that these rules must be changed so as to avoid a conflict which makes them utterly useless. His proposition attributes a major role to methodical reason in the pursuit of pleasures in reaching a decision, reason must anticipate the pleasure or pain that will result from obedience or infraction; it must examine every circumstance relating to pleasure—its intensity, duration, certainty, proximity—and consider its fertility (the possibility of its producing other pleasures) as well as its purity (a pure pleasure being one that has the good fortune of not engendering pain); finally, it must consider the scope of this pleasure, that is, the number of persons affected by it. Thus one can decide, after giving careful consideration to every possible pleasure as well as to every possible pain, in favor of the act which will produce the greatest excess of pleasure. By carrying out such an operation, Bentham thinks he can make morals and legislation an exact science like mathematics.

Penal law clearly springs from the same principle, since punishment is useful only to the extent that it enters into the calculation of pleasures and pains affecting the possible offender, offsets the pleasures resulting from his crime, and persuades him to follow the laws which the legislator deems to be useful to the greatest number. The important thing is to use sanctions to reconcile selfish interests and the interests of society, which, without them, would diverge: natural sanctions like the consequences of debauchery, popular or moral sanctions in the form of public opinion, political sanctions in the form of a penal code, religious sanctions.

Democratic radicalism was not connected with utilitarianism in Bentham's mind until 1808, when he became acquainted with James Mill. The "corporate spirit," he wrote then, is by definition hostile to the principle of general utility, and political aristocracy is "a closed corporation."[3] Utility is a principle of reform rather than of conservation, and the "felicific calculus" that he recommends would be completely useless if the interests of all were naturally identical. Consequently legislation, the penal code, must impose an artificial identity, and Bentham thought that this operation could be carried out only by having recourse to universal suffrage, in which all were represented.

v *Malthus and Ricardo*

Rigid application of the principle of calculation, which establishes the authority of the law by force, contrasts with the idealism of the rights of man, then represented in England by Paine. Yet William Godwin (*Political Justice,* 1793) used the principle of general utility to support the view that any law or government is evil; for the stability of laws contrasts with the continuous variation of utility and, consequently, with perfectibility; and Godwin criticizes not

[3] As quoted by Élie Halévy, *Le radicalisme philosophique,* III, 211.

only the institution of government but also that of property, which survives only by virtue of an artificial institution, inheritance. Godwin believes in the natural identity of interests, which is broken by institutions, and in the indefinite perfectibility of human reason.[4]

We have seen that Bentham denied any natural identity of interests and showed that one must have recourse to expedients and impose an artificial identity. Thomas Robert Malthus (*An Essay on the Principle of Population,* 1798; 2d edition, 1803), the economist, shows that an ineluctable natural law prevents happiness from increasing indefinitely. The famous law of population states, first, that when no obstacle checks increase, population doubles every twenty-five years and increases in geometric ratio from one period to the next; and, second, that for the same periods the means of subsistence can increase only in arithmetic ratio. Population is prevented from increasing beyond the limits of the means of subsistence by positive checks—mainly vice, misery, famine, war, and emigration. These checks do not prevent population from increasing as the means of subsistence increase, with the result that poverty becomes a necessity; the "law of the poor" tends to increase population without increasing the means of subsistence.

This "melancholic" doctrine had the same orientation, politically, as Bentham's democratic doctrine. Malthus used it as an argument against communism, which seeks to check misery by distributing land, only to bring about overpopulation and even greater universal misery, and against revolution, through which the people blame the government for their own misery (this was written after the revolts which followed the famines of 1800 and 1801), only to bring about repression and despotism.

The economist David Ricardo (*Principles of Political Economy and Taxation,* 1817), a friend of James Mill, also discovered an economic law which contradicts any so-called identity of interests: the landlord's rent increases as population growth forces people to have recourse to his land for their food. At the time when Fourier and Saint-Simon in France thought they had found a means to

[4] Élie Halévy, *Évolution de la doctrine utilitaire,* pp. 70–93.

overcome misery, Ricardo said that misery led inevitably to the ineluctable principle which became Marx's point of departure: wages tend spontaneously to fall to the lowest level at which life remains possible, and the profits of employers tend to be concentrated in fewer and fewer hands. Of course these laws are strictly true only if man's sole incentive is an economic one—the need to enrich himself. Only "economic man" is put in action on Ricardo's chessboard.

VI *James Mill*

James Mill, a follower of Ricardo in political economy, developed the philosophical theory of associationism, which he borrowed from Erasmus Darwin (*Zoonomia,* 1794) and from Hartley, and which he expounded in his *Analysis of the Phenomena of the Human Mind* (1829). In him, mental atomism finds its purest expression: the mind is reduced to its simplest elements or points of consciousness; combinations of these elements occur in accordance with the law of association by contiguity; association by resemblance is reducible to association by contiguity (the only type of association considered by Hartley). When a combination becomes inseparable, beliefs are formed in the mind. Bentham sought to base complex forms of legislation and social life on his oversimplified principle of utilitarianism (pleasure and pain are the sole motives of human conduct); in the same way, Mill's theory of mind, of graphic simplicity, found practical applications in ethics, logic and pedagogy. Contemporaries, like Macaulay, in the *Edinburgh Review* (1829), often called attention to the gap between the poverty of a principle and the richness of its presumed consequences, between the utilitarian principle, for example, and Bentham's admirable philanthropy; but the goal of these philosophers was to discover principles embodying barren, naked truths whose consequences would be all the more certain. The difficulty of achieving this goal led Mackintosh (*Dissertation on the Progress of Ethical Philosophy,* 1830) to the idea of transfer, which was to play an important role in associationist psychology. Reason shows us that utility is the sole primitive motive, but experience shows us that men are so constituted as to approve certain actions instantaneously, without referring to their consequences. This is because the approval that was originally given to these consequences has been transferred to the mental dispositions themselves, which, through association, have become the end of a particular action.

In its historical developments, utilitarianism appears to be truly a principle of universal application. It was linked (belatedly) to democracy by Bentham and to a kind of anarchy by Godwin. The jurist John Austin (*The Province of Jurisprudence Determined,* 1832), connected it with theological ethics, which seems utterly alien to it. Moral obligation has its source in the will of God, whereas duty springs from the rational pursuit of utility; yet if God is assumed to will only man's well-being, it follows that the good effects of a standard concerning happiness are a token of God's will. Unexpectedly, the pursuit of utility favors obedience to the law, which is the goal.

VII *The Romantic Reaction:*
Samuel Taylor Coleridge and Thomas Carlyle

This impoverished conception of the human mind was attacked directly by Coleridge (1772–1834), Wordsworth's friend. In his writings he maintains that reality is spirit and that man communicates with reality through immediate sympathy more surely than through science. He was a Platonist and a reader of Kant and Fichte, philosophers from Germany, a country declared by Mackintosh, in a letter to Dugald Stewart (1802), to be "metaphysically insane." In *Aids to Reflection* (1825) and *Confessions of an Inquiring Spirit* (1840) he uses his magical theory of inspiration and the "superhuman ventriloquist" to combat veneration for the Bible in popular religion, no less than mechanism, utilitarianism, and radicalism in politics—in short, everything that suppresses life in things. Plotinus rather than the Germans (notwithstanding his vocabulary) seems to have suggested the principal formulations of his ideas. With the Platonists he separates the understanding from reason: the understanding is a discursive faculty, which systematizes and combines what it has received from different sources; reason immediately provides the principles that permit the realization of understanding and do not have to be proved, for to require proof of the true facts inherent in the very nature of the inquirer is absurd. Like the Platonists, however, Coleridge uses reason to designate a kind of inspired and revealing insight into the heart of reality, a light inseparable from the feeling responsible for its realization; and since he had discovered or thought he had discovered, through Kant and Fichte, that practical reason reveals the essential nature of things, he uses the term to describe this higher form of reason. Moreover, in his view the vital heat of this reason is more important than the knowledge it provides, and even though he declares his own preferences for Platonism, which makes reason a true revelation, he leaves to professional philosophers the task of rebutting criticism which makes reason nothing more than a function of the mind.

Like the reactionary philosophers of his time, he rejects radicalism and Jacobinism in favor of a theory of history that perceives, in the success enjoyed by an institution, the philosophical idea and intelligibility that justify that institution.

Thomas Carlyle (1795-1881) exerted an influence similar to that of Coleridge, but greater and more far-reaching, not so much by his own doctrines as by the impetus he gave to a philosophical tendency which was on the point of becoming rigidified as spiritless utilitarianism or sanctimonious orthodoxy. He seeks to transform man's outlook on the world, which to him is not spiritless and gray but the strangest of all possible worlds, not a shop full of merchandise but a mystical temple. The most familiar facts become mysteries—the flight of time, for example, or the mysterious stream of existence. Carlyle censures not doctrines but attitudes, such as that of negation or doubt, which is linked to the purely intellectual contemplation of things. Trying to prove the existence of God intellectually, for example, is like trying to illuminate the sun by using a lantern. Knowledge of the laws of eternal justice is an affair of the heart and not of the head; these laws are seen from within and in action, not by reasoning. Utilitarianism, materialism, empiricism, atheism—all are negative doctrines, which grasp only the appearance of things. The natural attitude of the human spirit is affirmation, not negation; belief, not doubt; an affirmation or a belief which is not so much a well-considered system as a vital, almost unconscious action. We find in Carlyle the Romantic exaltation of instinct and nocturnal forces, which was then widely prevalent. Intuition is the only method of the philosopher; this is not the method of the vulgar logic of schools, in which all truths are laid out in sequence, each clinging to the coat-tails of the next, but the method of practical reason, which proceeds by embracing intuitively large groups and whole systematic kingdoms.

Carlyle boldly draws out the consequences of his thesis. He attacks Benthamism at its strongest point, its theory of punishment, and it is in the instinctive reaction of vengeance that he claims to have found its basis. He attacks liberal tendencies, popular sovereignty, and democracy, for he recognizes two kinds of men: inspired men, heroes, who possess wisdom and are destined to lead; and the masses of mankind, whose virtue is obedience to the law and who need an iron discipline. Universal history is essentially a history of the great men who have labored here in this world. They have been the leaders of other men, creators, models, and, in a broad sense, creators of everything that the mass of men collectively have managed to do or attain. The hero is a messenger sent from the heart of the mysterious infinite with news for us. He comes from the inner substance of things. In a word, Carlyle represents the British expression of the anti-Voltairian and antirevolutionary spirit which had been developing for a long time on the continent.

Bibliography

I

Stewart, Dugald. *Works,* ed. Hamilton, 2 vols. 1854–58.

II

Brown, Thomas. *Inquiry into the Relation of Cause and Effect.* Edinburgh, 1818.
——. *Lectures on the Philosophy of the Human Mind.* Edinburgh, 1920.
——. Selections from Brown appear in *The Story of Scottish Philosophy,* by Daniel Sommer Robinson. New York, 1961.

III

Texts

Hamilton, William. "On the Philosophy of the Unconditioned." *Edinburgh Review,* vol. 1, 1829, pp. 194–221.
——. *Discussions on Philosophy and Literature, Education and University Reform.* London, 1852.
——. *Lectures on Metaphysics and Logic,* ed. H. L. Mansel and John Veitch, 4 vols. Edinburgh and Boston, 1859–60.

Studies

Grave, S. A. *The Scottish Philosophy of Common Sense.* Oxford, 1960.
Mill, John Stuart. *An Examination of Sir William Hamilton's Philosophy,* 2 vols. London, 1865.
Rasmussen, S. V. *The Philosophy of Sir William Hamilton.* Copenhagen, 1925.
Stirling, J. H. *Sir William Hamilton.* London, 1865.
Veitch, John. *Hamilton.* Philadelphia and Edinburgh, 1882.
Wight, O. W. *Philosophy of Sir William Hamilton.* New York, 1854.

IV

Texts

Bentham, Jeremy. *Works,* 11 vols. Edinburgh, 1838–43.

Studies

Atkinson, C. M. *Jeremy Bentham.* London, 1905.
Everett, C. W. *The Education of Jeremy Bentham.* New York, 1931.
Stephen, Leslie. *The English Utilitarians,* vol. 1. London, 1900.

V

Malthus, Thomas Robert. *An Essay on the Principle of Population as It Affects the Future Improvement of Society, with Remarks on the Speculations of Mr. Godwin, M. Condorcet, and Other Writers.* London, 1798. Facsimile edition, London, 1926; paperback edition with introduction by K. E. Boulding, Ann Arbor, Mich., 1959.
———. *An Essay on the Principle of Population, or a View of Its Past and Present Effect on Human Happiness, with an Inquiry Into Our Prospects Respecting the Future Removal or Mitigation of the Evils Which It Occasions.* London, 1803; also in Everyman Library edition, London and New York.

VI

Bain, A. *James Mill.* London, 1882.
Halévy, Élie. *La formation du radicalisme philosophique,* trans. Mary Morris: *The Growth of Philosophic Radicalism.* London, 1928.
Mill, John Stuart. *Autobiography.* London, 1873.
Stephen, L. *The English Utilitarians,* 3 vols. Vol. 2. London, 1900.

VII

Texts

Carlyle, Thomas. The Century Edition, ed. H. D. Trail, 30 vols. (London, 1896–99; New York, 1896–1901) is the most complete edition of Carlyle's *Works.*

Coleridge, S. T. *The Complete Works of S. T. Coleridge,* ed. W. G. T. Shedd, 7 vols. (New York, 1853 and 1884), was very far from complete. Professor Kathleen Coburn is now in the process of preparing the first comprehensive edition of practically everything Coleridge wrote, apart from the *Collected Letters,* E. L. Griggs, ed., 4 vols., Oxford and New York, 1956–58.

FICHTE

KANTIANISM IS a system of criticism which conceals a dialectic. It is not only a determination of the limits of knowledge but also, within these limits, the a priori construction of objects to be known. Under different forms, this a priori construction is the focal point of the post-Kantian metaphysical systems of Fichte, Schelling, and Hegel.

Johann Gottlieb Fichte (1762–1814) was professor at the University of Jena from 1794 to 1799. Forced to leave Jena after the cry of atheism had been raised against him, he took up residence in Berlin (1799–1805), where he became acquainted with the leaders of German Romanticism, Schlegel, Schleiermacher, and Tieck. He lectured at the University of Erlangen in 1805 but left for Königsberg at the time of the French invasion, then returned to Berlin, where, in 1807 and 1808, while the city was still under French occupation, he delivered his famous *Addresses to the German Nation*. Finally he became professor, then rector of the University of Berlin. His principal work is his *Basis of the Entire Theory of Science* (1794), which was preceded by an *Essay Toward a Critique of All Revelation* (1792). Mention must also be made of works in which his theory of science is applied: *Basis of Natural Right* (1796), and related works on *The Closed Commercial State* (1800), *The Science of Rights* (1812), and *The Science of Ethics* (1798). He adopted a more popular style for *The Vocation of Man* (1800), a series of lectures *On the Characteristics of the Present Age* (1806), and *The Way toward the Blessed Life* (1806). His lectures on the *Theory of Science,* delivered in 1804, 1812, and 1813, were published posthumously (1834).

1 *Fichte's Concept of Freedom*

"If the theory of science is accepted," Fichte wrote in 1801, "and universally disseminated among those to whom it is directed, mankind will be delivered from blind chance; good luck and bad luck will no longer exist. Humanity altogether will be responsible for its own destiny and will depend on its concept of itself; it will have absolute freedom to do with itself whatever it may wish to do with itself." [1]

Fichte's philosophy is, by and large, a "scientific" demonstration of freedom. Hence the striking contrast between the breadth and scope of the end, which concerns all mankind, and philosophy itself, which is supposed to lead to it. Because of its abstract character, this philosophy, like higher mathematics, is restricted to a very small number; in 1813, according to Fichte, it had not yet been understood by anyone even though it was the goal sought in many different ways by the *Aufklärung.* Its aim is to liberate humanity, not by placing knowledge on the level of the common herd, but by means of an abstruse science, which requires a rare gift of intuition, utilizes concepts entirely different from those associated with common sense even though they are often called by the same name, and asserts its independence of knowledge, which belongs to life. His theory of science is the condition necessary for knowledge.

According to Fichte, science can be isolated from its applications just as mathematics is isolated from and independent of the engineer's art, or, more exactly, just as Socrates' dialectic can be isolated by abstraction from the moral betterment of a disciple. But in reality it has meaning and value only in terms of its fruits. During all the years when the young Fichte enthusiastically supported the cause of freedom, he considered science to be primarily a moral and

[1] "Sonnenklarer Bericht," in *Archives de philosophie,* 1926, p. 87.

spiritual ferment. At first his sole intention was to become the popularizer of Kant's philosophy and to elaborate all its practical consequences in his popular expositions.

This champion of action was not himself a man of action. He aroused consciences, stirred minds, gave encouragement, but he never had the precise programs and firm grasp of practical plans which mark true men of action. The contrast between the ardor of his intent and the meagerness of his results is characteristic of his whole life and perhaps of his whole philosophy. He is neither a reformer like Saint-Simon or Auguste Comte nor a statesman like Hegel or Victor Cousin. In his view, action is not in execution but in an inner disposition and inspiration. His only practical ideal is freedom, which discovers its own limit precisely in its own product. This freedom can surpass its product, however, only by using it as a means of advancement; otherwise freedom risks settling in its own creation and losing its indispensable power of advancement. But the impetus that carries freedom beyond the given does not involve any arbitrary, irrational activity. There is a material freedom which is simply opposition to the given,[2] but between the anarchical freedom of *Sturm und Drang* and true freedom there is an abyss. True freedom discovers its law in itself, is at once coherence and invention, is fidelity to reason and desire for independent thinking; but by the same token, it is also renewal of self. It is advancement of reason in itself but it is also education of others, for personal freedom is inseparable from the freedom of others, since "man is a man only among men." Consequently no need can be attributed it other than its own development or, stating the same principle another way, the development of humanity in oneself and others.

Any over-precise end would be incompatible with such an ideal. "My total and complete destiny eludes me," he writes in *The Vocation of Man.* "What I am to become, what I shall be, all this surpasses my thought."[3] This acknowledgment of a transcendent element is perhaps the essence of Fichtean freedom.

<hr/>

[2] Xavier Léon, *Fichte et son temps*, I, 513; 494.
[3] *Bestimmung des Menschen*, ed. Reclam, p. 147.

Fichte never considered the possibility of a spontaneous popular, democratic movement. He was never a liberal in the English or French sense of the word; he did not think that the people should be responsible for their own conduct. His *Contributions Intended to Rectify the Judgments of the Public Concerning the French Revolution* (1793, 2d edition, 1795) are not in any sense a defense of parliamentary institutions. He praises the abolition of the privileges of the nobility and the clergy, notably the repossession of church property by the state. In short, he praises everything that tends to insure civil and political equality, and he clearly sides with Rousseau rather than with Montesquieu. But to him the social contract (which he considers to be the juridical origin, if not the historical origin, of any society) serves not so much to stabilize and consolidate society as to permit changes in society; consequently it becomes a revolutionary principle. He is rightly credited with being one of the first to see that the contract should not check freedom in any way, since it originates in the freedom of individuals and therefore cannot be a principle of social restraint. Every individual has the right to break the contract at any moment.[4]

To the freedom of the individual he also sacrifices economic liberalism. *The Closed Commercial State* (1800) was inspired by the spectacle of misery which, in Prussia as well as in England at that time, existed alongside immense fortunes acquired through commerce. Fichte attributes this state of affairs to mercantilism, which sacrifices the interests of the many to the enormous development of foreign commerce, which profits the few. Because of the reforms he advocated, he is considered to be the first author of state socialism. The division of work is a necessity in human societies, he reasons, but it should be in harmony with justice. It is right for each man to be able to live from the work that he has chosen or that has been imposed on him, but he cannot, because of the fluctuations of foreign commerce, which is forever changing the value of money. If the state is rigorously closed to foreign commerce, a national medium of exchange with a constant value

---

[4] C. E. Vaughan, *Studies in the History of Political Philosophy*, II, 101.

can be created, and work will be remunerated justly and always in the same way. Closure implies that the state is a self-sufficient economic community, but this is true only if it has reached what Fichte calls its "natural frontiers"—that is, the frontiers inside which such a community is possible. No political tradition outweighs the demands of reason, but he concedes that his project is "without immediate application. Such projects are by their nature destined to remain purely abstract, unrelated to the real situation, where the political practitioner is in charge." [5]

Freedom is not something demanded by the people, not a limitation on the powers of the state (which, on the contrary, acquires even greater economic control). It is a rational imperative, one that first manifests itself and advances in an individual or a small group of especially endowed individuals. If there is a common trait to all of Fichte's activity, it is his attempt to establish around himself very small groups of reliable men to spread the spirit of freedom. His liberalism was so shallow that he had earlier, in 1792, been the apologist of the edicts of censorship (1788), which established a veritable inquisition in Prussia.[6] This was because he did not share the ideas of the *Aufklärer* and felt that it was dangerous to use popular instruction to spread "propositions which can be possessed with impunity only by a very clear, very cultivated brain." With perfect logic, a short time later, when he saw that Kant's treatise *On Religion* had been banned, he recanted and attacked censorship in his *Appeal to the Princes*. He was initiated into Freemasonry in 1800, for he considered it to be a sanctuary where "one must hide ideas which the public could not understand or might misuse." [7] He abandoned Freemasonry, however, as soon as he saw that it could not be an instrument for propagandizing his doctrine. It was in this spirit that he had prepared his lectures on *The Nature of the Scholar* (1794). To him the scholar is a social apostle, a "priest of truth," who teaches not only by words but

---

[5] Cf. Xavier Léon, *Fichte et son temps,* II, 60.
[6] *Ibid.,* I, 119.
[7] *Ibid.,* II, 55.

also, and more effectively, by example. The same considerations underlie the plan that he drew up, in 1805, for a model university, and especially the deductive plan of 1807; in both he rejects lectures, whether read or given from notes, in favor of a more direct form of instruction utilizing a Socratic interchange between the teacher and his students; in the second he insists that students, to be totally devoted to their task, must live in dormitories and practice celibacy. His theory of science "supposes no prior knowledge of any kind; it requires only a normally trained mind."[8] Yet "it involves an intellectual labor not of a degree beyond normal labor but of a wholly new *kind* and never before seen; to become proficient, one must work with appropriate data." The Critical Institute that he planned, with a journal which was to evaluate all scientific productions in the name of philosophy—a project inspired by Schelling —was an outgrowth of his self-assigned mission. "Science must be kept under strict supervision for some time," he wrote to Schiller in 1800, "or the small amount of good grain sown there will be destroyed by the growth of weeds."[9]

What he defended most vehemently was the freedom of his own mission. In 1798, at the University of Jena, a charge of atheism led to his dismissal, and only on Schiller's private advice was he persuaded to consider the one question of practical importance— that of the legality of the measures taken against him. He preferred to view the accusation as a pretext seized upon by his enemies, who wished to prevent him from imparting to his students the desire for independence. "I must defend my person as long as I can," he wrote, "for to me the triumph of right is surely tied to the liberty of my person."[10]

He delivered his famous *Addresses to the German Nation* in the winter of 1807–08, after the Peace of Tilsit, which destroyed the power of Prussia, and in Berlin, then occupied by Napoleon's troops. His patriotism was animated by the same spirit of freedom, for he

[8] *Sonnenklarer Bericht*, p. 72.
[9] As quoted by Xavier Léon, II, 229.
[10] *Ibid.*, I, 553.

thought that the Germans, among all nations, had the liberating mission that he and his circle had among all men: "You among all modern nations most clearly possess the germ of human perfectibility and have a role of leadership in the development of humanity . . . ; if you fail, all humanity will fail with you, without hope of future restoration." [11] His pan-Germanism contrasts sharply with that of Schlegel, whose lectures of 1803–04 were suffused with the medieval tradition of imperial and Catholic unity. Fichte looked only toward the future.

II *The Three Principles of the Theory of Science*

Is the reality of things, as conceived by the understanding, compatible with freedom? This question was the principal, if not the sole motive of Fichte's theory. To achieve his goal he had to discover the given factor in nature—a reality that can be penetrated by human action. "Nature, in which I have to act," he writes, "is not a foreign substance, produced independently of me, into which I cannot penetrate." [12] That is what he seeks to demonstrate, and for his demonstration he calls upon Kantian idealism. He can understand nature, he reasons, because "nature is formed by the laws of my own thought and must be in harmony with my thought. It must be absolutely transparent and knowable, penetrable even in its inward parts. It expresses nothing but connections and relations between myself and myself, and I can hope to know myself as surely as I can promise myself to examine nature." At first he does not consider Kantian idealism to be the solution of the problem of knowledge, as it was in the *Critique of Pure Reason,* but rather what it became in the *Critique of Practical Reason—* a means of reconciling freedom and the determinism required by the understanding. This reconciliation, according to many of the thinkers of his time, could not be effected by reason. Jacobi, in particular, maintains that reason alone, armed with the principle

[11] *Ibid.,* II, 68.
[12] *Bestimmung des Menschen, Sämmtliche Werke,* II, 258.

of sufficient reason, inevitably leads to Spinozism, which plunges us into an impersonal nature and annihilates the self. This course is opposed only by irrational beliefs founded on sentiment and justified insofar as they support our moral life. Thus the spirit is forced to waver between privative materialism and a kind of revelation of the heart which suppresses the exercise of reason. On this last point, Fichte set the stage for all his works by showing, in his *Essay Toward a Critique of All Revelation* (1792), that a revelation was unacceptable unless its content was wholly rational. Consequently he would have been forced back toward naturalism if he had not found support in Kant's idealism.

That support, however, proved inadequate. Doubtless the determinism of nature was no longer to be feared if it was only the projection of the conditions under which the human mind knows objects, but its positive relation to our freedom was still not comprehensible. Hence Fichte's ambition was to show, at the same time and by using the same series of proofs, that nature is the object of the self because it is the condition posited by freedom for its own exercise and advancement. There is nothing more transparent than that type of absolute moralism which tries to discover in nature an opportunity to act and accomplish its duty, and which deduces existence itself and the characteristics of nature from this very exigency—like an ascetic who brings about a situation which will put him to the test and lead him to perfection. The demonstrations of the *Theory of Science* center on this issue. Here Fichte's aim is not to have recourse to moral exigencies in order to stress the point but rather to demonstrate by purely speculative arguments that the problem of the production of nature is identical to the problem of the conditions necessary for the moral law.

Kant had discovered, behind and beneath the principle of causality or the other principles of pure understanding, the spontaneity of the *I think,* on which these principles were grounded. In the same way, Fichte begins with the principle of identity and seeks to show that the validity of this principle is grounded on the action of the *ego,* which posits itself for itself and which *is* because it posits itself.

Fichte's ego and its action, like Kant's *I think,* is not discovered by inner experience and reflection. This spontaneity and action are beyond consciousness, for they are the conditions necessary for consciousness.

There the parallel ends, however, for Kant never considered the transcendental deduction of the principle of identity, which is the first step taken by Fichte. According to Kant, the transcendental deduction is logical and proper only if the ego makes use of categories in structuring the diversity of sense data; strictly speaking, he deduces not the principle, but the use of the principle in conceiving an object; consequently the principle of identity cannot be deduced, and does not need to be deduced, since it has only a logical and not a transcendental use. Fichte does not hesitate to resort to an expedient in order to justify this deduction: the principle of identity states that A is equal to A; he restates the principle, saying that the A which is, is equal to the A which is posited, or that if A is posited, it is. Thus the principle of identity becomes a formula expressing the relation between the condition (positing of A) and the conditioned (being of A), and the bond of dependence between being and positing introduces the necessity of an identical ego, which posits itself as identical.

Furthermore, Fichte attaches so little importance to this expedient that he dispenses with any logical framework in his *New Exposition of the Theory of Science* (1797) and considers the pure activity of the ego—the self positing itself—to be an immediate fact of consciousness or primary intellectual intuition. Intuition rather than the Kantian transcendental analysis puts us on the level of the principle, and consciousness of the activity of the ego, which can withdraw from contemplation of external things whenever it wishes to do so, leads to this intuition; the intuition of the ego occupies a privileged position in that the being posited by the ego differs in no way from the activity which posits it.

This double entrance of the first principle leads to a question which is decisive for the nature of Fichte's idealism: Is the ego posited as an unconditioned or absolute principle, or only as an ultimate condition—one necessary and sufficient to construct the empirical given in which Fichte chooses deliberately to remain? In the latter instance, it would be a primary condition, but one which would itself be conditioned by its success in explaining the given (in somewhat the same way as Kant's *I think* is justified as a condition of the possibility of experience). It would seem that for at least two reasons Fichte should be inclined in this direction. First, if the ego exists only for itself and begins to be posited for itself only by virtue of the philosopher's reflection, it follows that the ego exists as a condition only in this reflection. As Fichte often states, the construction predicated on the principle that consciousness originates in the ego resembles, not a gnosogony which tries to describe the actual genesis of consciousness, but the construction of the mathematician, who uses a combination of ideal elements to arrive at truths concerning reality: "The determinations of real consciousness—to which the philosopher is compelled to apply the laws of the consciousness that he has freely constructed, like a geometer applying the laws of the ideal triangle to real triangles— are to him *as if* they were the result of a primary construction. . . . To mistake this *everything happens as if* for an *everything happens like this*—to mistake this fiction for the account of a real event which might have occurred at a certain time—is a gross error." [13] It seems that the ideal character of the construction does not apply to its principle.

A second reason for believing this, is the way in which the second principle—the *nonego*—is introduced. The ego is forever positing itself, and one can only go from the ego as principle to the ego; consequently a construction or deduction will be possible only if a second principle opposes the first, just as the geometer's limits make possible the deduction of infinite space. Fichte states that the second principle is completely independent of the first "with respect to its form," which depends on the opposition itself, although its content is conditioned inasmuch as an opposite term can be defined only in relation to a posited term. It is clear that

[13] *Sonnenklarer Bericht.*

the positing of this opposite term springs from philosophical reflection, which is incapable of constructing anything with the ego alone. Here, at higher level of abstraction, the nonego assumes the role played by the "manifold of sensibility" in Kant's transcendental deduction. Fichte does, of course, link the nonego to the principle of contradiction and use it to validate this principle, just as he used the ego to validate the principle of identity. But this expedient has no more importance here than it had earlier, for the act of opposing the nonego to the ego involves an intellectual intuition as primitive as the act of positing the ego.

We might assume that analysis of the conditions of these two acts would explain the whole chain of deduction which follows, that the hidden key to the whole problem is in the peculiar nature of the opposition between the nonego and the ego. These two terms are opposites, like the opposing terms white and black, or, better still, like the contradictory terms white and nonwhite. Contradictories can coexist but only if they are not applied to the same subject; thus there is opposition only where there is plurality and divisibility, for contradictories reciprocally limit each other. Similarly, opposition between the ego and the nonego can occur only if the sole reality posited up to this point, the reality of the ego, is divided, and nonego refers to the part of reality to which ego does not refer, and vice versa. "Over against itself the divisible ego posits its own opposite—a divisible nonego." This is the third principle of the *Theory of Science,* but the problem of ego and nonego cannot be resolved in the same way as the problem of the coexistence of ordinary opposites, such as white and black. Here the ego plays a double role: it posits opposites and is at the same time one of them; it is both the whole of reality and a part of reality.

Logically, it seems that we are in an inextricable situation, from which we can emerge only by sacrificing one of the two terms. This is the course chosen on one hand by Spinozist dogmatism, which attributes all reality to the nonego and makes the ego a product of this reality, and on the other by Berkeleian idealism, which reduces the nonego to an idea, a simple modality of the divine mind. Both solutions are logical but unacceptable, for they deny rather than explain the opposition between subject and object. But how can the logical incompatibility be resolved without eliminating one of the two terms? Since Fichte made a seemingly insoluble problem the pivot of his whole philosophy, behind his abstract formulations there must have been some concrete intuition to provide support and justification. He often mentions the difficulty encountered in trying to understand his theory of science by imagining as absent (*wegdenken*) the parasitic images which surround the concepts of ego or nonego; yet it is only by overcoming this difficulty that one can perceive intuitively the pure self-positing activity of the ego. But if the static images surrounding the pure activity of the personal self must be imagined as absent, it is all the more important for the dynamic image, which is at the heart of the theory, to be restored. The word "opposition" (*Gegensatz*), which expresses the relation between nonego and ego, designates not only a logical relation but also a dynamic, contentious relation between clashing tendencies seeking to annihilate each other; by the same token, the word "object" (*Gegenstand*) designates not only a term known by the subject but also that which resists the mind and is imposed on it. Fichte constantly shifts from the logical, static sense to the dynamic sense, with the result that his philosophy as a whole is like an abstract, schematic history of conflicts between two hostile forces determined to destroy each other. Here we have a kind of metaphysical Manicheism, which was to reappear in all the productions of a significant body of early nineteenth-century German philosophy. As with Meister Eckhart and Jakob Böhme, however, this Manicheism is clearly linked to a fundamental monism: an absolute, unique principle, which is realized only in strife, calls forth an adversary in order that it may substitute for its monotonous infinity the myriad concrete determinations of consciousness. The outcome of this struggle will always be the same: victory for the omnipotent principle and annihilation, sooner or later, of the opponent. In this context the Fichtean ego, which otherwise would be a logical monstrosity, is understandable;

it is the absolute limiting itself in order to have opportunities to struggle and, ultimately, to triumph.

Hence the design of his theory: theoretical philosophy, in which the nonego is progressively enriched and determined as it struggles with the ego, and in which categories replace the Kantian's "waffle-iron for forms"; and practical philosophy, which shows the progressive but never complete victory of the ego over the nonego. These are not two kinds of philosophy but two phases of the same movement. First the nonego, which begins by being the pure negation of the ego, must be given a reality, body, or solidity which will make it truly a resistant object. This is the role of theoretical philosophy, in which "the ego posits itself as determined by the nonego." Once this task has been accomplished, the reverse phase begins—that of practical philosophy, in which "the ego posits the nonego as determined by the ego." We saw earlier that a choice between dogmatic realism and idealism would have been the logical solution of the conflict; instead, Fichte substitutes a movement alternating between realism and idealism, which are like the two unattainable limits, never reached, between which philosophy fluctuates. Theoretical philosophy tends toward realism, determining the ego by the nonego; practical philosophy tends toward idealism, determining the nonego by the ego. But the final victory goes to idealism—not dogmatic idealism, which dissolves the nonego in the ego, but a practical idealism of action, which has the infinite task of affirming the sovereignty of the ego over the nonego, of spirit over the universe. "That the opposite must be denied until absolute unity is produced" is the condition specified by the first principle, which, if truly infinite, can posit its opposite only in order to deny it. For Fichte admits that the philosopher could never emerge from the ego by pure speculation if he did not add a practical datum—the feeling that the ego, insofar as it is practical, depends on a nonego which is not under our control. But this practical datum must be checked by another—the feeling of a necessary subordination of the complete nonego to the practical laws of the ego, progressively and through our own efforts. Thus the alternation between realism and idealism is a practical measure, for the nonego is posited as an object of knowledge only to support the practical activity of the ego. But this vast oscillation between realism and idealism, which is the heart of the whole, is also mainifested in detail.

III *Theoretical Philosophy*

Theoretical philosophy has as its starting point the synthesis of the nonego and the ego expressed in this proposition: "The ego posits itself as determined by the nonego." Thereafter, its course is dominated entirely by the principle that analysis must be used to determine whether this synthesis contains opposites (antithesis); if so, they must be bound in a new synthesis, and if this synthesis in turn contains opposites, they must be bound in a new synthesis, and so on until one arrives at opposites which can no longer be bound in a new synthesis; then comes the practical part, which by action resolves a problem that speculation cannot solve. In other words, we must strive to conceive what is conceivable in the primitive synthesis.

Our first synthesis includes two conflicting propositions: "The ego posits itself as determined" and "The nonego (active) determines the ego (passive)." One of the two propositions is idealistic, the other realistic; they destroy each other if there is no synthesis; but there should be one if the primitive synthesis from which these contradictories originate has been posited by the ego.

By striving to contemplate the primitive synthesis, we can witness the emergence—the appearance and disappearance one after the other—of every possible doctrine relating to the determination of the ego by the nonego. This determination implies that an inner affection is posited in the ego; for the nonego can be posited only in relation to something which is in the ego. But the ego can explain this affection in two ways: first, as the effect of the causality of the nonego on the ego. Here the real ground of this affection is considered to be the nonego, which changes qualitatively according to its effect. This is qualititative realism. Second, it can be seen as the effect of a diminished activity, equivalent to a passivity, posited in the nonego by the ego. Here the ego is a substance, its affection is a mode, and the nonego is no larger the ideal ground of this affection. This is qualitative idealism.

But we cannot contemplate qualitative realism exhaustively without taking the initiative from the nonego, that is, without attributing to it an activity independent of the relation between its action on the ego and the affection which causes it. Nor can we contemplate qualitative idealism without attributing to the ego an independent activity or absolute spontaneity through which it limits itself.

To say that the passive affection of the ego supposes an independent activity in the nonego is to predicate Spinoza's thing in itself and his fatum; to say that the ego produces its own affections in itself by its own spontaneity is to acknowledge, with the Leibnizians, an arbitrary unfolding of representations whose correspondence to the affections of the nonego are due to a law of preestablished harmony not posited by the ego. Spinoza's fatum is offset, however, by an absolute requirement imposed by the ego: nothing in the nonego can be real unless it has been transported there by the ego. On the other hand, against the Leibnizians it can be said that absolute, unlimited spontaneity can posit a diminished activity in the self only by excluding the rest of the whole, and since this part of the whole is posited as not posited, the diminished activity or affection of the self is posited only mediately.

This brings us to the synthesis of realism and idealism which constitutes Kant's critical idealism. The activity of the self or ego which produces a passive nonego is exerted only to the extent that the active nonego produces an affection in the passive ego; on the other hand, the activity opposing the ego is identical to that which the ego transports into the nonego; the result is a quantitative idealism which posits the limited activity of the ego—that is, the activity by which it posits only mediately—as absolute, and a quantitative realism which posits the nonego as the foundation of the limitation of the ego. These two doctrines concur in interpreting the opposition between ego and nonego as opposition between subject and object, each posited only by the negation of the other.

But this reciprocal causality is incompatible with the first principle, which states that the self alone must posit everything contained in it; in other words causality, the principle of realism, always opposes substantiality, the principle of idealism. How can the affirmation of a causal exchange between the ego and the nonego be reconciled with the absolute activity of the ego? Idealism provides a solution by attributing to the activity of the self the positing of subject and object in a reciprocal relation, making it the source of representations; but this solution is inadequate, since it does not explain why the self should posit an object. Consequently Fichte chooses a form of realism which attributes to an external reality the self's reason for limiting itself, and this reason can only be a *shock* or an obstacle (*Anstoss*), preventing the self from spreading further. We should note that this inexplicable obstacle is not an object but that which gives the ego an opportunity to construct an object and use it to determine itself; the self is posited as determinable. This realism in turn destroys the absolute character of the self-positing activity of the ego, for one can imagine that a simple resistance gives the ego the task of limiting itself only if it originates within the ego. It is clear from the outset that the ego could not limit itself if it were not infinite and did not contain what is outside its limits as well as what is inside them. Alternatively, it would not be infinite if it were not limited. This proposition seems strange at first, but it is wholly in keeping with Fichte's notion that an infinite thing can apprehend itself only in action— that is, only as it continuously shifts the limits it has posited. Thus the obstacle restricting the activity of the ego is not independent of it but conditions its absolute activity as it posits itself infinitely. The ego's absolute activity, which is forever substituting one limit for another, one representation for another, is the imagination—the same faculty that Kant thought capable of uniting the pure data of sensible intuition and the spontaneity of the understanding. According to Fichte, it is the "faculty that wavers continually between determination and indetermination, the finite and the infinite." In this way the theoretical problem is resolved, for now one can imagine, without contradiction, that "the ego posits itself as determined by the nonego."

The theoretical part of Fichte's philosophy is completed by the deduction of representation, which shows the genesis of the different representative faculties—sensation, intuition, understanding, judgment, reason. Here, in keeping with the very nature of the imagination, the limit between ego and nonego alternately becomes stable, wavers, and becomes stable again: in sensation (*Empfindung*) the ego finds itself (*sich empfindet*) limited by a nonego; in intuition the ego attributes the positing of the limit to its pure activity discovered by sensation, and this limit therefore becomes contingent; in the faculty of understanding (*Verstand*) the ego discovers the principle of the limitation of its pure activity in the determination of fixed objects considered as real—that is, the understanding confers stability on the products of the imagination.

IV *The Practical Part of the Theory of Science*

The self or ego, as intelligence, is the cause of every form of representation, but it is not the cause of the obstacle, brought forth by the nonego, which has caused the construction of its forms. Since the ego is absolute, it must be posited independently, and its dependence as intelligence eliminated; this happens if the ego determines the unknown nonego to which the resistance is attributed. But this causality of the ego over the nonego seems both necessary (since the ego can contain nothing not posited by it) and impossible (since the nonego then would cease being nonego and become ego, inasmuch as the absolute ego can posit everything that it posits only as ego). The problem, then, is to understand how the ego can exercise its causality over the nonego without losing its absoluteness, how its "objective activity," which supposes an object—that is, a being opposite to itself—can be linked to its absolute activity, and how the third principle (determination of the nonego by the ego) can be reconciled to the first (absolute self-positing of the ego).

At once impossible and necessary, the determination of the non-ego by the ego is accomplished by striving (*Streben*). According to Fichte, it is only in its striving that the absolute ego can know itself as such; if this striving should come to an end, all consciousness, all feeling, all life would disappear. Here we see clearly the frequently remarked trait which links Fichte to ascetic and cynical moralists.

This striving would lead only to inertia if it met with resistance equal to itself. It gathers strength only if allowed to reproduce itself continually. In the impulse to reproduce itself (*Trieb*) the ego always discovers its limits; but the feeling of being restricted, far from being a sense of powerlessness, is "a feeling of strength," since the self is conscious of its bounds only because it aspires to surpass them. Impulse can assert itself only against its restrictions, and that is why it urges the ideal activity of the ego to produce the object which imposes these restrictions. Here we see the roots of the faculties of representation studied in the theoretical part of Fichte's system. Because our striving must be limited in order to exist as such, it encounters an existing matter or immutable reality that restricts it; but because our aspirations are unlimited, and because we are unable to transform things, we strive to transform representations. Consequently the reality of the external world is posited in its entirety as the ground for the preservation of the tension underlying our striving.

Impulse is fully comprehensible, however, only if it becomes an absolute or moral impulse. To the extent that an impulse is linked to a particular object, it is satisfied by this object; but for this very reason aspiration ceases, and with it, all consciousness is annihilated. The ego is therefore truly reconciled to itself only if its impulse excludes any particular object, seeks only itself, and is satisfied with itself. Here reflection discovers Kant's categorical imperative, a purely formal law, which does not require that an act be directed toward any particular end. An act satisfies an impulse when it, too, is absolute—that is, when its object is such that it does not limit the impulse.

The nonego is posited only as a condition necessary for the existence of moral striving, and this moral striving in turn is desired unconditionally and for itself. When Fichte says, "The ego determines the nonego," he is not referring to any external, mechanical causality or to any material transformation of the external world through man's industry; he means that the nonego is posited as the means to an absolute end—moral striving. The infinite distance that separates moral striving and its total satisfaction, the ego that posits itself as limited by a nonego and the ego that posits itself absolutely, provides an infinite field for impulse and moral action.

v *Right and Morality*

The practical philosophy to which Fichte's *Theory of Science* leads consists in determining the conditions of moral freedom. The rhythm of its development is similar to that found in the exposition of his theory of science. If freedom is to be realized, there must first be a multiplicity of subjects whose freedom is limited reciprocally in a society governed by a state: this is the thesis of *The Science of Rights*. Then, through a reverse action, these multiple wills must be reduced to the supreme unity of reason and the union of the consciousness in the community realized in them: this is the thesis of *The Science of Ethics*. Thus human activity should proceed from the juridical society to the ethical community. Whether he is considering right or duty, Fichte does not think that the individual has his own destiny, apart from that of others: "Man is a man only among men." The gap between his theory of right and juridical individualism is as wide as that between his ethics and Kant's ethical individualism.

In the problem of right, in particular, Fichte contradicts the ideas which were generally accepted during his time: on one hand, the classic idea of a natural right, inherent in the individual, who brings it into his society and demands respect for it; on the other hand, the theory of right grounded on the duty to respect others, which entails the restriction of the freedom of each insofar as it is incompatible with the freedom of others. In one sense Fichte links right to the idea of the individual, but to him the individual is neither a primary nor an isolated datum. There are individuals because reason and self-consciousness can be realized only through individuality, which is therefore a means to a universal end; and reason can be aroused in each individual only through the influence of other individuals, for individuals can exist only in a society. To reach its goal (the development of each individual's inner conscience), society must restrict the liberties of each individual, and this imperative is the basis of the eternal law of right. Far removed from juridical individualism, the theory of right nevertheless does not point to Hegelianism state socialism, which confers an absolute power on the organized state, but to what has ingeniously been called juridical transpersonalism or theory of social right.[14] Fichte maintains (in direct contrast to Hegel) that society (*Gesellschaft*), the national unorganized community, is superior by far to the state, which is only its momentary expression. From it springs the demand for social justice, which must be realized by the state. Although his views are unquestionably socialistic, Fichte comes much closer to being a libertarian or associationist than an advocate of state socialism. In *The Closed Commercial State* private property is preserved, but only on condition that all property be distributed among corporative associations which jointly control production, so that the state has only to regulate and guarantee arrangements created by economic needs.

Still, juridical individualism persists. Each individual must have a sphere of action in which he has full mastery of himself. This indispensable means of purposive activity is the human body, from which Fichte sedulously deduces the characteristics of the role it must play—that of an instrument of freedom. Furthermore, rights

<hr />

[14] G. Gurvitch, *L'Idée du droit social* (Paris, 1931), p. 148; cf. pp. 407–42.

exist only where there is continuity to compel the respect of each individual; consequently there is a supraindividual power, the power of the state, to encourage respect for rights; but this power is legitimate only if created by a social pact specifying the distribution of property and the means of protecting it. In this way the individual becomes a citizen, and society is truly an organism in which "each part constantly supports the whole and, by preserving it, preserves itself."

The Science of Rights sets forth a state of dispersion and mutual opposition among individuals. Unitary reason demands, on the contrary, a union or community of rational, finite selves, and this idea is expounded in *The Science of Ethics*. The unity of reason is conditioned by the causality of reason, which is manifested in the categorical imperative and in duty. Reason dictates the realization of humanity which, in Fichte's view, is not and cannot be the achievement of perfection in an isolated, transient individual; humanity is mankind as a whole, and each individual should desire the moral advancement of all mankind or universal progress. Consequently the individual should attach equal importance to education and to moral perfection; it would be contradictory for him to separate concern for his own perfection from concern for the community of rational men, since the moral will tends always toward the universal rather than the individual. Finally, as we have already noted, the scholar's mission is important, for he has the special task of advancing reason and freedom.

VI *Transformation of the Theory of Science*

In Fichte's doctrine we can identify at least two radical ambiguities, which were the cause of its subsequent transformations. First, the conflict between the ego and the nonego continues endlessly, whereas, according to the first principle, the sovereignty of the ego ought to be completely restored. The practical self—free, forever militant, never triumphant—does not meet the requirements of the system. Second, the explanation of the determination of the nonego by the ego in the practical part of the theory of science is vague. We have noted the contrast between progress as the term was used in the *Aufklärung*—material progress through man's domination of nature—and Fichte's moral progress. The nonego whose limits are extended by the ego cannot be external nature (how could external nature resist our "moral" activity?) but what Kant calls nature in opposition to morality—the whole sensible part of our being. To be sure, in Fichte's inner feeling there is no ambiguity. The goal of human life is constant striving, and the only kind of progress that counts is self-mastery through an inner education, which is transmitted to others: an ascetic, cynical morality, perfectly clear and coherent. Between Fichte's faithfulness to himself as a moralist and his desire as a philosopher to create a system, there can be no reconciliation: as a systematic philosopher he requires an absolute as a starting point and, at the end, a return to the absolute; as a moralist he requires some kind of progress.

Schelling's objections incited Fichte to search for a system: the self or ego is an act of knowing or absolute knowledge, empty in itself; the absolute is prior to the act of knowing. A similar argument was used by Plato in the *Parmenides,* and by Plotinus in the *Enneads,* to prove the priority of the intelligible over intelligence; here we also see traces of the influence of ancient German mysticism, inherited from Neo-Platonism. In his new system of 1801, Fichte elevates the absolute, which in the first system was the ego, by one degree: he places it above the ego, just as Plotinus placed the One above intelligence. Is he moving toward emanationism? No, for his desire to construct a system is offset by his desire to safeguard freedom and moral activity. Whereas Schelling commits the old dogmatic sin of deducing thought and nature from the absolute, Fichte thinks that nothing can be deduced from it; consequently it is only by an absolutely free act that knowledge is posited for itself outside the absolute. We recall that it was this kind of detachment from the absolute, this will to be for itself, that Plotinus viewed as the fall of the soul. Here we find the same metaphysical myth, but now it is imbued with a totally different feeling—the feeling that being for itself is here at the root of the progress and edification of moral reality and, through it, the progress and edification of the material world.

But this radical freedom is still not moral freedom, and Fichte has to show how it will construct for itself the material world necessary for the striving and moral asceticism which alone enable the ego to sense and savor its freedom. Here again the fundamental idea of the first system intervenes: at the lower level, the ego can be active only by positing a nonego as its opposite; here freedom can become knowledge only by positing its counterpart, which is non-knowledge. How can freedom continue to be knowledge and still posit within itself being or nonknowledge? The solution of this problem is in the dialectical movement of the successive syntheses, which alternately show us knowledge settling in being, then freeing itself from being only to settle again (like intelligence, which first attaches itself to a limited object, then goes beyond it to reach a new object); each synthesis marks an advance over the preceding synthesis until knowledge, like moral activity, perceives itself as realizing a plan which would eventually coincide with pure thought; thus the identity of knowing and being, the absolute transparence of being with respect to knowing is posited here as an ethical ideal.

Fichte's exposition of 1801 may favor the systematic side of his nature by setting the absolute above the ego, but it still leaves an important place for personal moral idealism, thanks to the hiatus introduced between the absolute and knowledge—freedom which is detachment from the absolute. There the situation was relatively unstable: the absolute, enclosed in itself and incapable of projecting outside itself any manifestation of itself, seems to be fitted only for imposing limits on freedom and, consequently, for making possible work and striving; thus the absolute is an inert being and does not meet the requirements of a principle, which is, before all else, activity; on the other hand, the dualism of the absolute and freedom is incompatible with systematic unity. Actually, under the pressure of Schelling's vehement criticisms, this situation could not endure.

In his exposition of 1804 Fichte leans decisively toward systematism, to which he sacrifices at least the theoretical basis of his practical idealism. This is how Fichte's new speculation originated. There is a kind of antimony between the nature of the absolute principle and the way it posits itself for us. It is the act of knowing which requires that there be a higher principle than knowledge, and this principle is posited only to meet the requirements of knowledge; consequently its knowledge is the true principle. The only possible way of resolving the difficulty would be to show that if knowledge is primary for us, the absolute is primary in itself; but this demonstration would be possible only if knowledge could be deduced with necessity from the absolute and only if this necessity existed for us. The exposition of 1801 excluded such an a priori deduction, since knowledge is posited by an absolute freedom; the exposition of 1804 is intended on the contrary to show that knowledge is the image of the absolute, that this image is a necessary product of the absolute, and by what dialectic the philosopher is enabled to apprehend it as such, without attributing to free reflection, formerly so productive, any other role but that of revealing this necessity. The problem is to show that the inner construction of reflection is the original construction of an image. If freedom continues to play a role, it is as a necessary means of reaching eternal knowledge, which is derived from the absolute. Fichte was acutely aware of the difficulty of fitting his former idealism into the new system. "Knowledge of the absolute inner necessity [which unites the act of knowing and the absolute] is something totally obscure to a consciousness here rebelling with all its might, refusing ever to abandon its freedom and trying, if it cannot preserve freedom for itself, at least to find a refuge for it in God." The image of being that is constructed in us is grounded, not in any so-called autonomous ego, but in being; through ignorance, consciousness or the act of knowing is made the first link in the chain of deduction. From a dialectical movement conditioned by a freedom which was at the root of eternal knowledge, Fichte now passes to an absolutely unconditioned necessity; from an absolute which remained outside knowledge and was for us only an object, he passes to an absolute from which we draw light and blessedness.[15] Now we have complete Neo-Platonism: an absolute activity manifested in a Word which is the light of finite spirits. Of course, Fichte is not a mystic. He does not think that philosophy should have its source in an intuition of the activity of God, nor that a finite spirit can be reabsorbed in God and ground its activity on God's; in a sense, he begins with the finite ego and remains in the finite ego; he begins with the finite ego in order to demonstrate dialectically that the identity of being and thinking which constitutes it, is the image of the absolute, and he remains in the finite ego because the affirmation of the absolute is accomplished in it by reflection; being is incomprehensible, and the multiplicity of finite selves is an infinite striving to understand being. Moreover, in this last exposition, becoming and freedom are but a manifestation of eternal necessity, and they are produced necessarily. This freedom is provisional and precarious; it is merely a means between an origin from which it emerges and an end situated in infinity.

With perfect logic, systematism won out. It forced Fichte first to put the absolute beyond the activity of the ego (1801), then to deny the ego any autonomy (1804). But this perfect logic is a betrayal of his strong original inspiration, which survives only piecemeal in the last exposition. Fichte suffered the fate of many of his contemporaries: few philosophers of his era failed to see their vigorous theories become imprisoned in a system, just as the heavy cloak of the Empire stifled the revolutionary fires of the past.

Fichte protested all his life against mysticism with its immediate intuition of God, against naturalism with its God immanent in nature, against a Catholicism which tried to bring the state under subjection to religion. The philosopher sees, from the outside and by reflection, the eternal production of the Word by the Absolute. He sees how this Word is reflected in individual consciousness, as in his own, and how the free aspiration of his consciousness toward the spiritual life is posited as moral obligation. But Fichte is neither

---

[15] Cf. Gueroult, *La doctrine de la science de Fichte*, 1930, pp. 148, 158.

a mystic nor a naturalist, and his thought finds its final expression in the fundamental dogma of Christianity, the incarnation of the Word. This incarnation is the progressive development of morality and reason in the world. Christianity confers a meaning on history, in which Fichte identifies three periods: that of instinct, in which the moral conscience still slumbers; that of the fall and sin, in which man resists the demands of spiritual life and is held back only by the external authority of despotism; and that of redemption and inner transformation, in which man becomes the instrument of God. Thus Fichte's philosophy, under external influences, tends toward restoration of a philosophical Christianity, which took numerous forms during the first half of the nineteenth century. We were invited to participate in a human undertaking but have become collaborators on a divine mission.

The direct, immediate influence of Fichte was limited by the brilliant success of Schelling, and later of Hegel. It extended hardly beyond the beginning of the century. The *Philosophische Journal,* edited by Niethammer (1766–1848) can be considered the organ of his school. Soon J. B. Schad (1758–1834), in his *Popular Presentation of the Fichtean System and of the Religion Proceeding from It,* drew out the religious consequences of Fichteanism.

Bibliography

Texts

Fichte, G. *Sämtliche Werke,* 8 vols. Berlin 1845–46.
——. *Nachgelassene* Werke, 3 vols. Berlin 1834–35; Berlin 1962.
——. *Grundlage des Naturrechts.* Jena and Leipzig, 1796. Eng. trans. A. E. Kroeger: *The Science of Rights,* Philadelphia 1869; London 1889.
——. *Popular Works,* ed. and trans. William Smith, 2 vols. London 1848–49; 4th ed., London 1889. Includes translations of *Die Bestimmung des Menschen* and *Die Anweisung Zum Seligen Leben.*

Studies

Adamson, Robert. *Fichte.* Edinburgh and London, 1881.
Everett, C. C. *Fichte's Science of Knowledge, A Critical Exposition.* Chicago, 1884.
Fichte, I. H. *J. G. Fichte's Leben und litterarischer Briefwechsel.* Sulzbach, 1830–31.
Gueroult, M. *La doctrine de la science chez Fichte,* 2 vols. Strasbourg, 1930.
Gurwitsch, G. *Fichte's System der konkreten Ethik.* Tübingen, 1924.
Léon, Xavier. *Fichte et son temps,* 2 vols. Paris, 1922–27.
Medicus, Fritz. *Fichte.* Berlin, 1905.
——. *Fichte's Leben.* Leipzig, 1914; 2d rev. ed. Leipzig, 1922.
Talbot, E. B. *The Fundamental Principles of Fichte's Philosophy.* New York, 1906.
Thompson, A. B. *The Unity of Fichte's Doctrine of Knowledge.* Boston, 1895.
Vaughan, C. E. *Studies in the History of Political Philosophy,* vol. 2. Manchester, 1925. Pp. 94–142.

137

SCHELLING AND
THE ROMANTICISTS

FRIEDRICH WILHELM SCHELLING (1775–1854) served as a private tutor before he was appointed to the faculty of the University of Jena (1798), where he remained until he was called to the University of Würzburg (1803). In 1806 he left Würzburg for Munich, where he was secretary of the academy of arts. He did not resume his professorship until 1820, first at Erlangen, then at Munich (1827), and finally at Berlin (1841). His principal works dealt, first, with the philosophy of nature (*Ideas toward a Philosophy of Nature*, 1797; *On the World Soul*, 1798; *Outline of a System*, 1799); then with the philosophy of identity (*Exposition of My System of Philosophy*, 1801; *Bruno*, 1802). During the rest of his life he published only two shorter works: *Philosophy and Religion* (1804) and *Philosophical Inquiries into the Nature of Human Freedom* (1809). His *Introduction to the Philosophy of Revelation* and *Introduction to the Philosophy of Mythology* were published posthumously.

1 *The Philosophy of Nature*

When he left Jena for Würzburg in 1803, Schelling was twenty-eight years old and had been famous for six years. In five years he had published no less than six systematic expositions of his philosophy, not counting his *Philosophy of Art*, largely completed in 1802. He was the outstanding philosopher of the Romantic school,

138

and had taken a decisive stand against Fichte. This explosion of youthful fervor did not continue. During the remaining fifty-one years of his life, except for two important tracts, he published little. Most of the significant works of this period are the manuscripts of lectures prepared for his courses at Munich, Erlangen, and Berlin. The source of his inspiration also shifted: in the first brief period, while he was in Leipzig and Jena, the life of nature—the hierarchy of the powers of nature, from the lowest to organic life—and art constitute the principal subject of his meditation; after 1803 he read Jakob Böhme, was strongly influenced by Franz von Baader, and formulated a concrete image of the action of spiritual forces in the world. His interpretation borders on spiritualism, for it was the result of a sustained attempt to envision the great divine drama of which nature and humanity are different phases.

Such a pattern of evolution is not surprising. The philosophy of nature is remote from Baconian or Newtonian physics, remote from experimental investigation of the laws of phenomena. It resumes a Renaissance tradition which goes back through medieval alchemy to ancient philosophy. This tradition had flourished before Schelling, as early as the pre-Romantic period, particularly in Louis Claude de Saint-Martin, whose works were widely read in Germany.[1] According to Saint-Martin, material bodies change comtinuously and are the fleeting products of invisible, indestructible, immutable germs. Moreover, the philosophy of nature is closely tied to a theosophy. Rising above materialism, which confuses bodies—simple instruments of immaterial forces—with forces themselves, it attains a life closely related to spiritual and divine realities. The only cause for surprise is that the philosopher of nature waited so long to become a theosophist; contrary to the view generally held, it is not so much the evolution of Schelling's thought that needs explaining, as the slowness of this evolution.

The traditional outline of the philosophy of nature is fairly simple: Nature is independent and autonomous, thanks to an infinite rejuvenative power which restores the equilibrium between conflicting

[1] Cf. F. Lieb, *F. Baaders Jugendgeschichte,* 1926, pp. 169, 210.

forces whenever this equilibrium is broken by the ascendancy of one of them. This basic concept is found in the writings of Saint-Martin, who doubtless took it from Paracelsus, and it dominates the philosophical speculation of Schelling. Whereas mechanism (Cartesian or Newtonian) defines laws of correspondence, which enable the mind to pass from one part of reality to another in accordance with precise rules, this philosophy views nature as an organic whole, which regulates the action of conflicting forces tending toward mutual destruction. Thus it is an offensive revival, during an age that witnessed many different revivals, of the ancient Ionian vision of a Logos reconciling contraries.

To complete this outline, Schelling borrowed images from the sciences of his time, particularly chemistry and biology. According to *Ideas toward a Philosophy of Nature* (1797), oxygen (like mercury in Paracelsus) is the rejuvenative principle that arouses the earth's dormant energies by means of the essential chemical action of combustion; this action constantly renews its own conditions by virtue of atmospheric air, the permanence of which is insured by the combined, opposing actions of the animal world, which corrupts it and the vegetable world, which restores its oxygen. This universal "oxygenism" (according to Novalis' terminology) is replaced in *On the World Soul* (1798) by the notion of splitting by polarity, exemplified in electricity and magnetism; like positive and vegetative electricity, solar light and oxygen are opposites in terms of their product, vital air; oxygen in turn contrasts with phlogiston, as positive to negative, and combustion is union and restoration of equilibrium between these opposing forces. The activity of living beings is due to compensating rhythms, which, as they establish equilibriums, revive oppositions. Thus oxidation in respiration is offset by the introduction of phlogistic matter in nutrition, and an excess of oxygen is counterbalanced immediately by an excess of its opposite. This is how a living being differs from an inorganic being, in which effect depends solely on the action of two opposing forces; in the living being there must be a power higher than the pair of opposing forces—a power which plays them like instruments, manipulating them in such a way as to sustain life.

In Schelling's *On the World Soul* we find a conception of the universe closely parallel to that of Ritter, who had just discovered galvanism in 1797 and who, in 1798, was describing all bodies as systems of innumerable and infinitely small galvanic chains. To Ritter the universe is an animal: the celestial bodies are its blood corpuscles, the Milky Way is its muscles, and the celestial ether suffuses all its parts, like nervous fluid.

The philosophy of nature may be of some value in interpreting phenomena, but this possibility did not interest Schelling. His attention was drawn increasingly to the close kinship he discovered between this scheme and Fichte's dialectical method in the *Theory of Science*: if nature is substituted for the ego, it clearly corresponds to the infinite activity which asserts itself by positing its opposite (as a force of expansion is opposed to a force of repulsion in Kantian dynamics), which is infinite in that it is forever restoring the oppositions it has destroyed. The idea that Schelling then pursued was that of constructing a philosophy of nature which would remain on the same level of abstraction as the *Theory of Science,* considered as a treatise on method, of which his philosophy would be an application. But this plan turned him aside from the mysticism to which traditional naturalism was leading him, and, while waiting to return to mysticism, he took a completely different direction— one that led him, in 1803, to his philosophy of identity. Such was the effect of the stormy, complicated intellectual relations that joined Fichte to Schelling and that weighed heavily on the thinking of both. They were hostile brothers, who could not be separated or reconciled, and their hostility, which was the inevitable consequence of the position taken by Schelling, beginning with his *Outline of a System* (1799), increased until they broke publicly in 1804.

In adapting Fichte's doctrine to his scheme, Schelling uses the stratagem of substituting the dynamic constitutive opposites of nature for the ego and the nonego. He assumes that these opposites are the source of an inner dialectic, which produces all natural phenomena through successive syntheses and new oppositions. Countering the tendency of the universal activity of nature to produce a homogeneous fluid, infinitely diffused, is a force of attraction which produces different degrees of cohesion in this fluid; activity and cohesion are synthesized in an organism which is at once activity and thing, a thing suffused with activity. But an organism requires a nonorganism for its activity; the organism's irritability is determined by the inorganic world, and, by the same token, the inorganic world is determined by the organism. In contrast to the world of organisms, the inorganic world is simple juxtaposition, simple mass, but it is itself actively involved in the production of antagonisms and relations. First, gravity—not Newtonian gravitation, which confers an inexplicable property on matter—but an attraction identical in nature to the attraction of opposite kinds of electricity, due to the reciprocal antagonism of masses: in gravity these opposites tend to interpenetrate, but the tendency ends in juxtaposition; in chemical combinations such interpenetration occurs, whereas in electricity, polarity reaffirms the dualism of opposites. The inner activity of the organism, in turn, is manifested in antagonisms and relations. It wavers between the extremes of sensibility and irritability: in sensibility the organic subject limits its activity by its passivity; in irritability or the power of muscles to contract, the cycle is from heterogeneity to homogeneity, for subjective activity tends to lose itself in the object.

Thus the productive movement of the forces of nature is an interplay of antitheses and syntheses, identical in its logical rhythm with the Fichtean genesis of consciousness. But Fichte considered his method inseparable from his doctrine; if the dialectic is productive, according to him, this is only because of the initial act of an ego, which posits itself for itself; substitute nature for the ego, an objective product for a vital activity, and you have no principle of movement. Schelling rejects this view and insists that nature, too, is a vital activity and not a dead product, as Fichte had thought. Fichte's theory assumes the heteronomy of nature, which could exist only as an object of representation, which could have no end but that of serving as a point of application for moral action, and which can be explained in all its details only by the most superficial finality. But everything is different if nature is self-constructive, autonomous activity. Still, one must have an intuition of this activity. We know that for Fichte, every intuition is linked to self-reflection; by introducing an intuition of nature or otherness, therefore, Schelling claims that he is returning to a dogmatism prior to Kant. He could not have been more faithful, and at the same time more unfaithful, to the Fichtean spirit.

Schelling's theory of science is a kind of metaphysical algebra made up of universal signs, which can be assigned concrete values appropriate to the solution of each particular problem. We should remember, however, that Fichte considered the theory to be a genesis of consciousness of self. Thus the idea of treating the genesis of consciousness and all its functions as a special problem—one distinct from the theory of science, of which it is an application—would have seemed incomprehensible to Fichte. Yet that is exactly what Schelling undertakes in his *System of Transcendental Idealism* (1800). How does he intend to do it? He begins with Fichte himself and tries to show the ego becoming conscious of itself in the process of resolving conflicts issuing from the limitation of an activity which is in itself illimitable. In the theoretical part, however, he adds to deduction of the representative faculties—sensation, productive intuition, reflection, judgment—deduction of the constitutive forces of matter: magnetism, electricity, chemism, organism. The moments in the construction of matter correspond exactly to the acts of intelligence; the dormant forces of matter are identical in nature with the representative forces and, as Hemsterhuys and Leibniz had divined, "matter is nothing but spirit in the equilibrium of its activities." The practical part is the same: just as a philosophy of nature is joined to deduction of the representative faculties, a philosophy of history is tied to practical philosophy. History is at once a manifestation of freedom and the progressive revelation of God, "for God never *is,* if by being one means that which is manifested in the objective world; if he *were,* we would not be; but he reveals himself progressively. By his history man provides a proof of God's existence, but a proof which can be completed only by history in its entirety." Thus Schelling links Saint-Martin, then Herder, with Fichte. But he goes further: in his *System of Transcendental Idealism* he adds two parts not even mentioned in the *Theory of Science,* his lectures on teleology and his lectures on the philosophy of art. Why the new addition? The ego's penetration of the nonego remains an exigency of will, a principle rather than the object of intuition. Schelling seeks to identify an object actually realizing this essential requirement for intuition, and in which the ideal penetrates the real—for example, the living organism in nature and the work of art in the realm of mind or spirit. In inspiration the artistic genius perceives unconscious, impersonal powers uniting with his conscious powers in the production of a work of art. Art bears witness to the oneness of spirit and nature, the conscious and the unconscious, the ideal and the real.

II *Philosophy of Identity*

This influx of new thoughts—this combination of the Fichtean method with a philosophy of nature, of history, and of art—necessitated a systematization of ideas known as the philosophy of identity, which Schelling undertook to accomplish in his *Exposition of My System of Philosophy* (1801), in *Bruno,* and in *The Method of Academic Study.* At the summit of the universe is the absolute, which is the identity of subject and object; at the summit of philosophy is the intellectual intuition of this absolute. The absolute is neither subject nor object, neither spirit nor nature, but rather the identity or neutrality of the two opposites, like the One of Plato in the *Parmenides,* or of Plotinus. It is not a synthesis of being and knowing, which would imply that being and knowing first exist independently, whereas all being is already knowing since it is self-affirmation, and all knowing is already being since it asserts itself and posits itself. But if the source of all activity is in opposition, as Fichte teaches, do we not risk going beyond Plato and Plotinus to Parmenides' inert, sterile being? The derivation of nature, spirit, and their manifold determinations from the absolute is both an addition to the system and its most vulnerable point. Schelling refuses to acknowledge any emergence from self, any transitive activity, any true production in the absolute. Others made this mistake, in his view, because they considered spirit the subject and divine nature the object, like two fragments of the absolute. But the philosophy of nature demonstrates that nature, like the absolute, is subject-object, and transcendental idealism demonstrates that the same is true of spirit; like the absolute, nature and spirit are not a synthesis of two terms which first exist separately but the identity of both terms. How do they differ, then, from the absolute? They differ in that there is an excess of objectivity in nature conceived as subject-object—as if an intuition merged and became solidified in the being contemplated by it—and an excess of subjectivity, turning inward, or reflective activity in spirit. But the deviations of nature and spirit balance one another perfectly in relation to the absolute (the "potencies" of the absolute in Schelling's terminology), and in their totality are nothing less than the absolute itself. We see clearly that the same applies to the relative identity represented by nature as well as to the relative identity represented by spirit, and that the excess of subjectivity or objectivity applicable to each will delineate the diverse facets of both.

Philosophy never emerges from the absolute or from reason, and it is the organon of the absolute. Schelling seeks to prove that Spinoza and Bruno (the Renaissance Platonist) were his forerunners. In *Bruno* he constructs a most unusual system of metaphysical astronomy, making each of the great celestial bodies—the planets and the sun—a free, autonomous absolute, containing in itself the law of its movement; in these pages, more clearly than anywhere else, we see how far his philosophy of nature, which tries to establish a link between the absolute and each part of the universe, deviates from Newtonian science, which defines beings only in terms of their mutual relations. The philosophy of identity is in fact an attempt to solve an old problem, which Aristotle was unable to resolve, which science had abandoned, and which Schelling took up again in his *Philosophy of Nature*: the problem of the specific determination of living beings. For the old method of classifying concepts, the philosophy of identity substitutes a method of intuition, which traces the transformations of one thing in another, as Goethe traced the transformations of a leaf in every organ of a plant. Schelling's system of identity is only the ultra-abstract and completely general expression of a tendency, then widely prevalent, to seek what Leibniz called the "continuity of forms" rather than the spatiotemporal relations connecting phenomena.

Still, Schelling boasts of leaving nothing arbitrary in this intuition but of giving it a true method, thanks to his notion of potencies: each trinity of potencies brings out successively, in the subject-object under consideration, the real or objective aspect, the ideal or subjective aspect, and their identity. Thus the real, objective aspect of nature is gravity and cohesion, its ideal aspect is light, and identity is gravity suffused with light, or organization. By the same token, the real aspect of spirit is knowing, the ideal and subjective aspect is action, and the identity of the two is art.

Each of these potencies is itself a direct expression of the absolute, and in each, the same triplicity of potencies must be repeated. This is the starting point of the *Philosophy of Art* (1803), which contains —along with all the results of the aesthetic education Schelling received in Jena, where German Romanticism was in full flower—the final form of the system of identity. The total absence of a musical tradition, exclusive devotion to Italian painting of the sixteenth century, the ideal of architecture as represented by the Greek temple, veneration of the epics of Homer and Dante, which could be revealed only by the novels of Cervantes or Goethe and the dramas of Calderon or Shakespeare—everything bears witness to an artistic taste of astonishing narrowness, yet he had no other materials at his disposal. Just as he discovered the scheme for his philosophy of nature in Fichte, he turned to the theories of the Schlegel brothers in an attempt to find support for his system of aesthetics. In his view, art is the expression of the infinite in the finite; the eternal Idea becomes alive in the imagination; consequently mythology is the basis of art if it is truly, not an arbitrary creation, but a kind of systematic symbolism, in which Gods are in the imagination what Ideas are in thought. Of course Christianity is hostile to mythology; as a necessary reaction against the tendency to rigidify the infinite in finite forms, it abases the finite in the presence of the infinite; the finite no longer expresses the infinite by what it is (as Minerva expressed wisdom directly), but by what it signifies (like the Cross of Christ, which, degrading in itself, is glorious); Christianity and Protestantism are freedom from and the destruction of forms. Like Schlegel, Schelling believes in the impending birth of a new mythology, which will inspire a new art; his philosophy of nature, with all the mysterious correspondence it introduces into things, restores to the world the depth and the power of imagination it had lost with Christianity.

Thus pagan mythology, Christianity, and the new mythology mark the three stages in the history of art—its past, present, and future—or the return to pagan affirmation of the divinity of nature after its denial by Christianity. Moreover, this historical scheme has no decisive influence in the systematic determination of genres. The identity of the infinite and the finite, of subject and object, is a master key, which has just revealed the genesis of mythology and Christianity in history, and with which Schelling will be enabled to show the profound unity of art. The genres of art derive from a kind of law of compensation for excesses, from which all the potencies of the absolute are deduced. Plastic arts and poetry are the two limits of art: plastic arts capture and immobilize aesthetic intuition in the marble of a statue or a temple (excess of objectivity); poetry attempts to internalize aesthetic intuition in the continuous movement of an epic or drama, which exists only for the reflective spirit (excess of subjectivity).

III *Schelling's Later Philosophy*

Only the monotony of his ready formulas and his preference for the concrete, which so radically separated him from Fichte, could have persuaded Schelling to turn his attention to a treatise by Eschenmayer (*Philosophy Becomes Non-Philosophy*). The latter complains that the radiation of absolute identity blots out both God's consciousness of himself and individual finite beings, along with their wills and, consequently, their morality; in short, he reminds Schelling of what had caused Jacobi vehemently to deny Spinozist rationalism. In *Philosophy and Religion* (1804) Schelling already admits that finite beings cannot issue from the absolute, which remains in itself, and must therefore posit themselves by a pure act of freedom similar to the act attributed by Plotinus to souls that desire to live for themselves and detach themselves from the world soul. Among spiritual beings, this free act or breaking away from the absolute is the fall, and history with its double epic—the Iliad, in which history moves away from the center and the Odyssey, in which it returns to the center—contains the consequences of the fall and the final restoration. Schelling was beginning to emerge from his exclusive preoccupation with the absolute. "Since Jena," he wrote in 1806, "I have seen that religion, public belief, and the life of the state are the fulcrum of the lever which must unsettle the inert mass of humanity." *Philosophical Inquiries into the Nature of Human Freedom,* published in 1809, following Schelling's study of the writings of Böhme, marks the completion of the reversal. He no longer deduces, he relates; but his narrative is a systematic account of a mystical drama which takes us back through the centuries to Böhme and Eckhart. First there is a ground of existence (*Grund*) with neither light nor consciousness but only empty, impoverished desire; then God's spirit, moved by love, tempers understanding with desire, which, pregnant with every form of existence, becomes the creative will of nature—cosmogonic becoming; finally, at the high point in the drama, comes man. In natural beings the will peculiar to each being remains united to the universal will. In man, an intelligent being, this individual will, developed and enlightened, desires to exist for itself and to become its own universe; this is the origin of evil, rooted not in the ground of nature but in an enlightened will, which cuts itself off from universal love. The fall of man marks the beginning of the theogonic process or history, which is his return to God. Thus the universe is the revelation of God; in God the ground of existence is bound immediately to existence; apart from God it achieves existence only through the intermediary of nature and history. A creative God, a free man, and final union of man and God were the three articles of a theism—"the official belief of all constitutions in which justice and order reside"—from which Schelling was never again to deviate.

The Ages of the World (1815) is suffused with the same spirit. In this work, however, Schelling follows the example of Böhme and relates not only the evolution of man's nature but also that of God himself. Every act of becoming is a victory, representing a triumph over the blind, destructive forces which serve as its ground. There is no conditional, absolute affirmation; an affirmation is grounded only on negation, on an act relegating to an eternal past the dark, chaotic forms which tended toward being; nothing, indeed, is more dismal or surrounded by more dangers than an incipient life. But this victory is itself made possible only by renunciation of primal forces, which surrender their will to be for themselves, and become the organ of a higher will. This becoming is at first that of God himself; it can be only if it comes from nonbeing, from the primal germ, which is its first potency; in opposition to that germ, God is being which is (*das Seiende*), and this is its second potency; finally it is the hierarchical union of being and nonbeing, and this is its third potency. Each of these potencies desires to be, and in turn drives back the other two, as in the circular process of becoming, which goes from seed to plant, then from plant to seed; this rotation will cease only if there is a common will to surrender to a higher will—a will which is not that of any form of being and which desires nothing because it is above any possible difference. This is superdivinity (*Übergottheit*), which is based on nature, constituted by the three potencies. God is absolute freedom—freedom from any form of being or nature.

This completes the becoming of God and initiates that of the universe. The three divine potencies, liberated by their renunciation, become the matter of future creations: the first becomes the matter of nature, the second of spirit, and the third of the world soul. Even before any process of becoming was completed, an ideal hierarchy was established between these three powers, so that each is necessarily the image of the one superior to it. Nature produces a profusion of forms to reflect spirit, and spirit produces in it, as a series of visions, images of the ideas which are in the universal soul; thus by a kind of theurgy, the higher power inclines toward the lower one and determines it. Such is the ideal plan of creation, but this ideal plan contains no force to make possible its realization. Furthermore, absolute freedom or superdivinity has no creative will, since it is beyond all determination. Creation originates in the obscure, inexplicable will of the first power, the creative power of nature, whose awesome, destructive forces give birth first to the stars of the universe, then to organic life. Nature is the fruit of wrath or the negative power of God; love or the affirmative power of God is the creator of the world of spirits, which Schelling interprets here in the spiritualistic sense—beings capable of communicating by means of mysterious powers of which conscious life has only a vague notion; finally, love embraces wrath and creates the wisdom of the world soul.

For the static God depicted in the rational theology of the two previous centuries—the universal, immutable being—Schelling substitutes the God of mysticism and inner development. A being evolves because the forces which constitute it are not in their true place and must be driven back; the theogonic process through which God realizes himself is a kind of see-saw movement (*universio*), in which being that should remain potential is initially actual, whereas future actual being is repressed; the history of our universe is contained in this process.

Schelling's theosophy is confirmed by the study of mythology, in which he became interested as early as 1815. Previously, Schelling had been satisfied with the teachings of Schlegel, but mythology was beginning to assume a role similar to that played today by the sociological study of primitive religions. In his *Symbolism* (1810–11), Creuzer, again taking up a traditional theory that myths are really doctrines derived from an original monotheism, which has disappeared, tried to confirm his views by conducting detailed investigations of Egyptian, Asian, Greek, and Italian religions. From his friend Görres, the mystic, he took a thesis vehemently rejected by philologists, but adopted by Schelling, who saw in mythology a history of the human conscience: in the history of the human conscience mythology is the phase of hostile forces bent on mutual destruction and must be followed by the phase of Christian monotheism and spirit; the god of primitive humanity is an undifferentiated being who is neither one nor many; humanity breaks away from this amorphous state by means of polytheism, which, as a consequence of the diversity of beliefs, produces diversity among peoples and races.

Opposing this polytheism or natural religion which apprehends God in the diversity of his potencies is Christianity, a supernatural religion or revelation of the unity that surmounts his potencies. Christianity is not a definitive state; once polytheism has been overthrown, it becomes stable and restricts its own freedom in the Catholic Church, a force as blind as paganism. Philosophy should surpass it and originate a thoroughly spiritual religion.

Thus, to express his own views, Schelling successively used the language of Saint-Martin, Fichte, Schlegel, Jakob Böhme, and Creuzer. He began with the idea that reason, with intellectual intuition, could construct all forms of being, nature, and spirit. After 1806 he became aware of the distinction between universals, which are constructed by reason and individuals, which actually exist. This distinction led him to conceive existents as radically contingent and free in relation to essences and possibles. It also explains why, at the end of his career, he separated two philosophies: "purely rational philosophy," which constructs the possible, and "positive philosophy," which originates in the pure fact of absolute freedom —a principle of existence for oneself and others. Still, one trait common to every phase of this long evolution is worth nothing, and that is what we have called Fichte's Manicheism. Nothing posits itself except by a struggle and a victory over its opponent; the immediate can only be emptiness and nothingness.

IV *The Romanticists*

German metaphysics was strongly influenced by the personal ties linking the Romanticists to Schelling and Hegel. At Tübingen, Hölderlin was a childhood friend of the two philosophers, and he became an admirer of Fichte. The Romantic circle of Jena, at the beginning of the century, linked Schelling and Novalis, Friedrich Schlegel and Tieck. Ideas were constantly exchanged between men of letters and philosophers.

"The true essence of Romanticism," wrote Novalis (*Works,* ed. Minor, III, 343), is in making absolute, universalizing, and classifying the individual moment or situation." That is why, in the hands of the Romantics, the novel, short story, or poem acquires a philosophical value.

Between poetry and philosophy Hölderlin (1770–1843) sees an intimate bond. Poetry is the beginning and end of philosophy: "Ultimately that which is incompatible, philosophically speaking, is reunited in the mysterious source of poetry. . . . Philosophy does not originate in pure understanding, for it is more than limited knowledge of the given; it does not originate in simple reason, for it is more than a need for unceasing progress in union and distinction [this is obviously aimed at Fichte]; but clarify the divine word ἐν διάφερον ἑαυτῷ, and then it does not make demands blindly, for it knows what it requires and why" (*Selected Works,* ed. Schwab, pp. 234-35). Thus for Hölderlin philosophy, like poetry, is Heraclitean knowledge of the unity of contradictories. The organ of this knowledge is spirit, which justifies everything. "O friend," says Hyperion, "finally spirit reconciles us with everything." Again, its organ may be nature, "rude nature, which laughs at reason and is linked to enthusiasm" (p. 415), or perhaps a kind of harmony of spirits, which reunites what nature joined and understanding separated. A state of innocence and love, in which everything is united spontaneously, a state of dispersion, in which everything is separated, a final state of return to promitive union—this is the view expressed by Hölderlin, who was profoundly influenced on one hand by German mysticism and on the other by the Hegelian triad. The second stage is simply a prelude to the third: "We separate only in order to be more closely united, to have a more divine peace unite us with all things and ourselves." With Hölderlin this peace seems to signify the pure, abstract sentiment of life and being: "To be, to live is enough; therein is the honor of the gods; all who merely live are equal in the divine world, and there we find neither master nor slave; natural beings live for each other, like lovers; they have everything in common—spirit, joy, and eternal youth" (*Ibid.,* p. 284). Hölderlin's Romanticism is the wish for a complete, harmonious life in contrast to dispersion, the dominant defect of Germany, where "one sees professionals but not men, thinkers but not men; . . . one must already be intelligent before bringing his sensibility to perfection, . . . a skillful man before being a child."

Novalis (1772–1801) provides a Romantic interpretation of Kantian criticism. "There are unilateral, antinomical judgments," he writes, (*Works,* ed. Minor, III, 306), "and they are the ones in which realism conceives one species and idealism its opposite. There are synthetic judgments, which are the products of genius, and these are the ones conceived by criticism. There is also a common criticism, which sinks to academism or eclecticism as well as a higher criticism, which rises to syncretism." This higher criticism is the one responsible for the communication of all reality. For Novalis, "the nonego is the symbol of the ego and is useful only in enabling the self to apprehend itself; inversely, however, the nonego is represented by the ego, and the ego is the symbol of the nonego. . . . The world is a universal trope, a symbolic image of spirit." [2] Fichte discovered the unconscious magic capable of causing the external world to appear to be a reality independent of the mind that produced it. This magic should become conscious and voluntary.

This Romanticism, particularly in Novalis, is inseparable from the religious awakening and the reaction against the encyclopedic spirit manifested in France and Germany in the illuminist movement. We need only read Novalis' inspired sermon, *Christianity or Europe,* in order to discover the same spirit that produced *The Genius of Christianity* and *St. Petersburg Evenings:* "Will there not soon be, in Europe, a host of truly pious souls? Will not all truly religious men be filled with the desire to see heaven on earth? And will they not assemble and begin to sing the sacred choruses? . . . From the bosom of a European council Christianity will be reborn."

The career of Friedrich Schlegel (1772-1829) is typical of the Romantics. It progresses from an ideal of unbridled freedom, exempting the genius from all laws because the divinity speaks in him, to a conversion to Catholicism (beginning in 1804). The characteristic attitude of genius is irony, a mental disposition "which surpasses everything, rises above anything conditioned." In his *Philosophy of History* (1829) he goes so far as to uphold the philosophy of revelation, which apprehends the living God in the Church, in the state, and in art. In Romantic irrationalism, extreme license can be associated with extreme discipline.

v *Systems Related to Schelling*

Active all around Schelling were philosophers of nature in whom illuminism and occultism were blended, in diverse proportions, with the scientific spirit. Lorenz Oken (1779-1851), who glimpsed the cellular structure of organisms as early as 1805 (*Reproduction*),

---

[2] As quoted by C. Estève, "La poésie magique dans Novalis," *Revue philosophique* (November, 1929), pp. 410-11.

was violently opposed to Schelling's theosophy, but in his *Textbook of Natural Philosophy* (3 vols., 1810–11) he expounds a pantheism closely related to that of *Bruno*: everything is God's thought, and philosophy perceives, across nature and man, the transformations of this thought. An eternal world, whose development is God's consciousness of himself, assimilation of the great forces of nature to the moments of this consciousness (ether is the self-positing activity of God, light the act of consciousness), man considered the perfect animal—the seat of divine understanding, of which all animal species are dissociated parts—these are well known fantasies, and they lead to the conclusion that the warrior hero is a superior, divine man, just as in Carlyle and Nietzsche Romanticism led to the superman.

Gotthilf Heinrich von Schubert (1780–1860), on the other hand, inclines toward the theosophical and mystical side of Schelling's system (*Views of the Dark Side of Natural Science,* 1808; *The History of the Soul,* 1803), and the physician Andreas Justinius Kerner (1786–1862) interprets the state of hypnosis as a form of possession or inspiration. Karl Gustav Carus (1789–1869) seeks the origin of conscious phenomena in the subconscious region of the soul (*History of the Evolution of the Soul,* 1846; *Psyche,* 1851). He tries to apprehend the moment when consciousness emerges from unconsciousness: consciousness of self is preceded by the feeling of self, which, at its lower degree, is hardly distinguishable from its object; this unseparated consciousness is consciousness of the world (*Weltbewusstsein*); its development requires a concentration of impressions by the nervous system, the afflux of new impressions originating in the external world, and their consolidation by the memory.

Others, like Henrik Steffens (1773–1845), who provides a vivid description of the intellectual milieu of his time in *What I Experienced* (10 vols., 1840–45), went to great lengths in describing the complete evolution of the solar system until the appearance of man, as Schelling did in *The Ages of the World*. A mineralogist and geologist, Steffens (like Spencer later on) shows evolution tending toward individuality, which is realized fully in man. The violence of man's desires gives rise, in nature, to a conflict, which is put down only by grace.

When Franz Xaver von Baader (1765–1841) met Schelling in 1806, he found him too close to Fichte and Spinoza, just as Schelling accused him of being too close to Jakob Böhme and Saint-Martin. Baader nevertheless thought that *The World Soul* "had awakened physics from the death sleep of atomism." Schelling corrected his philosophy of nature along the lines indicated by Baader when he assumed, in addition to the two opposing forces in nature—the positive force and the negative force—the necessity of a third force to keep them together. Furthermore, Baader's description of divine evolution is quite similar to Jakob Böhme's.

Karl Wilhelm Ferdinand Solger (1780–1819) brilliantly illuminates an essential aspect of the philosophy of his time in his theory of tragic irony (*Erwin,* 1815; *Philosophical Conversations,* 1817): the whole world is the revelation of God on earth; consequently religion is the negation of the individual as such, and the beautiful is the most perfect expression of God in phenomena. But a complete union of the idea and the terrestrial element is impossible; therefore art, religion, and morality deny God even as they reveal him, and therein lies the essential irony of human existence.

BIBLIOGRAPHY

Texts

Schelling, F. W. J. *Sämtliche Werke,* ed. K. F. A. von Schelling, 14 vols. Stuttgart and Augsburg, 1856–61.
————. *Werke,* ed. M. Schröder, 8 vols. Munich, 1927–56.
————. *Über die Gottheiten von Samothrake.* Stuttgart and Tübingen, 1815, trans. F. de Wolfe Bolman: *The Ages of the World.* New York, 1942.
————. *Philosophische Untersuchungen über das Wesen der menschlichen Freiheit,* trans. J. Gutman: *Of Human Freedom.* Chicago, 1936.
————. *Über das Verhältnis der bildenden Künste zu der Natur,* trans. A. Johnson: *The Philosophy of Art: An Oration on the Relation between the Plastic Arts and Nature.* London, 1845.

Studies

Studies
Bréhier, Émile. *Schelling.* Paris, 1912.
Cassirer, Ernst. *Das Erkenntnisproblem in der Philosophie und Wissenschaft der neueren Zeit,* vol. 3, *Die Nachkantischen Systeme.* Berlin, 1920.
Copleston, Frederick C. *History of Philosophy,* vol. 7. London, 1963.
Fischer, Kuno. *Geschichte der neueren Philosophie,* vol. 7, 3d ed. Heidelberg, 1902. (A Study of Schelling's life and work.)
Hartmann, Nicolai. *Die Philosophie des deutschen Idealismus,* 2d ed. Berlin, 1960.
Hirsch, Eric D. *Wordsworth and Schelling.* New York, 1962.
Jaspers, Karl. *Schelling: Grösse und Verhängnis.* Munich, 1955.
Kroner, Richard. *Von Kant bis Hegel,* 2 vols. Tübingen, 1921–24.
Noack, Ludwig. *Schelling und die Philosophie der Romantik.* Berlin, 1859.
Read, Herbert. *The True Voice of Feeling.* London, 1953. (Schelling's influence on Coleridge.)
Schneeberger, G. *Schelling: Eine Bibliographie.* Berne, 1954. (An extensive bibliography.)
Watson, John. *Schelling's Transcendental Idealism.* Chicago, 1882.

HEGEL

GEORG WILHELM FRIEDRICH HEGEL (1770–1831), Schelling's classmate at the University of Tübingen, lived in Berne from 1774 to 1779 and in Frankfurt until 1800. In 1801 he became a university lecturer in Jena, remaining there until 1807. From 1818 to 1831 he was professor at the University of Berlin, where he began to win many adherents. Hegel's early writings (*Life of Jesus* and *First System,* written in 1795 and 1800) were published only recently. He achieved recognition in 1801 with his dissertation *De orbitis planetarum* and *The Difference between Fichtean and Schellingian Philosophy,* but his first great work, the *Phenomenology of Spirit,* was not published until 1807. Between 1812 and 1816 he published the three volumes of his *Science of Logic,* and in 1817, the general exposition of the *Encyclopedia of the Philosophical Sciences* (2d edition, 1827). The only other work of note to appear during his lifetime was his *Philosophy of Right* (1821); his lectures on aesthetics, the philosophy of history, and the philosophy of religion were published after his death.

1 *The Divisions of Philosophy*

If we approach Hegel after Fichte and Schelling, we are struck by the extreme density and depth of his speculations, for he was never satisfied until he had reached the concrete in nature and history. He was older than Schelling, but since he did not begin to publish until many years after his classmate, he had time to acquire the culture that Fichte had declared to be completely useless to the theoretician of science. An excellent Hellenist and Latinist, he was acquainted with mathematics and natural sciences, making it a practice, until he reached an advanced age, to record all kinds of facts acquired through his readings. Thus Hegel, like many philosophers living in an age determined above all not to let any positive element of human culture escape examination, based his philosophy on encyclopedic knowledge. Mind was defined less by abstract analysis of the conditions of knowledge than by synthesis of its positive products.

Hegel was an encyclopedist but at the same time a systematic philosopher. The encyclopedist does not want to let any positive reality go to waste; the systematic philosopher wants to retain only the product of a rational speculation. Hegel's ambition, from the beginning, was to fuse encyclopedia and system so intimately that the system would retain the positive reality in its entirety—but not as if this reality were at first given as a mass outside thought to be absorbed gradually by thought, since philosophy would then have only a formal function of organization. Reality must be posited in and by the system, for the philosopher seeks to conceive being and must be able to justify passage from concept to being or from being to concept. Furthermore, there is no hope of reconciling the two terms once they have been posited as external to each other; then empirical science can only add the finite to the finite, leaving philosophical speculation empty and without subject matter.

The philosophical problem, the rational determination of all being and all reality, is therefore insoluble unless it is resolved, in one sense, at the outset—unless at the start we are in possession of the thought, identical to being, which Hegel first called transcendental or intellectual intuition, then concept (*Begriff*). It was such an intuition that Fichte, and later Schelling, had opposed to Kant's formalism, and in his first published works Hegel criticizes the inadequacy of their solutions. Fichte's system does assume the identity of subject and object, but only as a postulate or ever receding ideal behind action. Fichte does not go beyond the kind of reflection that opposes the absolute ego to the ego of empirical consciousness and to the nonego, but in this way he isolates it in emptiness and abstraction. Hegel is even more displeased with Jacobi, who in principle denied reason the right to penetrate to existences and realities, and who conferred upon a completely heterogeneous belief in reason the mission of guiding us in the world of belief. On the other hand, Schelling (the Schelling of 1800) is at first in Hegel's good graces, for he asserted the identity of subject and object, and he never separated them after uniting them by intuition; according to Schelling, nature does not oppose the self as object to subject; nature is a subject-object, and so is the ego; each of the two terms contains the principle of the other term; each is an absolute of which every determination is immanent.

Hegel remained faithful for a while to Schelling, and in his qualifying Latin thesis at the University of Jena, *On the Orbits of the Planets* (1801), he criticized the Newtonians, who used the mathematical hypothesis of central forces (which are simply names) to reconstruct the solar system piece by piece, whereas he deduced from it the laws of "the oneness of reason and nature." But in due time Hegel abandoned Schlegel, and the Preface to the *Science of Logic* marked a definitive break. Schelling's absolute remained formal, uniform, sterile. "It is not yet science, any more than an acorn is an oak; it will be science when this concept is in turn resolved into its stages." The system of identity creates the illusion of deducing nature and spirit from the absolute, thanks to an excess of objectivity or subjectivity in the subject-object, but "it is simply the repetition of one and the same principle, which is merely applied externally to different material. . . . To pit this one piece of information, that in the absolute all is one, against all knowledge, which is distinct and complete and which seeks and requires content, to pass off one's absolute as the night, in which, as they say, all cows are black—that is the naïveté of the emptiness of knowledge." From this moment on, Hegel sets conceptual constructions against intuition (*Anschauung*), comparing the latter to feeling (*Gefühl*), "which jumbles ideas and tends more toward edification than speculation." This kind of philosophy likes to receive more than to give, to feel more than to express, to dream more than to think. It is a formalism which excites admiration by uniting terms that seem to be far apart and by teaching "that mind is electricity or that an animal is nitrogen. . . . But the petty trickery of such a procedure is soon discovered; it is like a picture consisting of only two colors . . . and the end result is a single picture since the two terms of the schema are in turn fused in pure identity."

What does Hegel offer to replace Schelling's sterile absolute? To appreciate the precision and import of his criticism, we must recall the deep-seated image we discovered at the root of the philosophical speculations of Fichte and Schelling: being is determined only by opposition and struggle against its opponent—a struggle ending in victory and subjugation. Schelling criticized Fichte only for delaying this victory infinitely; he himself tried to show that the different aspects of his absolute could be interpreted as alternate victories of subject and object; thus Schelling and Fichte clearly introduced into philosophy what Hegel calls the "negative"—the obstacle that the infinite current strikes against, producing a diversity of vortices. Hegel criticizes them (and we saw the extent to which Schelling was influenced by his criticism after 1811) for "not taking it seriously enough." In Hegel's estimation, "the idea of God becomes insipid in their speculation, for seriousness, pain, patience, and the *work of the negative* are missing." The life of God is an untroubled unity, which takes neither otherness nor self-estrangement (*Entfremdung*) seriously. But the three philosophers were separated only by minor differences, which their unending polemics tended to accent. Each accused his adversary of coming finally to the immobilism of the Eleatics (Schelling leveled against Hegel the criticism Hegel had directed at him), but each took images from the same source to introduce life and mobility into the absolute. These were the theogonic images which had again become prevalent during the critical stage of eighteenth-century illuminism: a God coming to birth and realizing himself by struggling and suffering;

a militant period preceding victory. This image and others of the same kind enable us to grasp one of the central notions of Hegel's system—the notion of *concept* (*Begriff*). How can I succeed in conceiving myself as I am? When my being and character have been developed in the context of a thousand circumstances associated with my life, for life is the mirror which "reflects" what I am in myself and offers this reflection to my thought as an object or being; I must seize its being in the reflection of nature if I am truly to possess it; the concept is this mediate knowledge or return to self in a roundabout way—by means of an emergence from self and an externalization of self.

The principle of the concept accounts for the great divisions of Hegel's philosophy: phenomenology of mind or spirit, in which he shows consciousness rising gradually from elementary forms of sensation to knowledge; logic, in which the concept as such is defined; philosophy of nature, which marks the moment when mind becomes alienated from itself; and philosophy of mind, which shows the return of mind to itself in law, morality, religion and philosophy. Consequently the system is a vast epic of mind or "an experience," to use Hegel's own words.[1] In its effort to know itself, mind successively produces every possible form of reality—first the frames of its thought, then nature, then history. These forms cannot be apprehended in isolation but only in the process of evolution or development that produces them.

II *The Phenomenology of Spirit*

How philosophical speculation originates in man and how it is the consummation of knowledge are the issues studied in the *Phenomenology of Spirit,* which Royce calls the autobiography of the world spirit (*Weltgeist*) and rightly compares to novels such as Goethe's *Wilhelm Meister's Apprenticeship.*

The *Phenomenology* describes a double equilibratory movement:

[1] See N. Hartmann, "Hegel et la dialectique du réel," *Revue de métaphysique,* 1931, p. 295.

one by which the subject seeks certainty in an external object and finally discovers it in itself; and one by which the subject, seeking to assert itself, first opposes the other subjects, which it destroys or subjugates, then becomes reconciled with them in mind or spirit. On the whole, it presents the history of the spirit's wanderings outside itself before it recognizes itself for what it is.

Hegel's aim is to determine what the mind should contribute in its own right ("take upon itself," in his energetic language) to the certainty it has of the objects of knowledge. Nothing, it seems at first, if we start from the certainty of our senses; everything, if we accept his final demonstration. The mind starts from sense certainty "the concrete content of which makes it seem like the richest kind of knowledge, like knowledge infinite in its richness." Actually this is the poorest kind of knowledge, for it is limited to a *here* and *now;* the *here* and *now* are not even in the object, which changes, but in the permanent self, which predicates each *here* and *now.* But the knowledge that the self has of the *now* is always mediate, for it rests on the negation of a preceding *now.* The act of knowing that contains negation is perception (*Wahrnehmung*).

Perception apprehends a single thing, endowed with diverse qualities. The uniformity of the object (or its unity) persists whether or not there is apprehension; consequently the certainty of perception is attributable exclusively to the object. But qualities both simultaneous and mutually exclusive contradict the unity of the object. To safeguard this unity, the perceiving self "takes upon itself" the qualities of the object; a thing, in itself, is red only to the eye, sweet only to the tongue. But the object is still responsible for its simple unity or relation to itself, and this uniformity with itself can be known only to the extent that it is compared with other objects—to the extent, therefore, that it has a distinct quality. From the moment when unity is distinguished from multiplicity in the object, when there is a separation of points of view which at the same time invoke each other, the object is no longer perceived but thought: we have reached the sphere of understanding or intellect.

But even though the object is thought rather than perceived, it is still an object. The relation between unity and diversity, as it is known by thought, is the relation between a constitutive force and its manifestations. On one hand the force cannot exist without manifesting itself, and it invites solicitation since it can manifest itself only if solicited; on the other hand, however, solicitation always comes from a second force alien to the first, and it therefore appears to be accidental. Such a contradiction can arise only if the two forces (for example, positive and negative electricity) actually express only one force; then the difference manifested is posited as inseparable from the thing in itself. A being which manifests itself in the form of differences that enable it to recognize its oneness with itself, is a concept (*Begriff*). The object which remained opposite consciousness in sensation, perception, and understanding, is no longer different in any way from consciousness, since it is now a concept; the alternating movement between identity and difference, difference and identity, is the concept in which consciousness rediscovers itself.

Victorious over the objective reality in which it has rediscovered itself, consciousness splits into distinct consciousnesses, and collisions between the individual consciousnesses initiate the second movement. This mysterious, hostile, impenetrable world of consciousnesses alien to my own must disappear. We should not overlook the fact that the very positing of the problem implies that Hegel already has the solution, and that his statement of the problem can be illuminated only by an idea formulated in advance: the union of consciousness and the universal spirit in religion by means of the Church. This is his proposed solution, and his aim is to show the dialectical necessity of the steps leading to it.

The destructive rage of the warrior, who destroys the hostile world, is the first step. But this destruction contradicts itself, for it eliminates other consciousnesses, which, by contrasting with its own, make possible its individuality. Destruction gives way to subjugation; the vanquished becomes the slave. The relation between master and slave is that in which the vanquished serves as an instrument for the victor's will, making him vividly aware of his self. This mutual bond of dependence between slave and master must in turn be destroyed, and it is destroyed by Stoicism. The Stoic, drawing support from his link to the universal reason, can declare his indifference toward any situation in which he finds himself—that of emperor as well as that of slave—and thus gain inner freedom. But this course leads him to the skepticism of the Cynic, to a purely formal freedom, which struggles against social conventions of every kind only to find at last a poor, empty life.

The skeptical notion that life has little value leads to the feeling that there is no hope of finding anything of value in the present life and to our stark recognition of the radical separation between our existence and the universal, perfect life. This is the first form (not the higher and definitive form) of the Christian conscience, forever nourished by the hope of a salvation which forever eludes it. The Jewish prophet begins his lamentations as soon as he recognizes his God, humbling himself as he exalts God; but he also exalts himself as he humbles himself, for this God is his own essence, which, as such, is hidden from him. Christianity has the same kind of theme: meditation on a dead God, whose tomb is discovered to be empty. The soul believes that it has assured itself of the fusion of the universal and the particular in the Christ it adores, but passion, death, and resurrection reveal individuality in the process of disappearing again. The Christian theme recalls the alternation between union with God and the barrenness characteristic of the life of the mystic.[2]

There is no solution unless the individual turns back toward the world, the civilized society which the Cynic and the monk had abandoned. There, like Faust (Goethe's first Faust, the only one then known), he seeks each moment's pleasure, which at each instant is destroyed by a blind necessity, alien to men's desires. This is the Romanticist's disillusion, the bitter aftertaste of passion. He is overcome by ardent longing for the ideal, which Hegel calls

[2] J. Wahl, *Le malheur de la conscience dans la philosophie de Hegel* (Paris, 1929), especially pp. 158–93.

the "law of the heart"—that of the reformers. The result is a kind of psychologically contradictory state, in which the humanitarian becomes a robber, as in Schiller's *The Robbers,* and in which his will to carry out reforms is insincere because he takes special delight in his rage against the baseness of the world, which he pretends to want to destroy. Opposing this humanitarian anarchism is the self-styled knight errant, who thinks he can overcome perversity and selfishness by his own loyalty and self-sacrifice; but he is suffering from a profound illusion, for it is this self-centered world that accomplishes every important task of humanity.

Over against such ineffectual heroes of Romanticism as Faust, Karl von Moor, or Don Quixote are those who narrow their ideal to a cause they can effectively serve or a limited end they can attain—those whom Hegel facetiously calls "intellectual animals," and whose cause is like the air they must breathe in order to live. Their numbers include every professor or artist who arbitrarily attributes an absolute value to his own task without noticing that for other individuals it is an alien reality, for which they will try to substitute their own cause. This was the situation that inspired dread in the specialists of the period, including Schopenhauer and Nietzsche.

To widen the cause to the proportions of the nation and the social order to which one belongs is to return from the illusory universal to the true universal; the citizen is the new embodiment of spirit. The city, however, is still not the universal with which the finite ego can identify itself. There are still conflicts between the individual and the city, typified by the tragic conflict of Antigone and Creon over the body of Oedipus. It would seem that they could be avoided by an imperialistic system, in which appropriate laws would regulate the antithesis between society and the individual, but imperialism founders in individualism. In fact, we discover that the state simply incorporates the particular wills of subjects; spirit, instead of being an absolute, is simply a multitude of equal individuals. The conflict, which found expression in the French Revolution, is resolved in favor of individualistic anarchy—

primitive anarchy, which reduces consciousness to the state of its origin.

Belief in the city of God compensates for this failure of the human city. The divine city is a region in which absolute, universal right is supposed to triumph completely, but at this stage we see the resurgence of the "unhappy consciousness," with the feeling that the universal city cannot be incorporated into the human, individual city. Any determination of the individual will necessarily fail to achieve the universality of a moral law. "Love they neighbor as thyself," says the moral law, but love for one's neighbor must not be so unreasonable as to be hurtful. Thus one must know in each instance what is good or bad, and that depends on innumerable circumstances.

After so many hopes followed by so many failures, spirit finally discovers itself in religion. What is religion for Hegel? It is essentially Christianity, with its dogmas of the incarnate Word and the remission of sins: the Word becomes incarnate, that is, the separation between the human consciousness and the universal spirit comes to an end in Man-God; sins are forgiven, that is, failures and imperfections are considered to be conditions determining the advent of the spirit. Thus the Christian revelation enters into the substance of Hegelian philosophy; it was there from the beginning, for the image permeating the whole system is a God whose passion is a necessary precondition to his subsequent triumph. But by a system of allegorical correspondence, dogma becomes a philosophical truth. When Hegel tells us that "religion is spirit knowing itself" or that "nature and history are the progressive revelation of spirit," he insists that his statements (one of them goes back to Aristotle's conception of God as pure thought thinking itself, and the other is a religiously inspired variation of the theory of indefinite progress associated with the Enlightenment) refer only to the incarnation of the Word and the remission of sins. Self-contemplation and progress are dependent on "negativity," for one can identify oneself only by returning to oneself after realizing oneself in every possible manifestation; consequently the history of

humanity is the reality symbolized by the incarnation of Christ—
God becoming conscious of himself. Thus the world is the spirit
revealing itself to itself, and in this way the world is justified.

III *The Hegelian Triad*

Hegelian thought subsisted freely in the nebulous atmosphere,
characteristic of the age, in which religion and true knowledge were
one; religion was no longer an absolute faith, outside progressive,
relative human knowledge; religion and knowledge exchange characteristics, religion transmitting its absolute quality to religion, and
knowledge inbuing religion with its rationality. Hegel's philosophy
reproduces, sixteen centuries later, the Gnostic revelations, in which
the elect boasted of apprehending in their rational and necessary
concatenation all the progressive segments of the divine life, of
which nature and human life are but one aspect. "The closed being
of the universe contains no force capable of resisting the passion
for knowledge; it must open and expose its wealth and depth to
the quest for knowledge" (*Encyclopedia,* ed. Lasson, p. lxxvi). Philosophy is consciousness of one's own essence, a "sacred light," which
has disappeared from the memory and sentiment of other nations,
and which Germany is committed to safeguard. Hegel opposes the
philosophy that seeks truth in the platitudes of the *Aufklärung* and
in the renunciations of criticism.

Philosophy grasps the inner "truth" of nature and history—that is,
it interprets them as a means of realization for a spirit, which becomes conscious of itself in and through them. The announcement
of the coming of the divine spirit, and the conviction that the event
provides an exhaustive explanation of reality in its entirety—these
elements of his thought place Hegel decidedly among those who
proclaimed the Advent and transformed the obscure dogmas of
Christianity into translucent ideas. "That which previously had
been revealed as a mystery and remains a mystery for formal speculation in the purest forms of revelation, and even more so in its
obscure forms, is revealed to the mind that exercises its absolute

right to freedom and asserts its firm will to accept reconciliation with the content of reality only if this content can assume the form most worthy of the mind—that of the concept of the necessity which binds all things together and in this way frees them" (*Encyclopedia*, p. 21). His aim is the "translation of reality into the form of thought" (*Ibid.*, p. 35), and it recalls the invention of mystical languages, brought back into fashion during the period. Along with Hegelian "translation," the period also witnessed the emergence of theories such as that of J. A. Kannes. In 1818, after Saint-Martin, Kannes advanced the notion (previously held by Plotinus concerning hieroglyphics) that Hebrew was "the language of the spirit, for a single word expresses several things which appear from the outside to be separate but are tied together by an inner kinship." [3]

Hegel's philosophy is a vast alchemy designed to transmute sense data and representations into thoughts, to introduce universality and necessity where we are given individuality and juxtaposition. To understand the system clearly, one must become accustomed to the idea that the same reality can be situated at different levels; for example, in Platonism the sensible world is the image of the intelligible world, and with Leibniz the aspect of the world changes according to the point of view of a monad. "Reflection (*Nachdenken*) brings about a change in the situation of the content in sensation, intuition, and representation; it is only by means of this change that the true nature of the object reaches consciousness. . . . Our big mistake is in seeking to learn the nature of thought from the form which it assumes in the understanding. To contemplate the empirical world is in essence to transmute (*umändern*) its empirical form and change it into a universal world" (*Encyclopedia*, pp. 56, 76).

The Hegelian triad is the movement of a reality which is posited initially in itself (*an sich*) (thesis) then develops outside itself and for itself in its manifestation or Word (antithesis), and finally returns to itself (*in sich*) and is near itself (*bei sich*) in the form of developed and manifested being. Philosophy as a whole is the

[3] As quoted by Erich Neumann, *Johann Arnold Kannes* (Berlin, n. d.), p. 98.

exposition of the vast triad of being, nature, and spirit: being designates the totality of the logical and conceivable characteristics which
every reality has in itself; nature is the manifestation of reality in
physical and organic beings; spirit is the internalization of this
reality. But the triadic rhythm is reproduced in each of the terms
of this vast triad: within the domain of being there is a being in
itself, a being for itself or manifestation of being, which is essence
(*Wesen*), and a being in and for itself or concept (*Begriff*). In
nature there is a nature in itself, which is the system of mechanical
laws, a nature for itself or manifested nature, which is the system
of physicochemical forces, and a nature in and for itself, which is
the living organism.

In spirit there is a spirit in itself or subjective spirit, which is the
seat of elementary psychological phenomena; a spirit for itself or
objective spirit which manifests itself in right, customs, and morality; and a spirit in and for itself or an absolute spirit, which is
the seat of art, religion, and philosophy. Each term of the subordinate triad in turn develops in a triadic rhythm: being in itself is in
itself a quality, for itself a quantity, and in and for itself a measure;
being for itself or essence is in itself an essence, for itself a phenomenon, and in and for itself a reality; and being in and for itself,
or concept, is in itself a subjective concept, for itself an object, and
in and for itself an Idea. In the same way, nature in itself is in itself space and time, for itself matter and movement, and in and for
itself mechanism; nature for itself or physics is in itself universal
matter, for itself isolated bodies, and in and for itself a chemical
process; nature in and for itself, or organic structure, is in itself the
mineral kingdom, for itself the vegetable kingdom, and in and for
itself the animal kingdom. Spirit in itself, or subjective spirit, is
in itself soul, for itself consciousness, and in and for itself spirit;
spirit for itself, or objective spirit, is in itself right, for itself custom,
and in and for itself morality. Finally, absolute spirit is in itself art,
for itself revealed religion, and in and for itself philosophy. One
can easily understand how each of the twenty-seven terms of the
nine triads evolves into an equal number of new triads and yet be

unable to see clearly any reason capable of stopping this triadic analysis at ultimate terms. Taking these ultimate terms one after the other, we discover a series of terms ranging from abstract being to philosophical speculation and representing every possible form of the real world, from the logical forms of thought to the highest forms of spiritual life, and between them organic and inorganic nature. Here we recognize the idea of a chain or series of forms, which, since Leibniz, had dominated eighteenth-century philosophy.

This broad outline may provide a fairly clear idea of the external, triadic aspect of Hegel's philosophy, but it does not by any means correspond to his manner of exposition. He claims to have shown precisely how a chain or series is progressively engendered by the triadic rhythm: each term of the chain is not an inert term produced by logical classification; since it is in itself a positing of the spirit— or, in Hegel's words, a definition of the absolute—each term has the will to be near itself (*bei sich*) and therefore to overcome negation and externality. Consequently there is in each term a dialectical power causing it to negate itself in a second term in order to re-discover itself in a third, after this negation; the third term is the starting point of a second triad, and in this way the movement continues until it reaches the reality which contains all negations. It is like a series of pulsations, each of which is identical in form with the preceding, but which, when accumulated, nevertheless engender new realities.

The Hegelian method exhibits such clarity only on a purely ideal plane, however, and it is often difficult for us to follow this triadic rhythm clearly, especially in Hegel's system of logic.

IV *Logic*

According to Hegel's *doctrine on being,* philosophy originates in the most barren and abstract concept imaginable—being, a kind of universal predicate which can be asserted of everything. But to abstract everything is to deny everything; being is a pure abstraction and therefore a pure negation or nonbeing. Speculative logic cannot remain at this identity of contradictories and moves on to a new concept—that of becoming, or passage from nonbeing to being and from being to nonbeing, which links being and nonbeing together as its two necessary moments. This is Hegel's first triad, and it suffices to show that the third notion is not a simple composition or sum of the two preceding notions but rather a synthesis or original notion, richer than the first because it contains the negation of the first.

Contrary to becoming, which is forever vanishing and disowning itself, is determination or quality, which is always relative to another quality. Qualitative otherness in turn has as its opposite quantity, which consists in the reciprocal exclusion of qualitatively undifferentiated units. The opposition between quality and quantity is overcome by measure, a qualified quantum implying a limit, which, taken simply as such (as in the thermometric scale), constitutes a degree.

The way Hegel links essence with measure is very artificial. Measure or a qualified quantum joins the two elements in which being, or quantity and quality, was dispersed. Thus it brings pure being back to itself, through its negations. It is this relation of being to itself, this rediscovered identity with self, that constitutes essence; it is by virtue of this self-explication and this relation that essence is distinguished from being.

Hegel's *doctrine on essence* is a crucial point in his philosophy, and its general outlines are easily grasped. "Man is inwardly as he is outwardly, that is, in his actions," he writes. "If he is virtuous or moral only inwardly, in intention and feelings, if he is not identical outwardly, one is as hollow and empty as the other" (*Encyclopedia,* p. 144). This example shows us why Hegel refuses to concede that essence is pure internality. "The expression of the real is the real itself," he insists. "Consequently it contains the essential, and the essential exists only insofar as it is in an immediate external existence" (p. 145). The doctrine on essence consists, therefore, in showing how essence and its manifestation (*Erscheinung*) unite in actuality (*Wirklichkeit*). Hegel's essences are modeled not on

Aristotle's logical concepts but on Leibniz' compossibles. A possible defined by a noncontradictory or identity with self has, in this identity, the principle of its distinctness or characteristic difference; but at the same time this difference ties it to the other possibles or essences, which mutually determine one another; and this determination concerns possible existence. Once we accept these points, we can easily understand how manifestation is linked with essence in Hegel's thinking, and "how the external has the same content as the internal." It is this identity of content that constitutes actuality. Consequently essence is substance "which is only the totality of its own accidents," whose content is but the manifestation; it is a cause because it makes the possibility of being pass away, "because it destroys its simple possibility"; finally, it acts reciprocally with the other substances. All the details of this doctrine of essence obviously converge: their common goal is to show that logic (like Leibniz' divine understanding) manifests all the externality of existence.

The *doctrine of the concept* (*Begriff*) seems at first to comprise disparate elements whose common link is elusive: a treatise on formal logic, in which Hegel studies the concept as such, judgment, and syllogism; second, an indication of the conceptual frames of the philosophy of nature—mechanism, chemism, and teleology; finally, metaphysical speculations on the divine idea understood "as reason, as subject-object, as unity of the ideal and the real, the finite and the infinite, soul and body, as the possibility that contains its reality within itself, as the being whose nature can be conceived only as existing." The dialectical union of these three parts and the integration of the whole in the vast dialectical movement are not easily grasped. We are already sufficiently familiar with the mental attitude designated by the word *Begriff*: a kind of liberation and a victory over negation, an affirmation posited mediately by the negation of a negation. In this sense, all forms previously determined are already concepts, since they are the product of a dialectical movement, but they are definite, limited concepts; now the point at issue is the concept in general, as true freedom. In this sense the concept is the dialectical opposite of essence, which is necessity;

it is a recovery of initiative, as pure being passes into the state of logical otherness or essence.

This freedom is formally conceived by Hegel as being for itself what Spinoza's freedom is in itself. With Spinoza, freedom is the individual's awareness of being a mode eternally and necessarily flowing from the divine substance, and eternal bliss is linked to this awareness. Similarly, with Hegel the concept is linked to the joy of seeing the particular determinations of being—differences—originating in the dialectical movement which deposits them and developing until they culminate in the individual. This is how one should interpret the statement that "the concept contains the moments of universality [*Allgemeinheit*, since the dialectical movement is one in all its determinations], specificity [*Besonderheit*, or the determination produced in this movement], and individuality [*Einzelheit*, which joins the determination to the universal]" (p. 159).

Everything in the domain of formal logic originates in the distinction between, and union of, these moments. Judgment (formulated in the abstract as: The individual is the universal) compares and identifies the two extreme moments of the concept; it is like the union of the existence of things with their universal natures—their bodies and souls. The syllogism unites the two extremes by a middle term or mediate judgment; the individual is contained in the universal (conclusion) by means of a specific characteristic (middle term) or determination, which causes it to be contained there. This metaphysical interpretation of formal logic, though of great interest, is too vast for us to explore in detail.

Leibniz realized the absolute totality of the concept in his monads or countless independent objects, each containing the universe. This dispersion of the absolute totality in juxtaposed objects is a dialectical necessity, for the concept must be posited outside itself and subsequently rediscover itself. This external self-positing is a contradiction (obvious in monadology, where the independence of monads is denied by preestablished harmony). The different phases of the object develop this contradiction: to Hegel mechanism is the perfect model of juxtaposition or disconnected aggregation; but connections must be reestablished, first from without, in the physics of impact, and then from within, in the physics of central forces, giving rise to wholes such as the solar system. The chemical process, which is neutralization of differences or differentiation of a neutral state, reveals the separation of united terms. Finally, in organic finality, the end dominates and directs the activity of the parts; in some way a thought becomes corporeal.

The concept emerges from this dispersion and returns to itself in the absolute or divine idea. Subject and object are the two movements it identifies: "the idea is essentially a process" and exists only in the immanent dialectic which grasps all modes of being and reduces them to its subjectivity; consequently it is at once method and content, or a method capable of providing itself with a content. Interpreting Hegel's statements freely, we might say that there is no other reality but our mental attitude; first we expel everything that might provide an object with any content whatsoever; the result of this expulsion is the idea of being, which is identical with nothingness and is the annulment of the object. Thus we isolate the pure speculative attitude: positing an object only in order to make it disappear, and being enriched by these negations.

v *The Philosophy of Nature*

After studying rhythm in speculative logic, we turn now to the second stage of the rhythm of the absolute idea and find it in the form of otherness or nature. In short, nature is the divine idea in the form of otherness; it is a stage in the life of the idea, the stage of its externalization before its internalization in spirit. For nature is still the divine idea—not a world of realities but a reflection of the idea, a reflection in which the Romanticists traditionally saw an expression or the very reality of the divine life. We must therefore rediscover, in the production of nature's forms, the triadic rhythm of the idea.

A system of mechanics founded by Galileo and Newton, a qualitative physics, which studies heat, electricity, magnetism, and the other natural forces as irreducible realities, a biology suffused with the idea of finality—these are the data that Hegel borrows from the theoretical and experimental sciences of his time, but he transmutes them methodically into the stages of his dialectic.

To transmute them is to discover at the very heart of natural beings this speculative mental attitude which constitutes the divine idea. In a given form one must consider not what this form is to the understanding, which defines it, but the demands made by its internal nature. Take for example the inert mass of mechanics; its law is that its state of movement or rest can be changed only by an external cause. "Here only the selfless [*selbstlosen*] bodies of the earth are imagined, and these determinations clearly apply to them. But this is only abstract, immediate, finite corporality. . . . But the nontruth of this abstract existence is canceled in bodies that exist concretely [planets]; gravity is immanent in bodies and already announces this greater freedom consisting in internal determination." Consequently, what Hegel deems philosophical in mechanics is the gradation of interrelated forms, ranging from the simple reciprocal externality of parts, which constitutes abstract space, to planetary masses, whose spontaneous motions are described by Kepler's laws.

In the same way physics, the study of qualified bodies, should show the parallel growth of individuated bodies constituting wholes and the universal totality which includes them as moments, conforming to the speculative will to discover the identity of the individual and of the universal, a universal of which individual beings are the necessary moments. Physics starts from the abstract self (*Selbst*) of matter—continuous and universally diffused light. But dark, heavy bodies set themselves against this light as resisting individualities. Physics shows how these individuals contitute a subordination. The diverse elements find their common self (*den selbstischen Einheitspunkt*) in the planets—for example, the earth, in which there are differences such as those manifested in meteorological phenomena, themselves conditioned by light (*Encyclopedia*, p. 250). But these bodies seek to constitute specific, precise individualities, and they break away from universal gravity by specific gravity and cohesion. In turn, cohesion is resisted by heat, which tends to reduce bodies to universal fluidity. Bodies find their individuality impaired by forces which determine precise, rigidly limited forms for each of them. "Form [*Gestalt*]," writes Hegel incisively, "is the past activity in its product" (p. 273), typified by crystal. Form is determined first by magnetism consisting of reciprocal attractions and repulsions, "affections and aversions," which outline the form of the body. Individuality obtained in this way remains hostile to universality; chemical forces reintroduce universal animation, neutralize differentiated bodies, differentiate neutral bodies, making them appear to be moments of the universal process. "The individual body is destroyed as well as produced in its individuality; the concept is no longer an internal necessity, it reaches the level of manifestation" (p. 303).

The image of the earth as a universal organism, the mother of all other organisms, is of course widely prevalent in the natural philosophy of every age. It is with this image that Hegel begins the study of organic physics, for to him geology is a morphology of the universal organism. Goethe's studies concerning the metamorphosis of plants pointed to the idea of a kind of homogeneity among the several parts of plants, each capable of living separately. In contrast to the universal organism of the earth, Hegel sees the vegetable kingdom as a dispersion of life in the form of elementary, separate lives in which the total individual is "the common ground rather than the unity of its members." Opposing this dispersion is the organic individuality of the animal which possesses unity with respect to its constitutive parts; the animal has a definite form (*Gestalt*) whose elements are systems—nervous, circulatory, digestive—corresponding to the three functions of sensibility, irritability, and nutrition. But universality among the parts of an individual organism is matched by exclusiveness with respect to nature; hence the conflict and struggle with external nature, "a negative term to be overcome and digested." It is in this struggle that the animal confers "truth and objectivity on the certainty of itself, its subjective concept, insofar as it is an individual being" (p. 323).

This emergence of individual beings finds its opposite and its negation in the genus or kind—the "concrete universal" or "concrete substance" of individuals. The universality of the genus is posited by the negation of immediate individuality, that is, by the death of the individual. "The inadequacy of the latter in face of universality is its radical sickness and the germ of its death."

Such is the framework, bare indeed, of this mythology of nature, in which natural beings, instead of presenting themselves as ready-made realities waiting for experience to identify them and determine their relations, exhibit in themselves an urgent longing for universality or spirituality, which engenders its own forms by a progressive victory of internality over inert juxtaposition, the absolute externality of the parts constituting space. This natural philosophy may be wholly alien to the method of the positive sciences, but two features link it to philosophical speculation of the period.

To begin with, Hegel does not describe the universe but the hierarchy of forms in the universe, and his description follows a plan closely related to that of Auguste Comte's *Course in Positive Philosophy*: we find the same desire on the part of both to apprehend the growing complexity of these forms, the same affirmation that one form is not derived analytically from another. To Hegel (and here he differs radically from Schelling) the idea of the world as a whole is as alien as it is to Comte, for the concrete universality of a living being is in its notion and not in its so-called material extension. Hegel is remote from philosophies of nature inspired by Hellenic models, such as that of Giordano Bruno, who, seeing the world as a whole or, rather, *the* whole, representing the supreme divine creation, included the philosophy of spirit in the philosophy of nature. By contrast, Hegel makes as rigid a distinction between these two philosophies as that made by Comte between the social sciences and biology, interpreting history, right, and ethics as the characteristic creation of spirit, the workings of spirit in its own domain (*bei sich*), whereas spirit is external to itself in nature. A second trait (shared, moreover, by all philosophies of nature) is the importance Hegel attaches to the experimental discoveries of the scientists of his time. He is as critical of scientific theories (particularly Newton's), as he is attentive to the qualitative experiments then regenerating the different branches of physics; for example, in the *Encyclopedia* he cites, among others, Malus' researches on polarization, Heims' on crystals, Du Luc's and Lichtenberg's on the atmosphere, Rumford's on friction, Diot's on refraction, Berthollet's on electrical discharge, Pohl's on galvanism, Berzélius' on electrochemistry, Bichat's on the distinction between organic life and animal life, and Cuvier's on comparative anatomy. Attentiveness to experience is only natural, for, as we have noted, Hegel's philosophy is a "translation" in speculative language; he must have a text to translate, and this text can be given only by experience. But qualitative experience alone interests him; quantitative experience appeals only to one seeking to state laws and to predict specific phenomena. He scoffs at Krug, a Kantian who ironically asked natural philosophy to deduce his mere penholder, for philosophy is not supposed to deduce accidents resulting "from the powerlessness of nature to remain faithful to concepts. This powerlessness is responsible for the difficulty of deducing, from empirical observation, infallible differences for classes and orders. Nature always blurs limits by intermediate, refractory forms, which militate against any firm distinction."

VI *The Philosophy of Spirit*

Hegel's philosophy of spirit deals in part with the same subject matter as the sciences which in French are called moral sciences and in German *Geisteswissenschaften:* psychology, law, history, human conduct. The rest deals with ethics, art, religion, and philosophy, but it is important for us to note that he in no way changed his attitude as he passed from the first group to the second. Unlike his successors, he did not set one group against the other, as factual sciences against normative sciences, but studied the materials of both groups as necessary forms of the life of spirit. He did not try, in this second group, to set down moral, aesthetic, and religious precepts, but, to grasp, as in the first part, the cause and essence of these spiritual facts. The same period witnessed the establishment of the science of religions, the history of law, and the history of art, which studied their objects as facts and tried before all else to discover, in the study of these facts, a more real and concrete notion of the human spirit. That was exactly the method followed by Hegel, who dominated and shaped the intellectual currents of his time with astounding vigor. French positivism was also a manifestation of a similar intellectual state, but in a more precise way Hegel marks a transition from Romanticism to positivism—from Romanticism, which cultivates reverence for the past and immerses the individual in nature and history, to positivism, which records and classifies new riches unnoticed by the impassive rationalists of an earlier period.

These rationalists (Locke, Condillac, and the ideologists) limited their study of man to psychology, and general psychological facts in their entirety are, in effect, the universal form taken by spirit (subjective spirit). But that is an abstract universality; the nature of spirit must be discovered in its positive products—history, law, customs (objective spirit). These are the external workings of spirit which, at its highest degree, communes with itself and rediscovers itself in art, religion, and philosophy (absolute spirit).

The philosophy of spirit, the most admirable part of Hegelian doctrine, is less secure in its logical structure (the triadic form here becomes quite mechanical and artificial in its application) than in its perfect affinity with Hegel's genius. As we have seen, he tried to discover attitudes of mind at the heart of reality, with the result that his interpretation of nature and even of logic is very paradoxical and artificial. At each degree of being there is only desire for spiritual internality, and defeat only revives and intensifies ardor; consequently one must attribute to the logical concept and the forces of nature a kind of will to self-knowledge, which has a metaphorical sense, however, only in spirit. On this metaphor are grounded the first two moments of the doctrine. But when nature, internalized and unified in living beings insofar as anything external can be internalized and unified, passes into its contrasting opposite—spirit —the metaphor becomes the expression of reality. Then spirit is "in itself" rather than "outside itself," and the Hegelian method, in perfect agreement with its object, provides an analysis of spiritual realities which is at times profound.

In our examination of Hegel's *philosophy of subjective spirit,* let us consider first spirit in itself. At its lowest degree it is close to nature; it is soul and even natural soul, containing in its immateriality an echo of the life of nature in its entirety; climatic differences, seasonal changes, hourly changes constitute its natural life. The soul develops, matures, grows old with the body, and it finds (*findet*) in itself immediate, specific, transient determinations: it is sensation (*Empfindung*), "muffled agitation of spirit in its unconscious and unintelligent individuality." Opposing this state of dispersion is feeling (*Gefühl*), which properly designates a feeling of the internality of the soul, like a vague self (*Selbstischkeit*), "at a degree of obscurity in which determinations are not yet developed as a conscious, intelligent content." At its lowest degree this feeling is not even personal; it is the state of a child in the womb with its mother's spirit as its genius, or a hypnotically induced state of somnambulism, in which the waking self founders. This feeling becomes more specific in self-feeling (*Selbstgefühl*), which designates a personal, individual feeling but one that still is indistinct and uncoordinated; it leaves us isolated from the external world which consciousness sets in order in its own world. Considered as a regression and not as a moment in a progression, it is the state of madness. By habit the soul frees itself from this self-feeling, which excludes it from the universal; due to habit, the soul has this whole life in itself, yet is not immersed in it, and remains open to a higher activity.

Natural life of the soul, sensation, feeling, habit—this whole initial phase of spirit constitutes what Hegel calls "corporeality of spirit," and what was later called the unconscious. It is a kind of twilight life, above which consciousness rises.

Consciousness is certainty of oneself, but it is an abstract and formal certainty, which leaves the whole natural life on the outside, as if it were an independent object. This was the aspect of consciousness—the absolute ego, which leaves the thing in itself outside itself—studied by Kant as well as by Fichte. But in its progression, consciousness must gradually assimilate these things, or appropriate them to itself, and pass "from subjective self-certainty to truth." This is the process of evolution which Hegel had described in the *Phenomenology of Spirit*, and which he summarizes here. At its lowest degree, consciousness is sensible consciousness, originating in the sensible world of immediate data; as it develops, it passes through perception, which seizes the relations and interconnections between these data. This is the domain of experience (in the Kantian sense of the word) of objects, which link sensible and changing individuality to the universality of the substances subtending their properties; it leads to understanding (*Verstand*), which grasps the permanence of the laws behind this change. At a higher degree, consciousness withdraws into itself and becomes self-consciousness; the ego posits itself as its own object, but this object is empty, "it is not a true object, since it does not differ from the subject"; therefore the ego can posit itself as its own object only by being egotistical and destructive—that is, by denying the existence of every independent object—but the egotistical tendency reappears as soon as it has been satisfied. We saw in the *Phenomenology* how war in all its cruelty, then slavery, and finally familial, amical, and civic relations gradually assimilated the egotistical individuality of the self to its essential universality. This assimilation is an operation accomplished at the highest degree of consciousness, which is reason (*Vernuft*) or "the certainty that the determinations of consciousness are also objective determinations, that they are by the same token determinations of the essence of things, and that they are its own thoughts" (*Encyclopedia*, sec. 439).

The spirit (or reason) is at once self-certainty and truth. Its development is at once internalization and externalization, or, putting it another way, theory and practice. Theory frees knowledge from any alien presupposition; it is the thoroughly penetrated and translucent object. Practice (always interpreted according to the model supplied by Kant and Fichte) frees voluntary determination from any subjectivity that may be in it, and confers on it universal validity. Theory reaches its goal through progressive internalization of the data of intuition, which become internal to spirit in representation; and the steps in the progress of internality are marked by recollection, then productive imagination, and finally memory proper (*Gedächtnis*). According to Hegel, memory is linked to the use of language, in which meaningful words allow us to think and understand things as we free ourselves from intuitions and images; this brings us to thinking (*Denken*), that is, "knowing that whatever is thought, is; and that whatever is, is insofar as it is thought." Practice, a part of subjective feeling and inclination, is always involved in the contradiction stemming from the desire to realize the formal universality of spirit in specific inclinations; this contradiction can be removed only by happiness or by universal satisfaction, conceived as being the ground or truth of partial, insufficient satisfactions, in which the individual is not yet assimilated by the universal. Theory and practice are united in free spirit—spirit which desires itself as an object.

It is obvious that this theory of subjective spirit consists, on the whole, in transforming psychology, which is the science of facts, into a philosophical science. Hegel reproaches the Kantians (the same reproach might be addressed to the French spiritualists of his time) for basing metaphysics on the study of the facts of consciousness, since in this way they renounced all rational necessity (*Encyclopedia,* sec. 444). Calling for a complete reversal, he seeks to derive the necessity of psychological realities from the very movement of philosophical speculation.

Freedom is still an inner determination of spirit, and this inner freedom is related to an outer reality, whether to external things or to individual wills. Freedom will reach its goal only when this reality becomes a world determined by it, a world in which it will feel "at home." According to Hegel's *philosophy of objective spirit,* it is this transmutation of the world by spirit that gives birth to all legal, moral, and political institutions. These institutions in their totality constitute the objective spirit.

Nothing is further from Hegelian thought than the eighteenth-century doctrines which reduced these institutions to simple psychological phenomena. Natural law deduced from innate dispositions, ethics based on selfish motives, the state built on a union of self-centered interests—these are the doctrines Hegel resists as firmly as Auguste Comte, notwithstanding the differences that separate the two geniuses. To both, the social fact represents a higher degree of complexity than the biological or psychological fact. With both, the eighteenth century is reversed.

They pose essentially the same problem as the eighteenth century —the agonizing problem created by the outpouring of individualism in the sixteenth century. Individualism originates in the concrete knowledge, painfully experienced, that society and the world fetter man: "Man is born free, and everywhere he is in chains." Hence the task of political philosophy is to give man reasons for clinging wilfully to society, for making the social bond a rational, voluntary bond. Paradoxically, eighteenth-century philosophers generally tried to find these reasons in individualistic tendencies themselves. Instead of accepting the notion that society conflicts with egotism, they sought to show that the restraints imposed by moral and juridical laws most aptly satisfy this egotism when it is clear and rational; furthermore, their demonstration became a practical standard for revolutionizing the moral or social codes that did not fulfil this condition. The revolutionary spirit, notwithstanding nineteenth-century views, was an attempt to preserve and stabilize society by making it conform to reason. In a sense Hegel extends the spirit of the eighteenth century, for he also sees law, morality, and the state as an expression of reason, in which there no longer subsists anything irrational imposed from without; but he reverses that spirit by trying to discover the rationality of these social forms in their intrinsic and necessary character rather than in their appropriateness to egotistical needs. He takes them as they are and as they should be in themselves, without allowing us to construct them with the help of egotistical whims. He, too, refuses to treat them as fetters or limitations and insists instead that they liberate man, even though the freedom that they confer is not the satisfaction of man's natural appetites. "The free personality," he writes, "is a determination of self by self, and this is utterly opposed to a natural determination" (*Encyclopedia,* sec. 502). Law, morality, and the state free man from his immediate nature far more than they issue from it. Hegel knows but one definition of freedom, and that is negation (just as Plotinus discovered freedom only in the One that surpasses determination). A free being "is one that can withstand the negation of its individual immediacy, infinite pain—that is, remain affirmative in this negativity." Again, he says that freedom is "the truth of necessity" and has as its essential form the a priori principle. The last two statements are equivalent to the first, for the a priori principle, identical with necessity, is a penetration of the immediate by thought, with the result that the immediate as such is suppressed and becomes a moment of this thought. Rights, morality, and political institutions are the progressive realization of this freedom.

Hegel's juridical theory tallies perfectly with the two correlative notions of person and property. Ownership of property is the affirmation of a person who seizes an outward thing that lacks a will, and makes it his own by putting his will into it. Yet property concerns not so much relations between a person and nature as relations between persons, for it is a means by which the rights of each are recognized by others. These relations are manifested in the contract of exchange, which Hegel defines as follows: a thing is mine only insofar as my will is inserted into it; it can become another's if I withdraw my will and another inserts his; but my right of property would be annulled if the other person did not act toward me as I act toward him, and refused to transfer his property to me; this reciprocal transfer is the contract that assumes the general motion of value, which makes properties comparable quantitatively.

Hegel bases the whole life of the law on this contract of exchange: first civil law, then penal law. Legal conflicts arise when several persons lay claim to the same property and when only one claim is just even though the others seem to be just. This plurality of legal grounds issues from the accidental, individual character of the contracting wills and can therefore be resolved only through the mediation of other personal wills. The interpretation of rights—in Roman law, the answers of prudent men—seems to be the sum and substance of Hegel's civil law. Furthermore, the formation of Roman law on the basis of the private interpretations of wise men must have given Hegel the paradoxical idea of constructing a theory of rights which would not depend in any way on the existence of the state.

The existence of established rights makes possible wrong, which is a manifestation of a conflict between a particular will or bad will and universal right. A wrongful action is an annulment, since it treats what is not mine as if it were mine; this annulment can take the form of private revenge accomplished by a particular will, but revenge simply repeats the wrongful act and in this way engenders an infinite series of new wrongs. The progression can be stopped only by punishment meted out by a disinterested judge who has the power to exercise control over persons and property. Thus punishment is above all restitution of the state of rightness.

What Hegel identifies as law is simply civil law and its dependencies—everything concerning the private lives of persons. But to him public or civic life is not, as the revolutionaries thought, a particular instance of the life of law. Few ideas stimulate more reflection on the profound meaning of Hegel's philosophy than this radical separation between the political order and the legal order.

The legal will is only an abstraction. The person, for whom freedom exists only in possession of an external thing, gives way to the subject, for whom freedom is internal—that is, for whom wilful determinations are truly his own. The passage is from abstract, objective right to morality. Here voluntary determinations have no place, regardless of the authority that prescribes them; here external activity has a place only if it corresponds to intention and is identified as belonging internally to the subject. In Hegel's *philosophy of morality* we can easily recognize the influence of Kantian ideas: a good will is the only thing that is good absolutely.

But the difficulties of the Kantian ethic are precisely those that give birth to the moral dialectic. Kant insisted on the impossibility of a perfect action—that is, an action which, in a particular individual and under particular circumstances, would fully meet the condition of universality set by moral law. That is why morality (*die Moralität*) is the domain of obligation (*Sollen*) or what ought to be. Following Kant's lead, Hegel shows how the harmony that exists between the particular conditions of an action (individuality of the agent, etc.) and the universality of Good is purely accidental, and how that which exists between the natural conditions of happiness and moral values is also accidental. He shows how disharmony gives rise to evil, which is nothing but spurious universality or an attempt of a particular will to pass itself off as the universal will (and this is possible because the abstract form of universality, self-certainty, belongs to the individual self). Doubtless this harmony ought (*soll*) to be realized, but it is incompatible with the conditions of moral action.

Speculations of this kind led Kant to the theory of postulates of practical reason and Fichte to the analogous theme of indefinite progress. It is here, perhaps, that the most distinctive trait of Hegel's doctrine comes into focus: in his view as in Schelling's, thought which reaches only obligation is not philosophical; consequently morality's point of view is inferior and should be surmounted. The abstract universality of the individual who tries in vain to achieve self-realization and always comes up against evil and nature should pass to the concrete universality of the social whole of which the individual is a part—the family and the state. Hegel's critique of individualism, initiated in the theory of law, is completed in the theory of morality. The dialectic forces the individual to proclaim his inadequacy, the yawning chasm which separates him from universality, and finally to discover his true freedom in society, whose moral institutions (*Sittlichkeit*) are the universality sought by the deficience of the individual.

The family, society (*Gesellschaft*), and the state are the three phases in the ascent toward the absolute spirit. The family originates in the transformation of the natural bond of the sexes into a spiritual bond by virtue of marriage and, more precisely, monogamic marriage. The existence of family ties and the education of children account for its material and moral continuity. Still this bond, which does not outlast the death of relatives, is accidental and transient; moreover, families themselves are like separate individuals, each having its own independence and self-interest.

This phase of separation, which Hegel expressly calls an atomism, gives rise to civil society (*die bürgerliche Gesellschaft*). Here Hegel is referring to the social forms studied by political economy and the juridical organism linked with these forms. The economic society created to satisfy the needs of individuals is therefore a necessary stage, but not the highest stage of objective spirit. Thus both Hegel and Comte are critical of economists, and both believe that political factors transcend economic factors. Hegel stresses the external nature of economic relations established to satisfy the needs of each through the labor of all. According to him the division of labor brought about by the diversity of needs doubtless increases the interdependence of men, but it makes their labor more mechanical and, in extreme cases, substitutes machines for human activities. In opposition to its mechanical and industrial aspects, Hegel, like Plato, sees the tendency of the division of labor to separate men into classes or states (*Stände*), each forming an organic whole or a moral unit with its own professional honor. But Hegel, absolutely faithful on this point to the tendencies of his time, does not think that economic factors spontaneously produce justice; on the contrary, he maintains that there must first be an authority to repress crime and an administration of justice which can insure respect for positive laws and legal formalities. Aside from this negative justice, however, Hegel seems to have had in mind a positive organization of work. We have already seen that the economic relation has the sole purpose of satisfying individual needs, yet a number of accidents make their satisfaction precarious and uncertain: changes in opinions and fashions, regional differences, differences in international relations, and especially inequality in the productive capacity of individuals. This instability can be corrected only if free men renounce their individualism. Here Hegel envisages strict regulation by a state or corporate system, which causes individuals to emerge from their isolation and reunites them to a universal reality.

The universal reality to which the necessities of economic organization lead is the state. According to the prevalent eighteenth-century doctrine, the state was the guarantee of freedom, and freedom meant subjective freedom, which referred to natural rights. To Hegel, the state is "objective freedom," that is, the phase in which spirit is in the domain of its social objective creations and no longer confronted by its opponent. Opposing the precariousness of family relations and the mass of individuals who make up economic society, in which spirit struggles with itself, is the state, in which all conflicts subside. To grasp clearly Hegel's celebrated theory, we should note that he does not follow the usual practice of envisaging the state in its relations with individuals, to whom it is a guarantee or a limit, but in itself, as a characteristic and radically independent manifestation of law and government. The unlimited powers of the state and its total irresponsibility are accepted as dogmas by Hegel.

This theory of the sovereignty of the state is clearly related to that stated by Rousseau in the *Social Contract,* if the contractual origin of the state is simply disregarded. Opposing the revolutionary Rousseau, who forges the general will from the harmony of individual wills, is the socialistic Rousseau, who declares that sovereignty is inalienable, indivisible, cannot err, and has no bounds, since the sovereign alone is judge of what he imposes on the community. Furthermore, with Hegel as with Rousseau, this unlimited law issues from the universal character of sovereign power. The state has the exclusive role of "bringing the individual, who tends to center his life on himself, back to the life of the universal substance," and therefore intervenes to prevent the spread of selfish interests and limit by law the arbitrariness of individual wills. In this sense the state, free since it is emptied of selfish interests, also makes its citizens free. The law is "the substance of free power." It is what a will freed from selfish interests desires, and once it has become part of sentiments and morals, it no longer is a coercive force.

The difficulty, with Hegel as with Rousseau, is in making the universal state function, since individuals are its only organ. There must be a constitution, that is, a way of articulating the parts of the state so that in its functioning, like an actual organism, it will constantly reproduce its organic unity. The Hegelian solution is utterly different from Rousseau's and initiates his apology for governmental absolutism, which, according to Hegel, can incorporate the universality of the state. The reasons underlying his predilection for absolutism—a predilection shared by many of his contemporaries—are diverse. First, his political experience. Hegel lived in a nation which was not a state. "Germany is no longer a state," he wrote in 1802. "The empire is divided into a number of states whose existence is guaranteed only by the great powers and is dependent on these powers rather than on its own might."[4] He blames this state of affairs as much on material weakening of the martial and financial power as on confessional and corporative particularism; but above all, he considers the vigor of the French state and complains that Germany has failed to find a Richelieu or a Napoleon—a single individual embodying its political principle.

According to Hegel, then, the absolutism of a single individual is the optimal means of guaranteeing the constancy and perpetuity of the state. But we should also note that the absolute sovereign represents the spirit (*Volksgeist*) of the people governed by him, that the reality of a constitution depends on its responsiveness to this spirit, and that the government exists only for the purpose of preserving the state and its constitution. According to the deep-

[4] *Die Auffassung Deutschlands,* manuscript published in 1822 by H. Heller.

seated religious image subtending Hegelian doctrine, the universal has its complete reality only if realized in an individual. That is why Hegel writes that "the monarchy is the constitution of fully developed reason; all others belong to a lower degree of evolution and realization of reason." He even goes so far as to specify that the monarchy should be a hereditary one, in which the universality of spirit is joined to the immediacy of nature.

The Hegelian theory of the prince closely resembles the absolutist idealism of the king as the "living law," which flowered in Neo-Pythagoreanism. Both theories assume that the prince's will embodies the universal will and that everything arbitrary is excluded from it. Hegel remains silent on proof of the grounds of his supposition, believing that he has done enough in demonstrating the rational and dialectical necessity which causes the prince to appear in nature and history. Here better than anywhere else we see the essentials of a method that requires experience to manifest what it decrees a priori; but here—if we consider the historical situation in which Hegel elaborated his political philosophy (after the treaties of 1815)—we also see better than anywhere else how the a priori decrees of the method correspond essentially to immediate, contemporary experience. Hegel's political theory belongs to a period when legitimacy and absolutism were being restored almost everywhere in Europe. It was the period when Francis I of Austria addressed these words to a convocation of professors: "I do not need scholars but good citizens. Those who love me should teach what I decree." It was the period when Ferdinand VII of Spain, speaking of the constitution of 1812, declared: "My royal will is not only to refuse to accept any decree of the Cortes but to declare this constitution null." It was the period when Frederick William III of Prussia postponed indefinitely his promise to bestow a constitution on his people. Hegel himself, professor in Berlin in 1818, interprets this absolutism as a reason for optimism, in contrast to his pessimism of 1803. "The German nation," he said in his inaugural lecture, "has saved its nationality, which is the seat of all life. . . . This state in particular [Prussia], having achieved its important place in politics by virtue of its spiritual superiority, has become equal in strength and independence to states which might have prevailed over it in external means."

Yet Hegelian absolutism is not hostile to a constitution. The prince is not a Machiavellian figure whose authority rests on force and cunning; he represents the spirit of the people and bears the same relation to them as God to his Incarnate Word—a radical unity of will. This is why Hegel introduces, alongside directly executive powers—judicial and administrative—a legislative power, in which he seems to assign the highest place to the class of citizens "whose particular function is to concern themselves with universal goals," that is, the class of professors and scholars; but he also acknowledges the other classes. This "legislative power" seems, however, to be nothing more than a consultative council. In any case, it can voice its opinion only on internal affairs of state, for in foreign policy not only decisions but also deliberations belong exclusively to the prince. This idea is thoroughly consistent with an era when Tsar Alexander I sought to base all international relations on a "Holy Alliance" between sovereigns.

This radical separation of internal and external policy is based on conditions which actually existed in Europe at a time when nationalities had scarcely freed themselves from the danger of domination by Napoleonic imperialism and were jealously guarding their independence. Hegel describes this situation perfectly in abstract terms: "As an individual, each state excludes other similar individuals. Their reciprocal relations are arbitrary and accidental, for universal law, which would make these persons an autonomous whole, exists not as a reality but as an obligation. This independence makes the conflict between states a relationship of violence or a state of war." To Hegel "obligation" is a sufficient reason for condemning an idea; philosophy does not speculate on anything that does not exist, and whatever exists is rational. "Philosophy deals with no being so impotent that it lacks strength to push forward to existence," he writes.[5] He dismisses summarily the idea of a society

[5] *Begriff der Religion,* ed. G. Lasson, 1925, p. 73.

of states or a system of universal law, which had appealed to many eighteenth-century thinkers, including Kant, and inspired many undertakings, by saying that such a society has no historical reality. The only social universe realized by history is the state; there is none above it, and what is set above it is a simple speculative game, unworthy of the attention of the philosopher, who must explain reality.

But the dispersion of individual states nevertheless remains a problem for the philosopher. Whenever he finds atomistic conditions, he knows in advance that these conditions are only apparent, for to assume that the individual is not identical with the universal is contrary to reason. But it would also be completely contrary to the spirit of Hegelian speculation to seek the solution in some superstate, which would absorb and annihilate individual states. History itself, in its concrete reality, provides the solution. What does history reveal to us? A series of civilizations and states appearing in succession in the foreground of the historical scene, reaching their apogee, and disappearing forever. This is the familiar theme of "epochs of history" or the supreme destiny which governs the formation and decay of empires; it is above all the theme of the Christian philosophy of history already foreshadowed in Philo of Alexandria and developed by Augustine and Bossuet. But in St. Augustine and Bossuet there was a double history: the history of the terrestrial city, that of the fall of empires, a history without progress, which culminated in destruction and annihilation; and the history of the City of God, advancing continually with the Jews, then the Christian church and predestination for eternity with the society of the elect. The Hegelian doctrine is a fusion of these two histories or, more exactly, an interpretation of the first by the second. There is no secular history distinct from sacred history; there is only one history, and that is sacred history. The eighteenth-century theoreticians of progress had tried to discover in secular history a form of intellectual, moral, and material progress, distinct from religious progress. Hegel follows those theoreticians and for this very reason contradicts the Augustinian tradition when he tries to discover progress in political history; but he contradicts them and follows St. Augustine when he sees in political history itself "the history of the degrees in the advent of the spirit" (*Philosophy of History*, ed. Lasson, 1917–20). Thus he explicitly rejects the notion of perfectibility, which had issued from the philosophy of the Enlightenment, and substitutes for it the notion of evolution (*Entwicklung*) or development of a spiritual germ, of which "the first traces already contain potentially the totality of history"—truly a spiritual history because it involves a perpetual victory of the spirit over its past.

History in the strict sense (excluding primitive or uncultured races) deals with races that have formed states, which are the terrestrial aspect of the Universal. Here history considers first of all the spiritual foundation of the state. "The substance of morality and the state is religion; the state rests on moral sentiment and the latter on religious sentiment" (*Encyclopedia*, p. 464). His thesis has many implications and is the condemnation of secular liberalism, an outgrowth of the French Revolution. To think that man can act according to laws which do not conform to the spirit of his religion is utterly absurd, according to Hegel, for such laws are certain to seem like purely artificial human fabrications. Hegel's criticism runs parallel to that of Auguste Comte. Once this thesis is accepted, history consists essentially in identifying the spiritual soul of each of the states which have by turns predominated in the world. The success of a state, its fleeting preeminence, is the success of a spiritual principle expressing the highest degree attained at a given moment by the divine spirit that permeates the world; the individual then represents the universal, but represents it imperfectly and is the cause of its fall, which derives from an immanent justice. Thus history is a theodicy.

Everything assumed by such a theis is obvious: exclusion, as we have noted, of any link with prehistory and uncivilized peoples; exclusion of any important role for accidents in history, of which the equilibrium cancels the effects. To maintain the opposite view—that possibilities always remain open—is to display insufficient maturity of judgment. "The real world is as it should be; the divine universal reason is the power of self-realization." (*Philosophy of History*, p. 74). Finally, the thesis excludes the rational, voluntary influence of men on the course of history. An action is the starting point of an infinite series of consequences, unknown to the one who has performed the action. The one who acts does not seek to impart anything "substantial" to his act; for example, Caesar thought he was acting against the law only to serve his personal ambition, yet he was preparing the way for the advent of a new world. There is a "cunning of reason," which makes the dominant passion of a great man serve its own ends, and history judges men and morals differently. The historical personage seems to be immoral because he lays the ground for the future and acts against the customs of his time, but even the criminal can be an instrument of history. By the same token, this thesis assumes complete harmony between nature and freedom. The spiritual principle represented by a nation is not "a matter of choice" but issues primarily from natural instinct.

This conception of the course of history might be termed the physicospiritualistic conception. Opposing it, according to Hegel, is the purely spiritualistic conception of the Catholics, then represented by Lamennais, Schlegel, and Rémusat. To these men an epoch originated in a decadent state and incorporated the remnants of a tradition going back to an originally perfect nation. We should add, moreover, that this odd and very ancient hypothesis supported fruitful investigations which were then being initiated in linguistics and comparative mythology. Hegel maintains that the original race could not be a part of the texture of history, since historical races are those that have formed states and possess knowledge of their own past, which they have passed on to posterity. But he is also, for the same reason, hostile to any form of comparative history which seeks to bring together different civilizations: Homeric mythology and that of the Hindu epics; Chinese, Eleatic, and Spinozist philosophy; or the ethics of the ancient world and Christian ethics. Hegel's aim—the postulate underlying his work—is to make each civilization a unit, which, if it reproduces details from another civilization, imbues them with its own spirit. The historian is not interested in the origin of an institution—for example the Christian origin of a pagan dogma (pp. 99, 101–12, 422).

These principles and exclusions finally raise the question whether Hegelian history is still history. It is history which is not interested in the past as such, or interested in the past only as it impinges on the present. "Since we deal only with the idea of spirit and consider everything in history to be its manifestation, when we survey the past we are concerned only with the present; for philosophy investigates truth and is concerned with the eternal present. Nothing from the past is lost, for the Idea is present, and spirit is immortal; . . . the moments that the *Geist* seems to have beneath it, are contained within its present depth" (pp. 124–25).

If we examine the concrete content of this history (embellished by Hegel's vast erudition and replete with remarkable pages on the geographic distribution of civilizations), we find that it is an attempt to apply his triad to the succession of the three great ages that he identifies in the history of the world: Asian despotisms, the Greco-Roman civilization, and the Germano-Christian civilization. Hegel here recalls the scheme he had outlined in the *Phenomenology*. The three phases of his scheme correspond to three degrees of freedom: the absolute freedom of the despot, based on the subjugation of every individual; the external freedom of the Greek or Roman citizen, based on the concept of right—a mental abstraction separated from nature; and the internal freedom of the Christian. The role of Germanism is to introduce the principle of internal freedom into the political reality. This last phase, corresponding to "old age" in human life, alone makes possible a comprehensive appreciation of historical evolution.

The Germanic race is the final chosen race of absolute spirit in its temporal march through the world, thanks to its affinity with the Christian spirit. "The pure internality of the Germanic nation has been the terrain suited to the liberation of spirit; the Latin nations, on the contrary, are still split to the very core; produced by a mixture of Latin and German blood, they still retain the mark of heterogeneity. . . . In them we find a penchant for separation and abstractions, an absence of the synthesis of spirit and sentiment that we call *Gemüt,* an absence of a spiritual sense; when they are most introspective, they are outside themselves; internality is a link, but its significance is not perceived by their sentiment, which is occupied by determinate interests that do not involve the infinity of spirit. . . . 'Well,' said Napoleon, 'we shall return to Mass. . . .' Here is the essential feature of these nations—separation of religious interest and worldly interest—and the reason for the split is in the spirit itself, which has lost all coherence, all deep-seated unity" (523–24). On one hand, the Catholic nations, the philosophy of Enlightenment, the Revolution; on the other, Luther and Protestantism. In the Catholic world two forms of conscience were recognized: piety and right. The notion of equality and the revolutionary spirit, which makes the state a simple aggregation of separate, independent wills, were based on this abstract, formal principle. Luther won spiritual freedom by asserting that the individual's destination is within himself; the reconciliation of religion and right was achieved by the Protestant church, which held that there is no religious conscience distinct from right and opposed to it.

The definitive superiority of Germanism is a spiritual superiority. The Germanic race possesses natural qualities which allow it to receive the highest revelations of spirit. It is not the superiority of the race as such that is proclaimed, but only its superiority relative to a determinate moment, the final moment, in the history of the world.

"God should be conceived as spirit communing with itself" (*Encyclopedia,* p. 554). This devout precept of Protestantism indicates passage from the theory of objective spirit (the state) to that of absolute spirit. To Luther, only one who adheres to Christ can know God, and the efficacious Word of God, Christ proclaimed, is found only in the Church. With Hegel the political aggregation, still external, passes to the spiritual aggregation, where, in the communion of the Church, that which emerges from the individual subject is fused with that which originates in the absolute spirit.

As its highest level, spirit, after returning to itself and its own home element, after positing itself in itself as subjective spirit and manifesting itself externally in the state and history, is religion, understood as unity of the inner spiritual life. In this notion of religion, the object is less to reach God than to consecrate man. God is not independent of spiritual communion, nor does he exist as such, as a self-knowing being, apart from this communion. Art, revealed religion, philosophy—all three moments in the development of the absolute spirit (and not just the second) belong to religion. Now we shall see how the theory of art and the theory of philosophy are a religious interpretation (in the sense we have given the word), a translation of our human activities into spiritual terms.

For this very reason, the theory of art can only be a philosophy of the history of art, the theory of religion a philosophy of the history of religions, and the theory of philosophy a philosophy of the history of philosophy. It is the real, concrete spiritual activity that must be interpreted in terms of its true essence; here as elsewhere, there can be no thought of a nonexistent ideal or a powerless obligation. One can follow Hegel's own example and generalize the observation he made concerning the theory of religion: "Particular religions are particular degrees of consciousness of knowledge of spirit; they are necessary conditions for the production of true religion, for true consciousness of the spirit. That is why they also exist historically. . . . In a true science—in a science of the spirit, whose object is man—*the evolution of the concept of a particular concrete object is also its external history and has existed in reality.*" A history of the human spirit subtended by a dialectic—this is the Hegelian theory of the absolute spirit. The human spirit is the universal spirit itself. "Man is a goal in himself; he has in himself an infinite value and is destined for eternity. He has his homeland in a suprasensible world, in an infinite internality, which he achieves only by breaking away from existence and natural will, and by striving to bring about this break."

Art, revealed religion, and philosophy mark the stages in the struggle to achieve internality: art, a sign of the divine Idea in external and sensible activities, still leaves nature outside the spirit; revealed religion, by virtue of the dogma of the revelation of the Father in Christ the man, brings about a reconciliation between God and man, who had broken away from the spirit; and philosophy, in the form of conceptual speculation, expresses what religion touched from a distance in the form of representation and "frees the content of religion from the exclusive form it had" (sec. 573).

That history and the dialectic have not worked together but hindered each other in the realization of the sciences of the spirit is made even more obvious by Hegel's knowledge of history and the abundance of historical materials, which were certain to cause the dialectical frames to burst.

We see this first of all in his theory of art, rooted in the twofold division between the material, finite, existing character of a work of art and the infinitude it expresses. In solving this conflict Hegel clearly uses two distinct dialectics: one is based on a simple ideological analysis and is aesthetic in the ordinary sense of the word; the other invokes history. The former shows how the external reality of a work is internalized, first, because it suggests subjective images and representations, which are linked with ideas by the intermediary of the imagination, second, because art imitates nature and evolves in the direction of forms which manifest the spirit more and more perfectly until it reaches the human form. In a word, since a particular form never achieves universality, art creates an indefinite multiplicity of forms to express God, and this is polytheism, which profoundly influenced the development of classical sculpture. The second dialectic seeks (but in vain) to define a progression of the arts which is at the same time historical: classical art, symbolic art, and Romantic art are its three stages. Classical art, which is primarily sculpture, immediately sees the finite as the sign of the infinite, without becoming aware of the opposition between the individuality of a work and universal being. In symbolic art, exemplified by architecture, awareness of the inadequation between form and idea leads to unending pursuit of an adequate form. The art of sublimity consists in using form to suggest the absolute idea, which is the negation of form. For example, in the Gothic church, painstakingly analyzed by Hegel, "the upward thrust manifests itself as the primary characteristic. The height of its pillars surpasses the width of their base to a degree beyond visual calculation; they rise so high that the eye cannot grasp their full dimensions immediately. It wanders here and there, leaps upward until it reaches the gently sloping curvature of arcs, which finally meet at one point and there come to rest; just as the soul, lost in restless, troubled contemplation, gradually rises from the earth to the heavens and finds its repose only in God." Finally, in Romantic art, God is no longer satisfied with any external form but finds his expression only in that which is spiritual—for example the arts of painting and music, in which externality, sound or color, appear to be wholly accidental in relation to their signification. Romantic art offers the supreme examples of internal forms. "Poetry succeeds in spiritualizing its sensible element, sound, to such a degree that this element becomes a mere sign, stripped of any particular expression."

A work of art has its truth only in the consciousness of the subject that contemplates it. It is like a character in search of an author, waiting for a consciousness to perceive it and confer meaning on it. Religion, on the other hand, is a relation between a subjective consciousness and God or spirit, which is realized in this very consciousness for which it exists. "God is God insofar as he knows himself, but his knowledge of himself is also the consciousness of himself that he has in man, and man's knowledge of God is continued in the knowledge that he has of himself in God" (*Encyclopedia,* sec. 564). Like primitive gods, who would die without the sacrifices of their worshipers, Hegel's God literally owes his existence to religion. For religion is God, no longer manifesting himself in his abstract, separate moments, but revealing himself as he is—that is, as spirit which can be revealed only to spirit.

But this revelation is accomplished only in the absolute religion known as Christianity. This absolute religion is the culmination of a long evolution, in which, down through historical religions, which mark its necessary steps, we see the concept gradually lose its fixity, its inadequation to itself, and reach true self-consciousness. In religion as in other matters, the concept can discover itself in its ideal state only by negating all finite forms. Moreover, the evolution of God as revealed in the history of religions is also the evolution of humanity itself: "A bad God or a natural God corresponds to bad, natural men without freedom; the pure concept of God—the spiritual God—corresponds to a free spirit. . . . Man's representation of God corresponds to his representation of himself and his freedom."

The first religions are naturalistic religions, in which consciousness knows the absolute spirit only as spirit immersed in nature and not as spirit endowed with freedom. This is the period of the Oriental religions: first, magic—hardly worthy of the name religion—in which man knows spirit only as a force capable of modifying nature directly; then the religion of "substantiality," typified, according to Hegel, by Buddhism. Here God is posited as an absolute power, and the subject or individual is assumed to be accidental, transient, and unreal; God is a spiritual being but lacks subjectivity and therefore has all the characteristics of a natural being. Then comes "the religion of abstract subjectivity"—the religion of Zoroaster—in which the subject seeks to assert his unity in the constant struggle of good against evil, light against darkness.

The second religions are those of "spiritual individuality," which raise the spirit above nature, subordinating nature to it as the body is subordinated to the soul. One example is the Jewish religion with its spiritual God, in face of whom all nature is without essence or substance—a kind of acosmic God with absolute omnipotence. This is the religion of sublimity. Opposing the Jewish religion is the Greek religion, characterized by the positive role of nature, which is the organ and expression of the spirit; the body is itself divine, but a finite body expresses a finite spirit. This is the religion of beauty. In the Roman religion, by contrast, nature again makes the spirit the center of the divine life; this utilitarian religion considers the human consciousness and its interests to be the end to which divine beings are the means.

Last in the series comes the absolute or true religion, in which the spirit is unveiled. "This is the manifest [*offenbare*] religion and not merely the revealed [*geoffenbarte*] religion." It is the religion of Christ, the religion in which "the universal substance" emerges from its abstraction, realizes itself in an individual act of self-consciousness, introduces the son of its eternity into the course of time, and shows, in him, the suppression of evil in itself. Further, this immediate, sensible existence of the concrete absolute is extinguished in the pain of negativity, in which, as infinite subject, it has become its own likeness; this absolute has become for itself because it is "the absolute return, the universal unity of the universal and the individual, the Idea of spirit as eternal, and nevertheless living and present in the world" (*Encyclopedia,* sec. 569).

We have been able to offer only the bare outline of Hegel's science of religions, in which he tests the validity of his ideas as he examines the most concrete details of religious practices which, in several instances, were being studied for the first time. His studies should not be disparaged, for in them he utilizes a wealth of historical material and, more important still, attempts to identify elements of originality in diverse forms of religious speculation instead of following the vague comparative methods previously held in esteem. Moreover, he performed a useful service by disturbing the quietude of those who accepted as a dogma the existence of an unbroken Judeo-Christian tradition, beset by pagan errors; thereafter the question of the origins of Christianity was raised in a new context.

The history of philosophy, which constitutes the heart of the Hegelian theory of philosophy, also commands respect. We noted its spirit in the Introduction to the first volume in this series,[6] and what we have already observed indicates that his absolute idealism is simply Christianity, and that he transposes it from the plane of

[6] Bréhier, *The Hellenic Age,* vol. 1 in *The History of Philosophy* (University of Chicago Press, 1963), p. 22.

representation to the plane of speculative thought; consequently there is a true philosophy just as there is a true religion; and just as religion contains vestiges of every earlier form of religion, philosophy, too, evolved only by virtue of a sequence of negations and oppositions, and the dialectical series contained in its evolution can be rediscovered in the series of historical systems.

Thus Hegel imperturbably completed the translation of all reality into speculative language. The spirit feels "at home" everywhere; nothing resists this victorious spirituality. But the spirit, in Hegelian doctrine, reaches its highest point in human culture. Religion itself is considered a product of culture, for religion is knowledge of God through self, and God knows himself only in and through this culture. The most obvious result of Hegel's philosophy is to confer the divine seal on every reality of nature and history: the terrestrial city is transmuted into a City of God. Antiquity and the Renaissance had known a naturalistic form of pantheism; in Hegel we have a cultural form of pantheism, linked both to German mysticism, which saw in humanity a part of the divine life itself, and to the intellectual situation of an age which sought above all to discover a concrete and complete definition of man in the moral sciences, then coming to birth. Remove the mysticism in Hegel and you have Comte's cult of humanity. It is this modern direction of his thought that the other mystically inclined German philosophers were unable to understand, and it is this that places Hegel beyond comparison with them.

BIBLIOGRAPHY

Texts

Hegel, Georg Wilhelm Friedrich. *Werke, Vollstandige Ausgabe,* 26 vols., ed. H. Glockner. Stuttgart 1927–40. (Vols. 23–26 are a *Hegel-Lexicon,* 1st ed., 1935; rev. ed., 2 vols., 1957.)

———. *Sämtliche Werke, neue kritische Ausgabe* (Jubilee edition), editing started by G. Lasson and J. Hoffmeister, continued after their death by various scholars. This edition contains Hegel's letters in *Briefe von und an Hegel,* 4 vols. (1952–1960). The unpublished letters prior to 1800 will appear in this new critical edition under the editorship of Gisela Schüler. There are numerous English translations of Hegel's works.

McTaggart, J. M. E. *Studies in Hegelian Cosmology.* Cambridge University Press, 1901.

———. *Studies in the Hegelian Dialectic.* Cambridge University Press, 1896, 2d ed., 1922.

Mueller, Gustave. "Hegel's Absolute and the Crisis of Christianity" in *A Hegel Symposium,* ed. D. C. Travis. Austin, Tex., 1912.

Mure, G. R. G. *A Study of Hegel's Logic.* Oxford, 1950.

———. *An Introduction to Hegel.* Oxford, 1940.

Popper, Karl. *The Open Society and its Enemies,* 2 vols. London, 1945.

Pringle-Pattison, A. S. *Hegelianism and Personality,* 2d ed. London and Edinburgh, 1887.

Stace, W. T. *The Philosophy of Hegel.* London, 1924; New York, 1955.

Serreau, René. *Hegel et l'hégelianisme.* Paris, 1962.

Wahl, Jean. *Le Malheur de la conscience dans la philosophie.* Paris, 1929.

Studies

Bosanquet, B. *History of Aesthetic.* London, 1892. Chaps. 2–12.

Caird, Edward. *Hegel.* London and Edinburgh, 1883.

Copleston, Frederick. *A History of Philosophy,* vol. 7, *From Fichte to Nietzsche.* London, 1963. Chaps. 9–11.

Croce, Benedetto. *Ciò che è vivo e ciò che è morto della filosofia di Hegel.* Bari, Italy, 1907. Trans. by Douglas Ainslie as *What Is Living and What Is Dead in the Philosophy of Hegel.* London 1915.

Findlay, J. N. *Hegel: A Re-examination.* London, 1958. (Emphasizes the Logic and interprets Hegel in somewhat nonmetaphysical terms.)

Glockner, Hermann. *Hegel,* 2 vols. Stuttgart, 1929. (These are vols. 21–22 of Jubilee edition of Hegel mentioned above.)

Grégoire, Franz. *Études hégéliennes.* Louvain, Belgium, and Paris, 1958. (Contains detailed and fruitful discussions of the central issues.)

Haering, T. L. *Hegel: Sein Wollen und Sein Werk,* 2 vols. Leipzig, 1929. (A leading authority.)

Hyppolite, Jean. *Introduction à la philosophie de l'histoire de Hegel.* Paris, 1948.

————. *Genèse et structure de la Phénoménologie de l'Esprit de Hegel.* Paris, 1946.

————. *Logique et existence.* Paris, 1953.

Kaufmann, Walter. *From Shakespeare to Existentialism.* Boston, 1959. Chaps. 7 and 8.

————. *Hegel: Reinterpretation, Texts and Commentaries.* New York, 1965.

Kline, George L. "Some Recent Re-interpretations of Hegel's Philosophy," *The Monist,* vol. 48, 1964, pp. 34–73.

————. *De Hegel.* Paris, 1929; 2d ed., 1951.

Walsh, W. H. "The Origins of Hegelianism," chap. 9 in *Metaphysics.* London, 1963.

Other Studies

Hegel-Studien, vol. 1 (Bonn, 1961), vol. 2 (Bonn, 1963), and Supp. vol. 1 (Bonn, 1964), ed. F. Nicolin and O. Poggeler.

Études hégéliennes (Neuchâtel, 1955), with articles by Alexandre Kojève, Georges Bataille, R. Queneau, Jean Wahl, and Eric Weil.

A Hegel Symposium (Austin, Texas, 1962), with articles by C. J. Friedrich, Sidney Hook, Helmut Motekat, Gustav E. Mueller, and Helmut Rehder.

DECOMPOSITION OF
HEGELIANISM

1 *The Hegelian Left*

Between Hegel's method and his system Friedrich Engels noted a contrast. This contrast, after the brilliant success of the doctrine between 1830 and 1840, was to bring about the fragmentation of Hegelianism and a split between its partisans. The system is the whole body of absolute, invariable truths which he thought he had discovered in art, politics, religion, and philosophy: the bureaucratic Prussian state, Romantic art, Christianity, idealism. The method is the conviction that philosophy is not a collection of rigid dogmatic principles but the process that prohibits any truth from being conceived as absolute, any social stage from being definitive. The system is conservative and the method revolutionary. Hence the division between the Hegelian right and the Hegelian left. Those who were drawn particularly to Hegel's system could believe that they had every right to remain conservatives in religion as well as in philosophy; by contrast, those who saw the essentials of Hegel's philosophy in the dialectical method could lean toward the most extreme radicalism in religion as well as in philosophy. Hampered by the necessities of the system, Hegel failed to draw out these consequences. The task fell to a group of young Hegelians who formed the liberal opposition party in Prussia, beginning in 1840, under the reactionary regime of Frederick William IV. "They drew out the true consequences, which Hegel himself dared not elaborate," one member of the group wrote. "It is the human consciousness that engenders everything assumed to be a reality, and while realities develop, contend with each other, and unite, consciousness remains *the one true* principle. All truths or realities are merely forms of absolute spirit and are in no way definitive; the spirit is perpetually creating new forms; becoming is the unique principle of any philosophy. Thus nothing endures except the action of the spirit itself, which will manifest itself in forms that are always new." This is a necessary consequence unless we accept Nietzsche's judgment that to Hegel the culminating and final point in the universal process coincides with his own existence in Berlin.[1]

The principle was first applied to religion, which could be discussed much more freely than politics. The works of David Strauss (*Life of Jesus,* 1835), Bruno Bauer (*Critique of the Evangelical History of John,* 1840, and *Critique of the Evangelical History of the Synoptics,* 1841–42), and Ludwig Feuerbach (*The Essence of Christianity,* 1841) all express the idea that the Christian religion is a product of the human consciousness. These works contain many statements similar to those found in the works of earlier writers, but they do not mark a return to the eighteenth century. The origin of man is no longer used to discredit religion but to make man aware of his inner resources. "Learning and philosophy," says Feuerbach, "to me are only instruments for gaining access to the treasures hidden in the heart of man." It is this trait that binds such men closely to Hegel, even though their attitude toward him is often critical.

The rhythm of Feuerbach's thought in *The Essence of Christianity* is thoroughly Hegelian. It consists in showing how that which seems external to us is in reality internal, how the God projected outside man by the theologians is in reality man himself. Return to self,

---

[1] Moses Hell, *Gegenwärtige Krisis der deutschen Philosophie,* as quoted by Groethuysen, "Origines du socialisme en Allemagne," *Revue philosophique,* 1923, p. 383.

identity of consciousness of God with self-consciousness—this is indeed the Hegelian spirit. Religion originates in a quality that radically separates human consciousness from animal consciousness: man's consciousness is split in two, for he is aware of himself as an individual and knows himself as a species. Man knows himself as such in thought, an inner language in which man addresses himself and is at once "I" and "thou." Thus he knows the infinitude of his species, his true being in contrast to the finitude of his individual self. God is nothing other than the totality of the infinite attributes belonging to the human species: wisdom, love, will. It would be impossible to find anything in religion that does not refer to man, for there is in God no attribute that is not specifically human; furthermore, religion has no goal but man himself, for man looks to religion only for his own salvation. "Man makes himself the goal, the object of God's thoughts. The mystery of the Incarnation is the mystery of God's love for man, but the mystery of God is only the mystery of man's love for himself" (*Essence of Christianity*). The theological illusion was necessary, moreover, since internality is always at the end of the process. "The historical progress of religions consists in the fact that the later religions always view as subjective or human what the earlier ones contemplated and worshiped as divine." Feuerbach believes that his doctrine is the definitive expulsion of all idolatry. Like Comte, he excludes the direct relation between God and nature, which, in the eighteenth century, had been the foundation of a form of deism tending toward atheism. "To discover a God in nature," says Feuerbach on this point, "we must first put him there. Proofs of the existence of God based on natural phenomena are only proofs of the ignorance and arrogance with which man makes the limits of his intelligence the limits of human nature." Thus he excludes any loop-hole: God exists only for man and in man.

Feuerbach intends not to destroy Christianity but to work toward its fulfillment, and he believes that his doctrine is a clear translation of a language written in cipher. It is "a faithful translation of the Christian religion, nothing but a literal translation from the dead language of fantasy, replete with images, into a good, intelligible modern language . . . a solution of the enigma of Christianity." In other words, since a translation retains the spirit of its model, Feuerbach claims to retain the spirit of Christianity in its entirety. His ambiguous stand was later adopted by Renan, who wanted to retain all the spirituality of the Christian life without its dogmatic affirmations. This religious atheism is the counterpart of the kind of idealistic sensualism that allows Feuerbach to confer on sensation the power to unite immediately with the inward nature of beings. "We see not only the surfaces of mirrors and colorful apparitions, but we also contemplate a man's look. Thus not only the exterior but also the interior, not only the flesh but also the spirit, not only the thing but also the self are the object of sense." [2] Interpreted in this way, sense enables man to escape from the isolation and limitation imposed on him by idealism. Union is the starting point of human infinitude and freedom, and religion is their affirmation.

David Strauss and Bruno Bauer were more concerned with history. They applied to the Gospels the principles of textual criticism which had been applied mainly to the Old Testament during the preceding centuries, but they retained the Hegelian spirit. To them the Gospel was a mythical invention traceable to the first Christian community. Strauss, in particular, found in the words of Jesus contradictions reflecting a conflict between Christians who were associated with Judaism, and Paulinism, which broke with Jewish practices. To him the Gospels contained the true history of the first Christian communities, reflected in the myth of Jesus. Thus the Hegelians were interested in Christianity as a phase in the evolution of spirit, and this is even true of Ferdinand Christian Baur, the orthodox Hegelian who tried, especially in his *Compendium of the History of Christian Dogma* (1847), to trace a continuous, organic development of the history of dogmas, showing that Christianity is "a new, distinctive form of religious consciousness, which ends the conflict between Judaism and paganism by reducing both to unity."

[2] *Grundsätze der Philosophie der Zukunft,* secs. 40–42.

But the relativism of the young Hegelians also applied to politics. They saw the state—especially the Prussian state, which, in contrast to other states, was not confined by any national tradition—as the vindicator of the new spirit. It was a Hegelian, F. Köppen, who wrote an admiring book about Frederick the Great. Disappointment caused by the reign of Frederick William IV, "that Romantic seated on a throne," who declared that "he would never allow a written sheet of paper to come between God and his person," and who exiled and persecuted all liberals, alienated the Hegelians and prompted them to become affiliated with revolutionary associations such as the League of the Just, which was then inspired by the spirit of Lamennais and the French socialists. Lorenz von Stein presented their ideas in his *Socialism and Communism in Contemporary France* (1842). As early as 1841, in his *European Triarchy,* Moses Hess, a Jew from Bonn, had said that the future lay in close union of German philosophy and French socialism. This was also the opinion of Karl Marx and, generally speaking, many Neo-Hegelians; bewildered by the failure of the Prussian state and finally convinced (like Bauer) that Hegelian relativism was nothing but a purely negative critique, they decided that the positive, constructive idea which they had been pursuing was to be found in communism.

Still, this union did not last, and as early as 1845, it was broken by both Hegelians and communists. Noted Hegelians—Arnold Ruge, the Bauer brothers, Buhl, Edward Meyer—seemed somewhat frightened. Their shyness in action, as Moses Hess charged, was equaled by their boldness in theory. For his part, Friedrich Engels, who had been associated with Karl Marx since 1841, reveals that he undertook with Marx, in 1845, a work "destined to show the antagonism between our [communist] conception and the German ideological conception, in fact, to liquidate our ancient philosophical conscience." This is the subject dealt with in their collaborative works, *The Holy Family or Critique of Critical Critique: Against Bruno Bauer and Consorts* and *The German Ideology.* "Until the present," writes Marx, "philosophers have merely interpreted the world in different ways. Now the object is to transform it." There could be no more incisive and exact criticism of the doctrines of Hegel and Feuerbach; as we have seen, they are literal translations rather than penetrations of a reality which is simply perceived by sight. Thus Feuerbach shows that man has been divorced from the object of religion—God—and his doctrine consists in healing the breach by bringing God back to man. "He does not see that after he has come to the end of his course, the main task still remains to be done. . . . This antagonism [between what appears to be the divine reality and its temporal base] must be understood if it is to be eliminated. For example, when the heavenly family is understood to be the reflection of the earthly family, it is the latter that must be subjected to theoretical criticism and rapidly transformed." Here we see clearly how the Hegelian dialectic is set in motion. Hegel showed that there was no *Seinsollen,* no independent ideal capable of inducing and directing action. Marx completes the thought by saying that no ideal is capable of preventing action, which therefore is freed from any kind of servitude to ideas. "All the mysteries which cause theory to fall into skepticism find their rational solution in practical human activity and in comprehension of this activity."

These criticisms, however, are aimed at the speculative attitude of the Hegelians rather than at the core of their philosophy. Marx accepts the Hegelian negation of an ideal distinct from reality, which, after 1848, assured the separation of socialistic materialism and French ideological socialism, but he does not offer a word of criticism for the central idea of the Hegelian dialectic—the idea of antagonism (negativity) as the condition required for the unfolding of reality, which was the obsession of German speculative thought.[3] Indeed, it is around this idea that Marx, a more energetic than original thinker, organizes the elements that he extracts in great quantities from English and French economists or sociologists. Without going into details which would exceed the scope of this work, let us recall how Marx reduced the whole moving force of

[3] Cf. Gaston Richard, *La question sociale et le mouvement philosophique au XIXe siècle* (Paris: Colin, 1914), p. 201.

history to a single antagonism—antagonism between the capitalistic or propertied class and the proletariat or working class; how this antagonism is completely independent of individual wills or conscience and is due to the conditions of production; how consciousness cannot and should not intervene except to identify and intensify this antagonism; how the role of the socialist party is to develop the class consciousness of the proletariat and transform it into a political party capable of seizing power and preparing for the dispossession of the capitalist class. Here we see the deep imprint of Hegelian thought. If Marx readily subscribed to the strange proposition that all moral, political, juridical, and intellectual relations among men living in a society are determined by its system of production, it was because he found support for his Hegelianism in a theory of political economy which made the mutual relations contracted by men in social production "independent of the will, necessary, determined." Socialism is the transition of society from existence in itself to knowledge of itself, like Hegelian philosophy.

The degree to which Hegelianism had become a kind of intellectual atmosphere is seen in Max Stirner's book, *The Ego and His Own* (1845). The author, whose real name was Johann Kaspar Schmidt, was born in Bayreuth in 1806. After 1842, along with many Neo-Hegelians, he frequented a group in Berlin known as the *Freien* (Freedmen), which is also the title of an important section of his book (pp. 117–82), devoted to the study and criticism of political, social, and human liberalism. The book as a whole embraces two antithetical parts: *Man* and *Ego*. The first part, which includes the section on the *Freien,* alludes constantly to Feuerbach's anthropology. Stirner's book, criticized by Marx immediately after its publication, obviously had an important part in contemporary discussions.

His attacks on the Neo-Hegelians of his time are pitiless, yet he is himself a product of Hegelianism. This is shown particularly in his attitude toward Bruno Bauer. The criticism of the editor of the *Litteraturzeitung* consisted in pushing the Hegelian dialectic to the extreme, considering "the thought process" to be the sole reality, and showing that any affirmation whatsoever in the sphere of ethics or politics was false and should disappear or crumble in the face of the sovereign advancement of thought. As Stirner remarks ironically, it is "the struggle of the possessed against possession," and in his view the "possessed" are those who accept as realities God, the state, or right. Bauer sees clearly that there is "a religious attitude not only toward God but also toward right, the state, law. But he tries to use thought (*Denken*) to dissolve these ideas (*Gedanken*), and then I say: 'Only one thing saves me from thought, and that is the absence of thought.' " Thus Hegelianism in its extreme form, after it has reached the relativity of all thought, must finally pass over to its opposite. Stirner had already said this in the style of Hegel, in an article of 1842, published by Karl Marx in the *Rheinische Zeitung* ("The Factitious Principle of Our Education, or Humanism and Realism"): *Science* itself must die in order to flourish again in death as *will*. Freedom of thought, of belief, and of conscience sink back into the earth's maternal bosom, enabling its quintessential juices to nourish a new freedom—freedom of will." [4] Absence of thought is pure, immediate, unique will as such, outside any kind of comparison. "I do not look upon myself as something peculiar but as something *unique*. To be sure, I bear a *resemblance* to others, but that applies only to reflection; in fact, I am incomparable, unique. My flesh is not their flesh, my spirit is not their spirit. If you put them in general frames, flesh and spirit are your ideas and have nothing to do with *my* flesh and *my* spirit." In the face of such aggressive nominalism not only old beliefs vanished but also the new universals, which the moderns had substituted for the old since the French Revolution: the State, Society, Humanity. The political liberalism of the middle class is grounded on the state. Is the freedom in question an enfranchisement? No, for it is obedience to laws, and the individual is simply linked directly to the law, which frees him from intermediaries exactly as Protes-

---

[4] As quoted by V. Basch, *L'individualisme anarchiste, Max Stirner*, p. 34.

tantism freed the individual not from obligations to God but from priests who stood between him and God. It is the state that is free, not I: *"Its* freedom is *my* thraldom."

Nor is the social liberalism of communism an enfranchisement. It eliminates private property, the foundation of the worker's thraldom, and substitutes collective property. Society becomes the sole possessor, providing me with everything and imposing obligations on me in return; still, "the socialists do not realize that society is not a self which can lend, give, or guarantee but an instrument or means which we can turn to our advantage, . . . and that we owe no sacrifice to society, for, like the liberals, they are prisoners of religious principles and search for a society which they can revere, as they once revered the state; . . . their society is still a phantom, a 'supreme being.'" Finally, in his criticism of "human liberalism" Stirner batters down the idol bequeathed by Feuerbach and Bauer—namely, man. Parting company with the socialists, Bauer saw the masses as "the most significant product of the Revolution, the duped crowd, which the illusions of the philosophy of the Enlightenment have driven to a boundless ill temper." He rejects the liberal ideas of 1789 in favor of a doctrine of internal liberation of the ego. According to Bauer, the egotism of the individual must be destroyed in order to make room for the man; thus he calls for separation of Church and state, since religious interests are considered to be egotistical and concern only the private life of man. In reality, however, man as Bauer imagines him is an unattainable ideal, and man still remains, for each individual "a sublime hereafter, a supreme being, a God," who merits no more consideration than the one rejected by Bauer's atheism.

"All these forms of liberalism are but the continuation of the old Christian contempt for the ego. . . . The religion of man is but the final metamorphosis of the Christian religion. For liberalism is a religion, since it separates my essence from me and raises it above me, since it elevates man just as another religion elevates his God and his idols." This idea is not without justification, for he heard Guizot express the wish, in a meeting of the Chambre des

Pairs, that the University of Paris might play the role of spiritual director which had formerly devolved on the Church.

The ever resurgent idea of the Hegelian dialectic, that of a fertile and productive antagonism, is pushed to its limit by Stirner. "Our weakness," he writes, "is traceable not to the antagonism between ourselves and others but to its incompleteness—to the fact that we are not separated from them. We search for a *community,* a *bond,* a single faith, a single God, a single idea, a single hat for everyone. . . . But the final, most decisive antagonism, that between one unique person and others, intrinsically surpasses what is called antagonism. . . . As a unique person, you have nothing in common with another person; by the same token, you are no longer separated from him or hostile toward him; you do not try to discover your rights against him in the presence of a *third party.* . . . Antagonism disappears in perfect *separation* or oneness." To push antagonism to such lengths (to emphasize it to the utmost is in keeping with the Hegelian spirit) is to suppress it and reduce it to its opposite— wholly unique persons.

Against the society or state, which destroys the oneness of the ego, Stirner, like Proudhon, sets association (*Verein*), which is my activity or creation—a means of increasing my power by uniting with others in a completely free association, which I can wilfully join or renounce. It seems that in Stirner's view the state is merely an association which has come into being, developed strength and stability, and become independent of me. His fundamental aim seems to be to reintroduce plasticity and mobility into these societies that have grown old.

Socialism and anarchy emerge as corollaries of Hegel's doctrine even though they do not originate in it. The young Hegelians were nurtured on the writings of the French socialists, and Stirner often quotes Proudhon; but here they took on the peculiar aspect of implacable rigor, "objectivity," and absence of sentimentality which they were to retain after 1848. Russia exhibits a similar pattern in the evolution of Hegelianism, in the person of Alexander Herzen (1812–70). In that country too, about 1840, Hegel's doctrine invaded the universities. Here we also find a Hegelian Right, which defends tsarism and Byzantine orthodoxy, and a Hegelian Left, which holds that "Hegel did not draw out all the results implicitly contained in his principles." In 1842, after reading the *Deutschfranzösische Jahrbücher,* the journal edited by Marx, Herzen wrote: "German philosophy is emerging from the lecture-room and entering life, is becoming social and revolutionary, is taking on flesh and undertaking to produce results in the world of events." [5] But the Russians are keenly aware of all the possible oppressive elements in Hegel's universal. "This universal," writes Belinsky, a friend of Herzen, "is a Moloch with respect to the subject [the concrete individual], which it uses to show itself off and then discards like a worn-out pair of trousers. . . . I hate the universal, the executioner of the poor human person." [6] Herzen and Belinsky incline naturally toward the point of view adopted later by Stirner and even go so far as to advocate nihilism, an expression apparently created by Herzen under the stimulus of Bruno Bauer's criticism. Yet at the same time Herzen links this doctrine to the idea of Russia's mission, and he remains a Slavophile in his own way, although he certainly is not a right-wing Slavophile—a reactionary, who favors a return to the past—but rather a Russian Hegelian. His philosophy of history is based on "prolonging the Hegelian scheme of universal history by a third epoch, in which the Slavic world ruled by Russia, will inherit the Romano-Germanic world, itself the heir to the ancient world." [7] Slavism is grounded on the principle of anarchy—the principle of *mir* or the peasant community. According to Herzen, this community should be transformed or modernized along the lines prescribed in Proudhon's doctrines. Thus nihilistic anarchy in no way prevents but, rather, dictates a form of Pan-Slavism identical with Hegelian Pan-Germanism—a cult of Holy Russia as the last stage of universal history. Moreover, Herzen delights in finding the expression of this cult in the Hegelian Bruno Bauer. After showing how

---

[5] As quoted by P. Labry, *Alexandre Herzen* (Paris, 1928), p. 248.
[6] *Ibid.,* p. 225; written in 1841.
[7] *Ibid.,* p. 27

Bauer arrived at nihilism, like Schopenhauer, though by a different route, he adds: "The Russians may be interested to learn that Bauer deems them to be the instruments predestined to reduce everything that exists to nothingness. This he explains in his book, *Russia and Germanism*." Furthermore, nothing is more Hegelian than his confidence in the ability of tsarism, and especially of Alexander II, to carry out a revolution which will free the peasant community.

In Russia as in Germany, Hegelianism took the place of a Schellingian Romanticism which had reigned supreme between 1820 and 1830, and which had culminated in a mystical type of nationalism. "German philosophy," wrote Kireyevsky in 1830, "cannot thrust its roots deeply into our soil. *Our* philosophy should emanate from the development of *our* life and answer the questions which are peculiar to us or fit in with the dominant interests of our particular existence. . . . Interest in German philosophy, which is just beginning to manifest itself among us, marks an important step toward this goal." [8] For the most part the transition from Schelling's influence to Hegel's is, as in Germany, the transition from nationalism to the revolutionary spirit—but to a revolutionary spirit radically different from that of the rights of man; one that seeks support as well as reality in a national tradition.

II *Orthodox Hegelianism*

Orthodox Hegelian ideas were strengthened and spread by several periodicals: *Jahrbücher für wissenschaftliche Kritik* (1827–47), A. Ruge's *Hallischen Jahrbücher für deutsche Wissenschaft und Kunst* (after 1838), *Deutsche Jahrbücher* (1841–43), *Jahrbücher der Gegenwart* (Tubingen, 1843–48), and *Jahrbücher für spekulative Philosophie,* edited by Nock (1846–48). J. K. F. Rosenkranz (1805–79) was Hegel's publisher, commentator, and apologist (see his *Defense of Hegel against Dr. R. Haym,* 1858). Among the Hegelians of the period we find several Protestant theologians who are concerned

[8] As quoted by A. Koyré, *La philosophie et le problème national en Russie au début du XIXe siècle* (Paris, 1929), p. 168.

with uniting Christianity and Hegelian speculation. Biedermann, for example (*Free Theology or Philosophy and Christianity in Conflict and Harmony,* 1845, *Christian Dogmatics,* 1869) incorporates into philosophy everything that is knowledge and representation in religion.

Like French eclecticism, the Hegelian school produced many studies of the history of philosophy. Karl von Prantl, the historian of logic (*History of Logic,* 4 vols., 1855-70) was first of all a Hegelian. The same is true of Johann Eduard Erdmann (1805-92), of Kuno Fischer, the historian of modern philosophy (*History of Modern Philosophy,* 6 vols., 1852-77), and even, when he was just starting his work, of Eduard Zeller, the historian of Greek philosophy. But in Germany as in France, historians of philosophy tended to devote themselves to pure philology.

Friedrich Theodor Vischer, the aesthetician, (*Aesthetics or Science of Beauty,* 6 vols., 1846-57) uses Hegel's dialectical method in his explanation of the arts. For example, he reconstructs the different "moments" in the work of the painter—drawing, light and shadow, perspective, color (secs. 664-70)—as a dialectical series, in which the complete, total appearance of the visible form is gradually engendered, yet he allows ample room for observation and induction.

Bibliography

Basch, V. *L'individualisme anarchiste: M. Stirner*. Paris, 1904.

Hook, Sidney. *From Hegel to Marx: Studies in the Intellectual Development of Karl Marx*. New York, 1950.

Kline, G. L. "Some Recent Reinterpretations of Hegel's Philosophy," *The Monist*, vol. 48, no. 1, 1964.

Lévy, Albert. *Strauss, sa vie et son œuvre*. Paris, 1910.

————. *La philosophie de Feuerbach et son influence sur la littérature allemande*. Paris, 1904.

————. *Stirner et Nietzsche*, Paris, 1904.

Löwith, Karl. *Von Hegel zu Nietzsche*, 4th ed. Stuttgart, 1958; trans. D. E. Green: *From Hegel to Nietzsche*, New York, 1964.

————, ed. *Die Hegelsche Linke*. Stuttgart and Bad Cannstatt, 1962.

Lubbe, Hermann, ed. *Die Hegelsche Rechte*. Stuttgart and Bad Cannstatt, 1962.

Lukacs, Georg. *Die Zerstörung der Vernunft*. Berlin, 1954.

Marcuse, Herbert. *Reason and Revolution: Hegel and the Rise of Social Theory*, 2d ed. New York, 1954.

Rawidowicz, S. L. *Feuerbachs Philosophie: Ursprung und Schicksal*. Berlin, 1931.

Rosenkranz, K. *Neue Studien zur Kultur- und Litteraturgeschichte*, 4 vols. 1875–78.

Sorel, G. *La décomposition du marxisme*. Paris, 1908.

Tönnies, F. *Marx: Leben und Lehre*. Jena, 1921.

Zeller, E. *D. F. Strauss, in seinem Leben und seinen Schriften*. Bonn, 1894.

FROM GOETHE TO
SCHOPENHAUER

POST-KANTIAN METAPHYSICS was not the whole of German philosophy between 1800 and 1850. Goethe's philosophical views differed radically from it, and Schopenhauer opposed it vigorously.

1 *Johann Wolfgang von Goethe*

A deep intellectual kinship existed, nevertheless, between Johann Wolfgang von Goethe (1749–1832) and the Post-Kantians, particularly Hegel.[1] Their common ties go beyond Kant to Herder: they overcame the Romanticism of their youth; they are hostile toward the mysticism of Tieck and Novalis, whether naturalistic or Christian; they believe that the supreme expression of the spirit is to be found, not in art or vague speculation, but in finite, determinate activity (for example, Faust's in the second part of Goethe's drama). To them, the highest art is not music but poetry, and the highest form of poetry is Greek tragedy, a synthesis of lyric and epic poetry. Furthermore, they distrust the two great movements of the eighteenth century, mathematical physics and revolutionary ideas. Unlike the Newtonians, what Goethe asks of experience is not confirmation of a law but revelation of the continuity of nature. He speaks scornfully of the method "whereby we claim to demonstrate a thesis that we posit by means of *isolated experiences,* and then somehow use

---

[1] See R. Berthelot, "Goethe et Hegel," *Revue de Métaphysique,* 1931, pp. 366–412.

these experiences as *arguments.*" Here his charge is leveled against the law of attraction, and he seeks instead to discover what he calls "observation of a higher order," that is, an observation embracing details observed in many different instances, arranged in a pattern designed to bring out the whole series of differences associated with the same reality. This is the basis of the experiments he undertook for his famous theory of colors.

In spite of this affinity, Goethe always remained aloof from philosophers. "For philosophy in the strict sense I had no tools . . . ," he writes. "*The Critique of Pure Reason* had appeared long before, but remained outside the limits of my intellectual horizon." The great philosophical problem of the objectivity of knowledge is not his problem. "To me," he says, "thought is not separate from objects; elements of objects or intuitions enter my thought and are permeated by it so thoroughly that my intuition is a thought and my thought an intuition." This is because Goethe is searching, not for a philosophy, but for what has often been called a kind of wisdom—an "experimental wisdom," in the words of M. Berthelot (*Revue de Métaphysique,* 1928, p. 12)—which first abandons man to his instincts, giving free reign in every possible direction to his tendencies, until reflection prescribes and justifies a precise, limited activity. Here we cannot even sketch the structure of this wisdom and its prodigious influence.

II *Karl Christian Friedrich Krause*

Karl Christian Friedrich Krause (1781–1832) studied philosophy under Fichte and Schelling but differed singularly from them both in his life and in his ideas. He was not able to settle down in Jena, Berlin, or Dresden. He taught at Göttingen but became involved in a revolutionary plot and had to leave the university. In 1831 he tried to obtain a professorship at the University of Munich but encountered the intransigeant opposition of Schelling. He wrote a great number of works, many of them published posthumously. His major work is *Lectures on the Basic Truths of Science* (1829).

Krause's inmost feelings set him squarely against Hegel and even Schelling, who do not share his sense of the importance and worth of the individual destiny of the person. In contrast to those two philosophers, he has no use for "concrete universals," which, like the state, oppress and annihilate any individual destiny as such.

The image that suffuses his whole system is that of the world as a cooperative system (*Vereinwesen*) held together by a higher term. For all the different states of consciousness, this term is the ego in each of us; for the organic whole formed by man and the universe, it is God. The Leibnizian character of his image is apparent. It is this special relation between unity and diversity that constitutes Krause's *panentheism:* the world exists as such only by virtue of the unending pursuit of virtue, the infinite activity or force, the holy will, which is God himself; God lives only in union with finite beings; that is why rational mankind, in which this union is best realized, is at the summit of reality.

The most vital part of Krause's work is his theory of human society, which is the core of his metaphysics. Krause is neither an individualist like Fichte nor a state-socialist like Hegel. In his view, rights exist within small groups of men and make clear the conditions under which human goals may be attained. In the broadest possible sense, therefore, human rights are the divine law or "the totality of all the external and internal conditions necessary to realize the rational life, insofar as these conditions can be produced by free activity." [2] Thus Krause hardly makes a distinction between rights and morality, but he places them clearly beyond individual arbitrariness.

Still to be determined is the nature of these associations or unions. Mankind as a whole is like a pyramid formed by associations, each endowed with an independent juridical life and related to all the others. Some associations—those based on friendship, the family, the commune, the nation—have a universal goal. Others, such as the Church, professional societies, and scientific associations have specific goals. The state is only one such association, and it has the limited

---

[2] As quoted by G. Gurvitch, *L'idée du droit social*, 1931, p. 455.

goal of realizing law. It is neither the whole of society nor the heart of society, but it corresponds to the nation, an association with a universal goal. Society as a whole consists of the federation of these associations. The federation is not hierarchically superior to the associations it integrates, leaving the independence of each untouched, but it is like their common spirit. This explains why the federations themselves band together, without creating a higher authority, until finally they constitute the global union of mankind as a whole (*Menschheitsbund*).

There is an obvious similarity between the Krausian spirit and Proudhon's anarchy. Krause may not have exerted a strong influence on Proudhon, but he had many other disciples. From 1836 to the present, beginning with his immediate disciples, Von Leonhardi and Ahrens, there has been a continuous stream of posthumous publications, and the source has still not been exhausted. Ahrens introduced Krause's philosophy into Belgium, where Tiberghien (1819–1901) was his principal representative (*Theory of the Infinite*, Brussels, 1846; *The Commandments of Mankind*, 1872); and in 1910 J. de Boeck, Tiberghien's pupil, published his *Theory of Determination on the Basis of Krause's Panentheism*.

III *Friedrich Daniel Schleiermacher*

Schleiermacher (1768–1834) was a preacher rather than a philosopher. While he was in Berlin, in 1797, he became acquainted with Friedrich Schlegel and the Romanticists. He taught theology at several universities and, last of all, at the University of Berlin. His doctrine is contained in *Discourses on Religion* (1799) and *Monologues* (1800).

To a certain degree his religious doctrine is related to Jacobi's or to Kant's theory of postulates. He insists that the religious life must not be dominated by arbitrarily imposed dogmas; that the religious life itself, as we know it by direct inner feelings or by the testimony of others, implies the necessity of positing a dogma; and that Christian dogmatics therefore embraces the minimum number of beliefs indispensable to the Christian life. Furthermore, the Christian life embraces two related feelings: the feelings of rising from a "lower consciousness" to a "higher consciousness," and the feeling that our elevation cannot originate within ourselves. This conjunction of plenitude and deficiency forces us to believe that our inward change is produced by the permanent influence of a person who, having reached the higher level of consciousness, where he remains forever, can serve as our model. Thus our aspiration takes us back beyond the historical person of Christ and his influence as it has been transmitted to the Church, back to the Christ of the Gospel of John, "the son who does nothing on his own, but what he sees his father do." This is the Christ who says, "Whoever sees me, sees my father," or "What is mine is thine, and what is thine is mine." It follows that the distinctive point of view of Schleiermacher, who differs from Jacobi on this point, is traceable to the conviction that our inner need is identical with a historical and objective datum. But it also follows that the religious life is wholly dependent on the findings of historical criticism. The situation is all the more perilous for Schleiermacher, since he exposes the Bible and the three synoptic Gospels to the attacks of critics. Still, he exempts the Gospel of John, the authenticity of which was considered highly doubtful by his contemporaries.

The fact that he questioned the authenticity of the synoptic Gospels is of great importance in the history of ideas. It tended to give first place to historical criticism, even in the context of the inner religious life, and to give direction to the works of Strauss and Renan.

Another striking consequence of Schleiermacher's conviction is that his Christology is distinct from his theology. He is vitally concerned with the personality of Christ, but does not care whether the supreme being on whom we feel ourselves to be dependent, through Christ, is or is not a personal being. Furthermore, in conformity with the doctrine of Schelling and Hegel, he thinks that God can be separated from the world only in an abstract way and that God and the world are but "two values for the same thing."

In fact, God is unity which surpasses all unities, unity without plurality, and the world is the totality of oppositions, plurality without unity. But the two moments are inseparable: God without the world remains an empty image, and his unity can be perfected and enriched only by natural forces and moral laws. Schleiermacher's religion is a religion without a personal God; the inner feeling on which it is based dictates nothing of the sort. According to him, religion is a feeling of absolute dependence, and God is the name that we give to the being on whom we depend. According to our religion, this God will be multiple or one, natural or supernatural, personal or impersonal.

IV *Wilhelm von Humboldt*

Wilhelm von Humboldt (1767–1835) was one of those who refused to be seduced by the dialectic of the post-Kantians. His ideal of human culture relates him to Schiller and Goethe. In 1810 he was given the responsibility of reforming the educational system of Prussia, and he developed the teaching of the humanities in the Gymnasiums (as in the French lycées of the same period). To him every man was the universal man, sensitive to every aspect of civilization. Humboldt was the prototype of the German philologist, who, like Renan at a later date, saw philology as an independent, self-sufficient discipline.

Like Hegel and all the Romanticists, he took up problems of evolution, but he did not claim that they could be resolved by a universal formula capable of accounting for every concrete detail. He assumed that individuals—unexpected, unforeseeable, and truly effective realities—have a part in evolution. The theory of individuality in history sets Humboldt apart from his contemporaries, although it bears a resemblance on many points to the Romanticists' ideas concerning genius.

Humboldt's ideas find their clearest expression in the studies of language to which he devoted himself almost exclusively after 1818. Progress in language is gradual but "thwarted by the action of new, incalculable forces." Language is not an invention of nations: "It possesses a spontaneous activity, but one that is essentially beyond explanation; it is not a product of this activity but an involuntary emanation of spirit; it is not a creation of nations but a gift conferred upon them by virtue of their internal structure; they use it without knowing how they made it." Language is given entirely and immediately; it is not fabricated in parts. The diversity of tongues originates in the obstacles or support that the universal force of language finds in the spiritual force inherent in each nation—a hidden, mysterious force, which is not part of the chain of causes and effects evident to reason. He is probably referring to Hegel when he says that our ideas, which purport to explain everything, must not be substituted for facts as they present themselves, and he uses the word "inexplicable" quite frequently. "Every process of evolution in nature, particularly organic and vital evolution, is hidden from our observation," he writes. "No matter how thoroughly we investigate the states leading up to a particular development, between it and the last state we always find a break separating something from nothing, and the same is true of disappearance. Man's comprehension is restricted to the realm of the intermediate." Thus we see in Humboldt the birth of the idea of a kind of creative evolution (even though he does not use the term) which the concept alone cannot penetrate.[3]

v *Johann Friedrich Herbart*

Johann Friedrich Herbart (1776–1841) was professor at the University of Göttingen in 1805, then at the University of Königsberg until 1833. His taste for pedagogy dates from his visit to Pestalozzi while he was a tutor in Switzerland (1797–1800).

One could hardly find a mind more opposed by natural inclination to the metaphysical doctrines then current. He sees the doctrines of Kant, Schelling, and Fichte merely as an episode

---

[3] See *W. V. Humboldts philosophische Anthropologie*, ed. F. Heinemann (Halle, 1929), especially pp. 126–38.

culminating in the failure of idealism. The history of philosophy recognizes necessity, but to a lesser degree than any other history. Its retardation or advancement depends on events which science can neither produce nor dominate.

Herbart's is a doctrine of understanding (*Verstand*). "The time is approaching," he writes, "when one cannot avoid the fundamental condition of comprehension [*Verstehen*], which is recognition of the contradictions inherent in the forms of experience." Logical analysis reveals that the data of experience are contradictory; *therefore,* Herbart reasons, they are not real, and philosophy has the unique task of discovering the true realities to which these appearances lead us, once they have been purged of contradiction. He compares his mode of thinking to that which led Greek philosophy from Heraclitus to Leucippus; the first proclaims the inner contradiction of change, and the second arrives at an atomistic theory—the theory of the absolute reality of any contradiction. Similarly Locke, seizing the contradiction between the unity of substance and the diversity of the independent qualities belonging to it, resolves things into an aggregate of characteristics which are only representations.

Philosophy originates in a form of skepticism concerned primarily with fundamental concepts. Each particular thing should be one and simple, yet we perceive only a multiplicity of its qualities; we maintain that events are connected by causes and effects, yet we see only a succession of events; we assert the unity of the self, yet we apprehend only a multiplicity of representations. Thus the Herbartian contradiction separates what is given and what is considered real.

Methodology teaches us how to discover a rigid procedure which will enable us to pass from the given to the real, as from a principle to its consequence. Generally speaking, this procedure involves substituting a collection or set of terms, each of them a simple being concerned with self-preservation, for the multiple unity (or unitary multiplicity) represented by the contradictory data of experience. It is the coexistence of simple beings that gives the appearance of a multiple unity. Hence, for the contradictory concept of properties inherent in a substance, Herbart substitutes the concept of accidental relation between one simple being and other simple beings, which coexist with it—but not by necessity—and make all so-called properties mere accidents. In this way he also explains the self, together with the multiplicity of its representations. If these representations were inherent in the self and defined by characteristic bounds, as Fichte said, the self would be a multiple unity; in reality, a subject is a simple being, and the series of acts by which it posits objects is a series of acts of self-preservation in the face of attempts by other beings to destroy it; consequently they are traceable to accidental relations with other beings.

This procedure constitutes the "method of relations," which Herbart sets against the spirit of the reigning philosophy of his time. If numbers, changes, and the development of new properties are known to be grounded on relations, ideas or numbers will not be mistaken for absolutes and principles of things. This was the mistake made by all those who, after Plato, imagined an intelligible or possible world and who defined existence as a complement of possibility. On the last point Kant, in Herbart's opinion, was the first to have seen the light, for Kant stated that existence could never be deduced from essence and could only be an absolute positing.

The method of relations gives rise to a representation of the universe as a collection of absolutely simple beings exhibiting neither diversity nor a principle of diversity. These beings are linked by no transitive causality, for each of them continues to be what it is; they have no immanent causality, for the act by which a being preserves itself is provoked by another being; a being has no tendencies, for the quality of a simple being implies neither need nor privation; finally, since each being has a determinate quality, causality is reduced to a union of opposing qualities, which seek to destroy each other and give rise to acts of self-preservation.

It follows that continuity does not belong to the real world of simple beings but to the imaginary forms of space and time. Space and time are not given facts, and Kant's great mistake (the one on which his idealism is based) was in assuming that continua are a law of the objects of experience. "Synechology" explains how the idea of continuous space can arise even though "intelligible space" consists of the places occupied by simple beings in juxtaposition.

Psychology is merely an application of the metaphysics of Herbart. He firmly rejects traditional theories of faculties or multiple immanent causes in a simple being, and he accepts only representations, which have the same role in psychology as the "fibers" with which the physiologist fashions bodies. When they are identical by nature, these representations resist each other and tend to destroy each other (for example, sweetness and bitterness, red and blue); if one of them is disturbed by a more powerful opponent, it gradually grows dim and becomes less and less conscious, until finally it is completely repressed and transformed into a simple tendency; it continues to exist and cannot be annihilated, but it is then below the threshold of consciousness. Thus Herbartian psychology is an investigation of the mathematical laws governing the dynamic conflict of presentations. He shows how this conflict results in the fusion (*Verschmelzung*) and reproduction of homogeneous ideas or presentations (*Vorstellungen*). Affective phenomena do not constitute a distinct species but are born of this interaction between presentations; for instance, grief occurs when an idea or presentation (that of a lost friend) is simultaneously evoked (by the idea of the places where we met) and repressed (by the idea of his death).

All in all, then, Herbart supported a precritical realism based on the view that reality itself is not given to us immediately, and that we know only certain general characteristics of it through the intermediary of phenomena. "We live in the midst of relations and actually require nothing else."

The Herbartian school had many adherents in the second half of the century, after the decline of the great metaphysical systems—for example, Bonitz (1841–88), the historian of philosophy; Drobisch

(1802-96), the psychologist; and Hartenstein (1808-98), publisher of Herbart, Lazarus, and Steinthal, who founded the *Zeitschrift für Völkerpsychologie* in 1859.

VI *Jakob Friedrich Fries*

Jakob Friedrich Fries (1773-1843) was professor at Heidelberg (1805), then at Jena (1816). The turn he gave to Kantianism (*The New or Anthropological Critique of Reason*, 1807) is quite similar to the direction taken in France by Cousin's eclecticism. To Kant, proving principles means showing that they make possible the objects of experience; to Fries, it means discovering them through introspective reflection. "Philosophical knowledge is hidden in common knowledge," he writes, "and philosophy has the task of extracting it; any philosophy is based on introspection." The three basic faculties—knowledge, feeling (*Gemüt*), and activity—have as their respective ends truth, beauty, and virtue. The understanding (*Verstand*) is not a specialized faculty but a certain degree of development of the three basic faculties—the degree at which rational knowledge is revealed to reflection.

Thus Fries rejected every constructive philosophy of his period. He did not go beyond Newtonian mechanics, and he refused even to accept the ideas on organic finality presented in the *Critique of Judgment*. In politics he was a liberal, and the Prussian government suspended him from his professorship at Jena in 1819. He went so far as to write that "our right is a right grounded on the brute strength of the rich." His philosophy of history denies that there is any end or finality associated with the development of humanity and insists that the victory goes to the strong and the adept.

The ideas of those who have supported Fries through the years and until the most recent period are presented in the *Abhandlungen der Fries'schen Schule*. After E. F. Apelt (1815-51) Hans Cornelius based philosophy on psychology (*Introduction to Philosophy*, 1903); and L. Nelson (*The Impossibility of the Theory of Cognition, Abhandlungen*, III) developed the idea, suggested by Fries, that knowledge is not a problem but a fact which can be known only through inner observation.

The post-Kantian metaphysicians found many other opponents in Germany. Bernhard Bolzano (1781–1848), known primarily as a mathematician and logician, set out to make a clear distinction between logical reality and any psychological process. He considered truths, presentations, and propositions to be realities existing in themselves, independently of the mind that contemplates them (*Theory of Science,* 4 vols., 1837).

Philosophers like Friedrich Eduard Beneke (1798–1854) were in contact with English philosophical thought, notably the ideas of Schaftesbury and Thomas Brown.

VII *Arthur Schopenhauer*

Schopenhauer (1788–1860), whose parents belonged to the liberal bourgeoisie, was born at Danzig in 1788. After completing his doctoral thesis (*The Quadruple Root of the Principle of Sufficient Reason,* 1813; 2d edition, 1847), following Goethe, he took up the study of colors (*On Vision and Colors,* 1815). In 1818 he published *The World as Will and Idea,* which was no more successful than his career as a lecturer at Berlin in 1820. From this time on he led the independent life of a comfortable bachelor, more or less idle until 1833. From 1833 to 1860, the year of his death, he lived in Frankfurt, where he wrote his principal treatises: *On the Will in Nature* (1836); *On the Freedom of the Human Will* (1839) and *On the Basis of Morality,* both published as *The Two Fundamental Problems of Ethics* (1841); and *Essays from the Parerga and Paralipomena* (1851).

The great systems fashioned at the beginning of the nineteenth century were doomed to collapse soon, for they emerged in the midst of many hostile forces concerned with the maintenance of the eighteenth-century traditions. The cold, realistic, analytical vision of man and nature contrasted sharply with the turgidity of the Romanticists, and those embodying that vision did not achieve immediate success. Stendhal wrote knowingly for the reader of 1880. Schopenhauer also wrote: "My ideas are certain to seem like mere verbiage to my contemporaries, but I am comforted by the fact that I am not a man of my time. . . . If this century does not understand me, many others will; *tempo è galant-uomo!*" [4] His Voltairian spirit causes him disdainfully to reject the Christian philosophy or philosophy of religion, which he calls a monster or a "centaur" (*Works,* IV, 169) and which then dominated the intellectual climate. His desire to translate formulas immediately into intuitions intelligible to everyone, makes him dislike great systems which aspire to the exact opposite: to translate immediate data— the natural, moral, or social reality—into a speculative language, replete with embellishments and obscurities. In the very first lines of the first edition of *On the Will in Nature,* Schopenhauer indicates the contrast: "A *system of thoughts* must always have an architectonic structure, which allows one part to support another, but not inversely; the foundation supports the rest without being sustained by it, and the summit is sustained without sustaining anything. By contrast, a *single thought,* no matter how vast, should preserve the most perfect unity; if it can be divided into parts for the purpose of communication, the link between these parts must be organic— that is, each part must sustain the whole insofar as it is sustained in return, no part can be first or last, the whole must be made more distinct by each part, and the smallest part can be understood fully only if the whole is understood first." Later, after he had lost all hope of being accepted in the intellectual circles of his time, Schopenhauer adopted the harsh, derisive style which he used against "academic philosophers." Here, however, we find everything that sets him against his contemporaries: the systematic philosopher is a man with a somewhat puerile talent for making us wait endlessly for the end by putting it off again and again, like the novelist of the same period who keeps introducing new episodes and leaving something unfinished, to whet the reader's appetite; the man "with a unique thought" is one who is brought back to his idea, as to a

[4] *Sämmtliche Werke,* ed. Grisebach, III, 284.

focal point, by any observation or reflection whatsoever. Nothing exhibits more variety, more dissimilarity, more incongruity than Schopenhauer's themes: art, fashion, women, gambling, second sight, telepathy, music; everything serves his purpose, for he is sure that he can discover "the unique thought" by probing each of these subjects. Methodical reasoning is scanty in his writings; in fact, no matter where we begin, we have the impression that we are being led almost immediately to the center of his doctrine. To him everything—the most trivial fact as well as the most abstract idea—is suggestion and revelation.

What is this unique idea? Schopenhauer's doctrine is like a vast magical evocation. Magic dominates the spirits of the earth, rendering them innocuous as it calls them forth; until called, they are obscure and injurious to the degree that they are hidden from sight. Similarly philosophy, the essence of the world or the x which sustains the world, "is revealed as will—like Mephistopheles [see Goethe's *Faust,* scene iii], who, by skillful attacks, is called forth from the dog, colossally enlarged, of which he was the essence." Once it has been revealed, this will, until then the cause of ever recurrent suffering, becomes innocuous.

Schopenhauerian philosophy is the totality of these "learned attacks." The first attack is Kantian idealism. It proves that the world known to us is merely our representation and has no reality in itself. It is only a "dream of our brain"—a richly textured dream, to be sure, but one that has no more substantial reality than dreams associated with sleep. The rich texture that distinguishes wakefulness from sleep derives from the nature of our intellect, which connects sensible impressions according to the law of causality, concepts according to the logical laws of the understanding, elements of intuitive knowledge according to the order of space and time, and voluntary acts according to the laws of motivation. Such is the "fourfold root of the principle of sufficient reason," which assigns a reason to each of the four distinct orders of representations: sensible becoming, judgment, being as the object of intuition, and will. So-called matter is only pure causality—the law of the understanding, which compels us to connect our representations. Thus Schopenhauer's phenomenalism is in a sense more radical than Kant's, for it no longer distinguishes sensibility from understanding or the given from the construct, and it considers categories not as concepts of object in general but as the inner structure of the understanding.

The second attack is also Kantian idealism. It does not allow us to be the dupe of this world, but it causes us to wonder "whether this world is nothing but representation—in which case it should pass before us as a dream without substance or an empty, ethereal vision—or whether it is not something else still." Our "metaphysical need" for a reality and the bewilderment resulting from our confrontation with existence urge us to see the world as an enigma to be deciphered. Inner experience begins to enlighten us, making us know ourselves as individuals with tendencies, needs, aspirations, or, in a broad sense, individual will; furthermore, it convinces us that the will is so closely linked to the body that any tendency or desire is translated immediately into a bodily movement. Thus a body, which was simply one object among other objects, now becomes the expression of a will, even more so than my will itself. The body is the will known from the outside, as representation. "The will is a priori knowledge of the body, and the body is a posteriori knowledge of the will; . . . my body is the *objectivity* of my will," this singular experience is "the supreme philosophical truth" (I, 153–54).

Will must simply be generalized and extended. Each human being has his own will, accompanied in general by motives. It is illuminated by the intellect, but in itself it is pure and simple tendency, completely blind and irrational. The essence is what Kant called our intelligible character—the basal, permanent, inexplicable part of us, of which the intellect serves as the instrument. Motives clearly define the particular circumstances of time and place associated with the active employment of a rational being's will, but "do not begin to explain the fact that this being wills in general, and wills in precisely this way" (I, 228). Consequently it is possible that each body is the objectification of a will wholly similar to our own, and Schopenhauer strives to transform this possibility into a reality.

His book *On the Will in Nature* brings together all the experiences which show that the will is the primary source of activity in organic and inorganic nature, and that it is identical with the body, which is simply its outer shell. "Each entity is its own creation." Centrifugal force, gravity, elasticity, vegetative force, animal instinct, all are tendencies whose affirmation, seen across the intellect, constitutes the bodies of nature. They are completely inexplicable, occult qualities; the fall of a stone is no more comprehensible than the movement of an animal (I, 181).

Representation causes us to see a great diversity of objects, but this plurality is its exclusive property, since space is its necessary condition. Space is the true principle of individuation sought by the Scholastics. How could there be plurality in will, "since the relation between the part and the whole belongs only to space and ceases to have meaning as soon as one abandons the form of intuition"? It follows that there is but one will, not a small will in a stone and a large will in man.

The individual objects that are represented are many, and they are arranged in a graduated series of types, from stones through plants and animals to men. These types are eternal, like Platonic ideas, and they remain fixed and permanent in the midst of the diversity of the individual objects which represent them (Schopenhauer is in no way a transformist, and he explicitly criticizes Lamarck). But these ideas also belong to the world of representation, which is the visible, objective world. Each type or force of nature is a certain degree of objectification of will and not, as Plato thought, the thing in itself. The thing in itself is one single will, blind, free, irrational, and not subjected to any of the forms of the principle of sufficient reason.

The essence of things has been evoked: an illusory perception produced by an absurd will. At the same time the root of the evil inherent in existence has been exposed: the will to live—absurd, irrational, infinite—which forever engenders new needs, and with them new sorrows. The whole range of human experience is illuminated, enabling us to understand at once hope and its vanity, striving and its necessary failure. Sexual love with its fury, its jealousy, its power, which ignores all rationality, and its tragic earnestness, is forever producing new beings for new pains. There is no end to the misdeeds of the "genius of the species" or of the skillful go-between (*Parerga,* chap. xliv). Hence Schopenhauer's famous diatribes against women, whose vaunted beauty is the bait dangled in front of us by the genius of the species. Has man finally satisfied his desires? If so, boredom ensues, the evil which he dreads as much as pain and which can lead him to despair. That is why he does his utmost to avoid it. "It is boredom that causes beings as little attracted by mutual love as men nevertheless to seek each other out, and this is the source of sociability." They must have *panem et circenses,* and the remedy for boredom is just as important as the remedy for famine. Humanity can have no hope of progress, for the same evils—sickness, crime, war—are forever recurring, *eadem sed aliter.* Only the Philistine believes that everything can be achieved within the framework of "a comfortable state, a good police force, and well equipped industries" (II, 519). The existence of pleasure cannot be used as an argument against pessimism, for sorrow, which springs from the will to live, is the only positive reality, and pleasure is felt only in the fleeting moment when sorrow ceases.

There is a remarkable contrast between the first two parts of Schopenhauer's work (what we have called his first two attacks— Kantian idealism and the discovery of Will as the thing in itself) and the last two parts, which concern art and the morality of pity. The first two deal with technical philosophy, and the last two concern the means discovered by humanity, apart from any philosophical speculation, to put an end to its anguish. The first means is art, which, by pure contemplation, frees us from the anguish associated with action; the second is morality based on pity, which culminates in negation of the will to live and, consequently, abolition of suffering. Art and morality are direct revelations of the essence of things—true gnostic insights which calm the will, independently and directly, without forcing the subject to pass through the circuit of philosophy. Here the philosopher has only to reflect on the experiences of the artist and acts of moral value. In the genius and the ascetic he will find direct knowledge of the essence of the world, but at the same time he will find (and this is not given in the simple philosophical knowledge of the second part) freedom from the injurious action of the will. The third and fourth "attacks" unveil the will and at the same time render it harmless. The vast influence of these two last parts made Schopenhauer, in the words of Nietzsche, the educator of the following generation.

Concerning art, Schopenhauer has a clear-cut theory, which is connected with the theory of archetypal ideas or degrees of objectification of will. Each of the arts has the mission of revealing one of these degrees or ideas to us, and the arts, like Ideas themselves, constitute a hierarchy. At the bottom is architecture, which facilitates clear intuition of the lower degrees: gravity, cohesion, resistance. To accomplish its mission it employs diverse means to check the downward impulsion of the mass: the entablature thrusts its weight on the ground by means of columns, the vault by means of pillars and flying buttresses; the conflict between weight and resistance manifests the force inherent in matter. At the top of the hierarchy are the plastic arts. Sculpture manifests the dynamic structure of the human form. Will triumphs over the obstacles posed by these lower manifestations, which are the forces of nature, as it becomes objectified in the individual. The body is an arrangement of parts, each of which should be developed precisely in the direction of this goal; in nature, however, the necessary conditions are realized in varying degrees of perfection. The artist does not imitate nature but creates a work of art in accordance with his intuition of the Idea. Whereas sculpture reveals man in general, painting represents character, that is, diverse aspects of humanity in different circumstances. It deals with particular events, expressions, and gestures, sometimes in the most meticulous way, as in the case of the Dutch painters. The aim of historical painting is not to represent the true course of past events but to extract from these events whatever reveals a particular aspect of humanity. The sculptor and the painter elucidate Ideas by intuitions; the poet suggests them by means of concepts designated by words, combining them in such a way as to achieve intuitive representations through them. Each poetic genre expresses different aspects of humanity: lyric poetry brings out human suffering, the will thwarted by obstacles, and, in contrast, the impassiveness of nature; tragic poetry, in its highest form, shows the drama arising from conflicts between characters, by a kind of logical necessity, when even the most trivial incidents occur. Finally music—an art which is independent of any spatial image or abstract thought, and whose form, like that of our inner life, is time— expresses the most abstract quality of sentiment itself. It expresses, not a particular joy or sorrow, but joy in itself or sorrow in itself, without the motives which produce joy or sorrow. By virtue of its affinity with our innermost being, it is no longer the image of a phenomenon but of will itself. "The world is incarnate music just as surely as it is incarnate will."

Genius is a development of the faculty associated with intuitive knowledge of Ideas. Through his work the artist communicates his intuitive knowledge to the spectator, whose state of pure contemplation causes him to forget his individuality and frees him from suffering. He is no longer an individual but "the sole eye of the world"; the objects represented by art no longer relate to will but to pure knowledge.

Art is only a fleeting sedative for will. The decisive "attack"—the one that will set us free—is knowledge of the absolute identity of all beings, and it is expressed in moral life. The single will is fragmented in the form of individuals, each with the absolute, unconditioned will to preserve its own existence. Selfishness is wedded to its very essence, for the will to be recognizes no limit or restriction. Everything that opposes it arouses anger, hatred, and malice, which would easily lead to crime and homicide if it were not held in check by fear, another form of selfishness. In our struggle against egotism we cannot count on so-called moral instincts, which consist mainly of fears, prejudices, or vanity. Morality based on the categorical imperative, in turn, is only a Prussian-type discipline without logical justification; it cannot dispense with a God who commands and wishes to be obeyed. Morality, like all the rest of philosophy, is not supposed to command but to make reality intelligible.

The egotism of each individual seeks to protect itself from the egotism of others, giving rise to the morality of justice, which uses the threat of punishment to prevent crime. The state, according to Schopenhauer, has the sole mission of limiting injustice; the state, therefore, springs from egotism and has nothing to do with the mission of education.

The morality of justice keeps intact the illusion on which egotism is based: the illusion of the plurality of beings. The illusion is destroyed by knowledge of the identity of individuals, which makes egotism something absurd and abominable, for it is the will devouring itself. This knowledge is accompanied by pity, which found its most complete expression in the Gospel and Christian holiness; still, Christianity does not go far enough, since it preaches the salvation of each person as an individual and leaves to God the task of saving the world. Hindu asceticism is different: in complete abnegation, manifested particularly in chastity and mortifications, the knowledge of the identity of individuals becomes the sovereign remedy. The will to live is stripped of its power and submerged in the state of Nirvana, which is the negation of the will to live and which, in its positive aspect, can have no meaning for us. Schopenhauer looks only to individual initiatives for the salvation of the world. One could almost say that the ascetic is the individual raised to his highest possible state, "the one who, by suppressing will, goes so far, in effect, as to suppress completely the character of his species." Against the Western notion of humanity as a whole dispersed in the form of multiple activities, he sets the Hindu notion of self-renunciation and withdrawal, which is the extinction of the individual's humanity.

VIII Christoffer Jakob Boström

The idealism of Christoffer Jakob Boström (1797–1866) might be presented in terms of the pains taken by the Swedish philosopher to escape from the naturalistic Romanticism of the post-Kantians. "All modern idealists, including Schelling and Hegel," he writes, "are only relative idealists. Schelling and Hegel tried to restore to so-called nature the substantiality that Kant and Fichte had removed. Their aim was right and proper, but their method was wrong. They assumed that nature, as we conceive it, and intelligence, which is its opposite, together exhausted reality. . . . But if we assume that nature as such exists only in us and for us, and that other finite, rational beings must also exist, we must imagine many similar natures. And the foundation of all these natures can only be God and his eternal ideas, of which they are phenomena" (from the German translation of Boström in *Philosophische Bibliothek,* I, Leipzig, 1923). On the whole, Boström is deeply indebted to Leibniz and Berkeley for his concept of the world as a hierarchy of persons, with God—the being endowed with absolute reality and perfection—at their head, and gradations among them ranging from a lower to a higher life and finally to life eternal.

Bibliography

I

Goethe, Johann Wolfgang von. A standard edition is *Jubiläums-Ausgabe,* ed. K. Burdach and others, 40 vols., Stuttgart and Berlin, 1902–07. Goethe's most important works, except *Zur Farbenlehre* and *Beiträge zur Optik,* have been translated into English.

II

Krause, K.-Chr. F. *Das Urbild der Menschheit.* Dresden, 1812.

———. *System der Sittenlehre.* Leipzig, 1810.

———. *Vorlesungen uber das System der Philosophie.* Göttingen, 1828.

———. *Abriss des Systems der Rechtsphilosophie.* Göttingen, 1828.

III

Texts

Schleiermacher, F. E. D. *Aus Schleiermachers Leben in Briefen,* 4 vols. Berlin, 1860–63.

———. *Sämtliche Werke.* Berlin, 1835–64.

———. *Schleiermachers Briefwechsel mit J. Chr. Gass.* Berlin, 1852.

Studies

Barth, Karl. *From Rousseau to Ritschl.* London, 1959.

Brandt, Richard. *The Philosophy of Friedrich Schleiermacher.* New York, 1941.

Dilthey, Wilhelm. *Leben Schleiermachers.* Berlin, 1870; 2d ed., ed. H. Mulert, Berlin, 1922. (Should be supplemented by Dilthey's articles in his *Gesammelte Schriften,* 2d ed., Stuttgart, 1959–60, vols. 4 and 12.

Niebuhr, Richard R. *Schleiermacher on Christ and Religion.* New York, 1964.

Süskind, Hermann. *Der Einfluss Schellings auf die Entwicklung von Schleiermachers System.* Tübingen, 1909.

Wehrung, Georg. *Die Dialektik Schleiermachers.* Tübingen, 1920.

IV

Humboldt, W. von. *Gesammelte Werke,* ed. Karl Brandes, 7 vols. Berlin, 1841–52.
———. *Gesammelte Schriften,* ed. Royal Prussian Academy, 17 vols. Berlin, 1903–36.
———. *Werke,* ed. A. Flitner and K. Giel. Darmstadt, 1960———. (Four of the projected five volumes are completed.)
———. *Humanist Without Portfolio: An Anthology,* ed. and trans. Marianne Cowan. Detroit, Mich., 1963.

V

Herbart, J. F. *Sämtliche Werke,* ed. Hartenstein, 12 vols. Leipzig, 1850–52.
———. *Sämtliche Werke,* 19 vols., ed. Kehrbach. Langensalza, 1887–1912.

VI

Elsenhans, T. *Fries und Kant,* 2 vols. Giessen, 1906.
Hasselblatt, M. *Fries: seine Philosophie und seine Persönlichkeit.* Munich, 1922.

VII

Text

Schopenhauer, A. *Sämtliche Werke,* ed. A. Hübscher, 2d ed., 7 vols. Wiesbaden, 1946–50. (The most recent edition of Schopenhauer's collected works in German.)

Studies

Copleston, F. C. *Schopenhauer, Philosopher of Pessimism.* London, 1946.
Gardiner, Patrick. *Schopenhauer.* Harmondsworth, England, 1963.
Taylor, Richard. Discussion in *A Critical History of Western Philosophy,* ed. D. J. O'Connor. New York, 1964.

RELIGIOUS PHILOSOPHY
BETWEEN 1815 AND 1850

1 *Pierre Simon Ballanche*

Between 1815 and 1830 (and, to a lesser degree, until 1850) social propheticism existed as a philosophical movement, linked more or less clearly to the illuminism of the preceding century and to the revival of religion. The tone was set by Pierre Simon Ballanche (1776–1847). "I wish to express the great idea of my century," he writes. "This leading idea, profoundly sympathetic and religious, has received from God himself the august mission of organizing the new social world, and I wish to search for it in every sphere of the human faculties, in every order of sentiments and ideas. This secret idea becomes assimilative, draws its substance from everything that has been, is, or will be, and tends by nature to become the first element of any civilization—that is, a belief."[1] Thus a thinker like Ballanche assumes the task of expressing a belief, which is an organizing force behind all spiritual and social life. The desire to believe, more than faith itself, is characteristic of his age. Ballanche notes that the desire is so deeply rooted that we try to satisfy it by asking society to impose it by force (*Dialogues, 1819*).

But Ballanche was an orthodox Catholic, even though he main-

[1] Written in 1827, *Œuvres complètes*, III, 6. With Chateaubriand, Ballanche frequented the Abbaye-au-Bois, the royalist salon of Mme Recamier. His principal works date from the Restoration (*Essai sur les Institutions sociales dans leurs rapports avec les idées nouvelles*, 1818; *Palingénésie sociale*, 1827).

243

tained ties with all the esoteric circles in France and Germany, and could not admit that belief derives from a social consensus and authority. "Society," he says, "cannot provide what you require of it." Still, to him as to De Bonald, society is the necessary intermediary between transcendent reality and the individual. Doubtless the end is religion, which seeks, before all else, the salvation of individuals, but society is a necessary means. "Outside society man has only potential being, so to speak; he is progressive and perfectible only by virtue of society" (*Palingenesis*). Thus society seems to him to possess a Messianic value; it "never retrogrades, remains essentially religious, more religious than individuals . . . and cannot fail to be religious."[2]

The fundamental belief that makes society live is faith in palingenesis. This faith affirms that imperishable, incorruptible being is contained in perishable and corruptible being. "Every creature must achieve the end to which it is suited and to which it has a right by virtue of its own essence" (*Works*, III, p. 11). Ballanche's religion is based on optimistic confidence, not in continuous progress, but in an unlimited possibility of renewal or regeneration. "Man fashioning himself through his social and individual activity" or "society fashioning itself" is the essence of religion—not the natural religion of the deist, who immobilizes everything in nature as well as in history, but traditional religion, of which Christianity is an expression. Its essential dogma is one that has persisted through the ages: the dogma of fallen man and his rehabilitation. This harsh dogma explains the whole course of human destiny as it is unfolded through successive initiations, each preceded by an ordeal which is like an expiation. It follows that history has a religious sense and is an "epic of thought," which describes the successive roles of the collective genius of nations in the progress of humanity. The genius of a nation—"a mysterious fact similar to a cosmogonical fact," which is manifested in its language and in the form of its government—has as its essence one of the forms of the fundamental dogma. "Each nation has a translation of the common traditions

[2] *Dialogues du vieillard et du jeune homme*, ed. Mauduit, p. 126.

of mankind." Like Eckstein and Creuzer, Ballanche devoted himself to the study of comparative mythology and symbolism, trying to discover vestiges of the dogma in Greek, Hindu, and Germanic myths.

Ballanche's doctrine of palingenesis was inspired by the theory of *corsi e ricorsi* formulated by Vico, whom he discovered in 1819. Both are in agreement on the idea of a perpetual regeneration or renewal, but one trait, common to every thinker of the period who drew his inspiration from Vico, sets them apart: Ballanche confers a religious sense on history, which Vico denies. Vico determines the natural laws of societies, exempting the development of Christianity, which is wholly supernatural; Ballanche makes no distinction between the natural and the supernatural, the historical and the religious.

According to Ballanche, society has a messianic value. What we observe in action, however, is not society as such but individuals, bodies, governments, and clergies, which serve to express the genius of the people. This genius nevertheless remains the judge and the measure of the fidelity of the expression. In "palingenetic ages" such as the age in which Ballanche believes that he is living—that is, in periods in which religious life begins anew—there is a struggle between faith, which is being regenerated and old expressions, which are becoming obsolete. "There is confusion about the religious center. Divine thought is no longer there where it is assumed to be, and it is not yet in the opposite center" (III, 108). Thus, according to Ballanche, the clergy remains behind in the performance of its task, and one should be at once religious and anticlerical. Any individual or corporative thought can draw its strength only from society, for "it becomes omnipotent, in a certain sense, only when it expresses a thought of the majority." The individual capable of assimilating the divine will or concentrating in himself the deep-seated feelings of a country is a hero, as in the case of Joan of Arc. The legislator is successful only if he can shape laws to fit the actual state of society. The multitude, which cannot create order, "has a remarkable instinct for adopting it" (*Dialogues,* p. 97). For this reason legitimate power is indeed based on the consent of the people, but not in the sense of a Roussellian contract, as if society resulted from the reunion of men at first separated or as if the people could exercise its sovereignty directly; the consent of the people is a moral unanimity, and it is identical with divine right. Here Ballanche discovers a criterion for the legitimacy of power which allows him to condemn Bonaparte, who, with his contempt for men, exemplifies human thought in contrast to divine thought.

II *Józef Maria Hoene-Wroński and Polish Messianism*

In the first half of the century long-suffering Poland witnessed the emergence of a current of religious thought in which the national ideal was wedded to a humanitarian Messianism announcing universal peace and the kingdom of the Spirit. The poet Mickiewicz, who lectured at the Collège de France from 1840 to 1844, believed that the Polish nation was the messiah of the people and the center around which peace should be organized. This fervent hope, which inspired some of Chopin's most beautiful musical compositions, is the particular form assumed in Poland by the religious enthusiasm then animating the world. It found expression particularly in the numerous works written in French by Hoene-Wroński (1778–1853), who sought refuge in France in 1803. It was Wroński who introduced the word Messianism, which he used in a letter written to Pope Leo XII in 1827 and in many of his books (*Introduction to Messianism*, 1831; *Messianic Metapolitics*, 1839; *Messianism or Absolute Reform of Human Knowledge*, 1847). This doctrine is replete with whimsical features, many of them common to the period; for instance, he expressed his ideas mathematically, believing that in this way he was confirming their scientific precision. He tried in vain to interest the great men of his time in his projects. In the medley of his thought we find one salient idea, which contains the essence of his doctrine. This central idea is that of spontaneity or creative potential—or, to use his expression, autocreation. Each being is eternal and has within itself the power to be its own creator; moreover, its spontaneity is in no way arbitrary, for Hoene-Wroński boasts of having found the mathematical formula for creation. His philosophy of history is simply an application of the formula. It announces a religion of the Absolute, in which the tendencies that heretofore, according to him, divided the world, will be conciliated: the tendency to pursue virtue, which gave birth to the theocracies of antiquity and the Middle Ages, and the tendency to seek truth, manifested in the Greco-Roman civilization and in Europe. This deep-seated antimony opposes Protestantism, which supports progress, to Catholicism, which supports order, and Christianity only prepares the way for the absolute religion, which will provide a scientific interpretation of such mysterious dogmas as the divinity of Jesus. Politically, Hoene-Wroński announces a federation of peoples, which was one of the basic ideas of Polish Messianism. In Towianski, Slowacki, and Mickiewicz we find the source of an idea popularized in France by one of Renan's famous articles—the distinction between a *people* or group with a common origin and a *nation* formed by the common will of men who differ by origin. The Polish nation, which then existed only by virtue of a common will, exemplified, through its woes, the transformation of a people into a nation. True nations alone can unite and give birth to humanity.

III *Soren Kierkegaard*

In Soren Kierkegaard (1813–55), religious speculation culminated in a kind of individualism and impressionism which proved to be as hostile to the Hegelian doctrine as Stirner's anarchism. The Danish philosopher is ill-disposed toward everything presented as objective, universal, impersonal, and therefore injurious to personal existence, which, because of his melancholic temperament, he places in the foreground of reality. Objectivity goes hand in hand with error, whereas truth resides in subjectivity. It might seem that subjectivity is typical of separation or isolation, but the systematic mind which unites and discovers mediations everywhere is superficial for the very reason that it disregards these profound, definitive separations. Life itself resists any attempt to enclose it in a system; it consists not in uniting but in choosing (see *Either/Or*, 1843) and it is characterized by decisive leaps rather than by gradual evolution. There are mutually exclusive types of life, in which no conciliation is possible: there is the aesthete, who enjoys the present, drifts along haphazardly, and ridicules any regular occupation; there is the moralizer, who chooses his life with all the obligations imposed on him by society and the family; finally, there is the religious man. Kierkegaard's religious feelings spring from his awareness of the insuperable gap which separates nature and spirit, time and eternity. Like the fideists in France, he rejects any attempt to rationalize faith, which involves paradoxes and absurdities such as that of a God who became man (*Stages on Life's Way*, 1845). All in all, we find in him a kind of negative philosophy, which, as in Plotinus, sets the soul opposite God in an absolute solitude. His last years were marked by a series of controversies with the official church (*The Moment*, 1855).

Recently, in Germany, there has been a revival of Kierkegaard's influence, particularly in the work of the theologian Karl Barth (see, for example, *The Word of God and the Word of Man*, 1924). For Barth, rough human attempts to worship God can be contrasted with the Church as pure spirituality and divine activity. The writings of Heidegger also reflect Kierkegaard's influence.

IV *Ralph Waldo Emerson*

By virtue of his influence and a great part of his life, Ralph Waldo Emerson (1803–82) belongs to the second half of the nineteenth century, but his ideas were largely shaped between 1832 and 1840. Born in Boston, he graduated from Harvard. Though destined, at first, to the pulpit, he brought his ministry to an end in 1832 and sought solitude in Concord; there, following a trip to Europe, where he met Carlyle, he resided until his death. His abhorrence of systems equals Kierkegaard's. "I need hardly say to anyone acquainted with my thoughts that I have no System, . . . " he writes. "No diligence can rebuild the universe in a model by the best accumulation of disposition of details." A system is useless because (and this is the essence of Neo-Platonism) the world "reproduces itself in miniature in every event that transpires, so that all the laws of nature may be read in the smallest fact. So that the truth-speaker may dismiss all solicitude as to the proportion and congruency of the aggregate of his thoughts, so long as he is a faithful reporter of particular impressions" (*Journal,* November 14, 1839). The natural form of his speculative thought is the essay, which enables him to see the revelation of an absolute law in commonplace facts. Everywhere in nature we see the individual and the universal bound together. Man should choose nature as his model and "strive to imitate, if he can, the silence of these lofty beings [trees], beautiful in their growth, their strength, and their decline." In 1836 he stated the principles of his transcendentalism thus: "There is a relation between man and nature, so that whatever is in matter is in mind. Underneath all appearances, and causing all appearances, are certain eternal laws which we call the Nature of Things" (*Journal,* October 15). It follows that we must try to discover our code of ethics within ourselves. "Whoso would be a man, must be a nonconformist. . . . What have I to do with the sacredness of traditions, if I live wholly from within? . . . No law can be sacred to me but that of my nature. Good and bad are but names very readily transferable to that or this; the only right is what is after my constitution, the only wrong what is against it" (*Self-Reliance,* 1841). Emerson's individualism is not Stirner's anarchism, for to him each individual is at the same time the universe, and great men (*Representative Men,* 1850)—Plato, Montaigne, Swedenborg, Goethe, Napoleon—are those who best incarnate this universe. Emerson represents in America a theory of genius derived from German Romanticism through Carlyle or directly through the reading of Schelling.

The word "Transcendentalism" embraces all these currents of philosophical speculation. It suggests that any experience, no matter how trifling, can lead us to a transcendent power, which will reveal the universe to us. Hence a type of fatalism reminding us at times of Stoicism, for since everything is contained in everything, our destiny is realized at each moment, and events are unimportant. Transcendentalism is a matter of faith and not of demonstration. Emerson may be compared with many of his contemporaries— the fideists, Kierkegaard, Newman—and has a place in the philosophical movement, continuing today, which is concerned with belief. By his temperament more than by his ideas, he exerted an influence on William James, the son of his friend Henry James.

v Fideism and Christian Rationalism in France

During the July monarchy and at the beginning of the Second Empire, under the persistent influence of De Bonald and Lamennais, there was a revival of the ancient discussion on the powers of reason. At the very core of Christianity there has always been a tendency for Christian rationalism (St. Anselm, St. Thomas) to reject authority as the sole source of knowledge of the supersensible. In recent years Rome has on several occasions condemned what it calls fideism, which consists in maintaining that faith, and not reason, is the criterion of certainty, that reason is incapable of establishing the existence of God, and that the authority of Scripture does not need to be proved rationally.

This spirit is seen clearly in Philippe Buchez (1796–1865), who received a Catholic education and at first espoused Saint-Simonianism. He abandoned Saint-Simonianism in 1831 to edit the Catholic Journal L'Européen until 1832 and from 1835 to 1838. His thought offers a rather whimsical mixture of Saint-Simonianism and the traditionalism of De Bonald and Lamennais. His *Introduction to the Science of History* (1833) is a kind of Christian philosophy of history, based on two great concepts assumed to be of Christian origin: the concept of the unity of humanity, expressed by St. Augustine in the *City of God;* and the concept of progress, which is found in Vincent of Lérins. To Buchez, progress is a kind of necessity, for an agent can act only by modifying a patient, and these modifications are certain to be cumulative; the system, the social world, nature are the patients which are transformed by human activity; according to him, social progress culminates in an authoritarian, centralizing type of Christianity, in which spiritual power belongs to the priest. In his *Complete Treatise on Philosophy* (1840) he tried above all to write a doctrinal catechism which would fulfil social needs and counteract eclectic philosophy. According to him, Christian philosophy has been misdirected since, beginning with St. Augustine, it introduced the dialectic and logic into Christian instruction. The *biblici,* who restrict themselves to explaining Scripture, prevail over the sententiaries and authors of *Summae.* In this spirit, Buchez recognizes no other criterion of certainty but morality, even in theoretical matters, and no moral authority but society, whose salvation is the supreme law.

But fideism often appears in Louis Bautain (1796–1867), who, first a disciple of Cousin and a professor at the University of Strasbourg, underwent a remarkable conversion and was ordained a priest in 1828. In the system of instruction then prevailing in the seminaries, Bautain found the very defects that Renan was later to discover: a mixture of Scholastic rationalism, Cartesianism, and philosophy of common sense, which could not fail to arouse doubt by subordinating the authority of the Church to general rationality, and he wrote his *Teaching of Philosophy in France in the Nineteenth Century* (1833) for the purpose of bringing about a reform. His overall doctrine, expounded in *The Philosophy of Christianity* (1833), issues from reflection on Kantian criticism. It seems to him that the "Analytic" struck a blow against the Scottish school by demonstrating the subjective, and consequently the uncertain character of first principles, and that the "Dialectic" utterly destroyed rationalistic metaphysics. Reason to him is only logic or the faculty of inference, and it cannot seize a single principle. He superimposes on this reason "pure intelligence," which comes into play only under the influence of the revealed world: the old doctrine of the Logos, restated by one of De Bonald's supporters. Bautain was condemned by Rome, and he yielded; but he continued always to advocate a philosophy which would serve religion and to insist that Catholicism should be the religion of the state.

The same fideism was the heart of the doctrine of Bonnetty, who founded the *Annales de philosophie chrétienne* in 1830. As Ferraz says,[3] "the Scholastic philosophers who were subjected to so much ridicule in the seventeenth and eighteenth centuries, and who were thought for so long to personify the spirit of immobility and routine, had come to be feared as freethinkers." Rationalism goes hand in hand with paganism, and Bonnetty's doctrine was also condemned by Rome in 1853. Still another doctrine, that of Ubaghs, was condemned in 1866. The Louvain professor maintained that God's existence could not be demonstrated, and he denied the spontaneity of reason, which could be put to use only by outside direction and authority.

The question of fideism was gradually reduced to a question of internal ecclesiastical discipline. But around 1840 there was a resurgence of Christian rationalism, which abandoned traditionalistic tendencies and resisted with all its might the official rationalism of the University of Paris. The leading participants were Abbé Maret (1804–88) and Father Gratry (1805–72). Maret's *Essay on Pantheism* (1840) develops a thesis stated by Bautain and traceable to Jacobi: pantheism is the great heresy of our time, and it is the necessary fruit of a form of rationalism that neglects Christian instruction. Maret claims that Schelling and Hegel, like Saint-Simon and even Cousin with his theory of impersonal reason and the necessity of creation are pantheists. His *Christian Theodicy* (1844) assumes that reason can apprehend the existence of an infinite, creative God, but only if it is shaped in a Christian environment; if reason reached the perfect being by itself, it would still be wrong for us to say that its natural product is pantheism, since this doctrine contradicts God's perfection by identifying him with the world. Maret's last work (*Philosophy and Religion,* 1856) tends

[3] M. Ferraz, *Histoire de la philosophie en France au XIX*[e] *siècle: traditionalisme et ultramontanisme* (Paris, 1880), p. 347.

toward an "ontologism," which makes the ideas of infinity and perfection proof of a divine element within us.

Father Gratry—an Oratorian who studied at the École Polytechnique, met Bautain at Strasbourg around 1828, and became chaplain at the École Normale in 1840—differs radically from Maret on one point: he believes that pantheism is contrary to reason. In his view, by jeopardizing reason the Reformation and the traditionalism of Lamennais struck a telling blow against faith, even as they were trying to serve it, and increased indifference to higher intellectual preoccupations. To him Hegelianism, with its identity of contradictories, is not a rational doctrine but truly a sickness of reason, for it denies the principle of contradiction.

Father Gratry rediscovered the rationalistic, mystical—one might say Platonic—tradition of his order. According to him, two processes are essential to the human mind: deduction, which goes from like to like; and dialectic, which goes from unlike to unlike or from the finite to the infinite, and which is possible only through love and a kind of summons from the transcendent being toward which it moves. But Plato's dialectic differs from Hegel's. The true dialectic begins with the limited perfections of man and attributes them to God, who is without limitations. Hegel's point of departure is essentially the famous Spinozist axiom, "Any determination is a negation." In abolishing limits, he abolishes qualities as well, with the result that he reaches only an indeterminate being, identical with nonbeing. The true dialectic was used by Plato, Aristotle, St. Thomas, Descartes, and even Pascal to demonstrate the existence of God. Gratry claims to show the excellence and universality of this procedure by comparing it, curiously, not only with poetry and prayer as in the *Symposium,* but also with scientific procedures of induction and the integration of integral calculus. His undertaking is analogous to Malebranche's attempt to show the Christian character of reason.

Gratry was vehement in his criticism of those he considers to be disciples of Hegel, Vacherot, Renan, and Scherer (*Study of Contemporary Sophistry; The Sophists and Criticism*). His violent criticism reaches its peak in the *Letter to M. Vacherot* (1851), written after Vacherot had published his *Critical History of the School of Alexandria*. This letter, which led to the dismissal of Vacherot, who was then professor at the École Normale, went so far as to censure the secret infiltration of pantheism and fatalism as well as the cultivation of the monstrous, the false, and the unintelligible in nature and the arts. Gratry prefers the sophists of the eighteenth century to those of the nineteenth: the former attacked faith in the name of reason; the latter attack reason itself. He appeals to the Voltairians among them who still believe in God.

From the very beginning of the July Monarchy, Bordas-Demoulin (1798-1859) insisted on freeing the Christian doctrine from the traditionalism and irrationalism of De Bonald and Lamennais. His *Philosophical and Religious Miscellany* (1846), as well as *Constitutive Powers of the Church* (1853) and *Essays on Catholic Reform* (1856), are the antithesis of Proudhon's book on *Justice in the Revolution and the Church*. He was convinced that the era of political liberties inaugurated by the revolution was a phase in the history of Christianity, and he sought in practice to free Catholicism from the influence of reactionary parties. Preaching the "conversion of the clergy to the Gospel," he expressed his disapproval of the Scholastic and medieval tradition, the infallibility of the pope, and overextension of the powers of the priesthood, which should be limited to teaching the Gospel and has no right to offer general instruction. He could hardly be understood at a time when friends and enemies agreed that the Church was essentially hostile to the revolution.

Bordas' reformist ideas were based on a philosophy opposed to the official doctrine of eclecticism. His doctrine draws from the philosophy of Descartes, particularly the theory of ideas: an idea is absolutely distinct, by its fixity and necessity, from an image; and even though it is a mode of thought—which makes man its master—it is at the same time, like a divine idea, the representation of a fixed essence; consequently, man is joined by reflection to divine thought. This theory, which is also that of Plato, Plotinus, and

St. Augustine, is opposed to three other theories, all equally false. Bordas designates them according to their origin: that of Epicurus, who identified ideas with sensation; that of Aristotle, who saw ideas as simple products of the workings of mind; and that of Zeno of Citium, who shattered the personality by fusing man and God in action and knowledge. The tendency of these distinctions is obvious: to preserve the role and independence of individual activity without falling into skeptical relativism. "Individuality is the crux of modern society and the source of all true progress, for it stimulates and develops all our powers. To shatter individuality would be to drive ourselves back to society as it existed prior to Christianity." [4] In the same spirit his theory of infinity, presented at the end of *Cartesianism* (1843), attempts to identify infinities of different orders in the universe and thereby to insure, along with creation, a kind of autonomy of the created mind, which is infinite in its own way and lacks none of the ideas found in God.

[4] *Œuvres posthumes* (1861), I, p. 153.

Bibliography

I

Texts

Ballanche, Pierre Simon. *Œuvres complètes,* 6 vols. Paris, 1932.
———. *Le vieillard et le jeune homme,* ed. R. Mauduit. Paris, 1928.

Study

Sainte-Beuve. *Portraits contemporains,* vol. 1. 1855.

II

Text

Wroński, H. *Le Sphinx.* 1818.

Studies

Augé, L. *Exposition du messianisme.* 1835.
Cherfils, C. *Introduction à Wronski.* 1898.

III

Texts

Kierkegaard, S. *Samlede Vaerker,* 2d ed., ed. A. B. Drachman, J. L. Heiberg, and H. O. Lange, 14 vols. Copenhagen, 1920–31.
———. *Papirer,* ed. P. A. Heiberg, V. Kuhr, and E. Torsting, 20 vols. Copenhagen, 1909–48

Studies

Bretail, R. *A Kierkegaard Anthology.* Princeton, 1946.
Geismar, E. O. *Lectures on the Religious Thought of S. Kierkegaard.* Minneapolis, 1937.

Hohlenberg, J. E. *Søren Kierkegaard.* London, 1954.
Jolivet, R. *Introduction to Kierkegaard.* London, 1950.
Lowrie, W. *Kierkegaard.* New York, 1938.
——. *A Short Life of Kierkegaard.* Princeton, 1942.
Swenson, D. F. *Something About Kierkegaard.* Minneapolis, 1941.
Wahl, J. *Études Kierkegaardiennes.* Paris, 1938.

IV

Text

Emerson, R. W. *The Complete Works of Ralph Waldo Emerson,* 12 vols., Centenary Edition. Boston, 1903–04.

Studies

Bishop, Jonathan. *Emerson on the Soul.* Cambridge, Mass., and London, 1965.
Pochmann, H. A. *German Culture in America.* Madison, Wisc., 1961. Pp. 153–207.

SOCIAL PHILOSOPHY IN FRANCE: CHARLES FOURIER

THE FIRST HALF of the century produced many social reformers, particularly in France. Charles Fourier, Saint-Simon, Comte, and Proudhon tried, each in his own way, to create a reflective social philosophy equivalent to the political transformations of the time.

1 Charles Fourier

Born in 1772 to a well-to-do mercantile family in Besançon, Charles Fourier lost his fortune at the siege of Lyon in 1793. He was a soldier from 1794 to 1796, then a traveling salesman, clerk, or broker in Lyon until 1815; later he worked in Besançon and Paris, but he was always sickened by an occupation based on "the art of buying for three francs something worth six and selling for six something worth three." Behind his counter he dreamed of a regenerated humanity.

Divine Providence established a perfect harmony in the material world, which makes the heavenly bodies move in unison. In this world there is a motive principle, which is God, a moved principle, which is matter, and a principle governing movement, which Fourier calls justice or mathematics. Without the last principle, the heavenly bodies would collide at random with each other and destroy each other. God introduced a similar harmony into the movements of organic life, which are subject to finality and into the movements of animal life, which obey instinct.

With respect to these three kinds of movements—material, organic, animal—which are kept in perfect order, the "social movement" or set of relations between men living in a society seems thoroughly chaotic, blind, irrational. Could Providence have relinquished all control over the social movement? Fourier's vital faith caused him to reject this possibility and to conclude that in the past the principle governing it has simply eluded men, just as the principle governing the stars remained unknown until Newton discovered it and stated it mathematically. Fourier boasts of being the Newton of the social world, that is, of having discovered the principle of harmony which governs social relations. The very statement of the problem shows that he is not concerned with inventing or imagining a rule to create the social order—any more than Newton created the harmony of the stars by formulating it mathematically. Nor is he any more of a utopian, by persuasion, than Saint-Simon. He searches for the principles of harmony that actually exist in human nature, just as attraction exists among the stars. The nature of man is not to be legislated but revealed.

Faith in Providence is our guarantee that man will achieve happiness by giving free rein to the primitive passions with which nature has endowed him. But human society is organized in such a way that man is everywhere in fetters: law, morality, religion press upon him from every side; work is a necessity, a painful state from which he seeks to free himself; and social reformers, in spite of secular experience, think only of substituting new rules for old ones. There is a sharp contrast—truly an anomaly, contrary to the divine will—between divine Providence, which is revealed to us by our own nature, and the present state of affairs. Fourier proposes to eliminate this contrast, but not because he wants to revert to the state of nature, like a new Rousseau. A regression in the Roussellian sense supposes a simplification of our passions, a reversion to primitive passions, which goes counter to Fourier's intentions. According to him, man naturally has numerous, complicated passions, which should be developed in conformity with nature rather than curtailed. The passions can lead to excesses or vices, of course, but they are the sole source of our activities. That is why, for example, Fourier censures the Saint-Simonians for trying to abolish property, the stimulus to activity, even though Rousseau had been against property and had called it a social institution superimposed on nature. "To preach the abolition of property and inheritance in the nineteenth century," he wrote in 1831, "is an anomaly which should provoke indignation!" What Fourier sees in the passions is what makes them the source of human happiness, whereas with Rousseau the development of sentiment led to a kind of idle contemplation. What Fourier stresses is not the passions themselves but passions with their infallible result—labor. The affirmation of a link between human passions and labor results less from a psychological analysis than from Fourier's conviction that Providence could not have separated the development of our nature, which is rooted in our passions, and the conditions of our existence and happiness, which depend on the productivity of our labor.

The watchword of the era was production or organization for production. Production depends on labor, and the only means of increasing the productivity of labor is by making it "attractive." Labor is attractive only if it is suited to the taste of each worker, and this condition can be met only in free associations large enough for each member to perform labor useful to all and suited to his taste, and small enough for each member to be acutely aware of the others and have a clear picture of their cooperative achievements. In our huge societies the individual is relatively unimportant, so that he fails to see his relation to the social whole. This is the origin of Fourier's idea of the phalanx or small cooperative group of workers numbering 1,620. He proposes to organize an experimental phalanx in the midst of our civilized society. It is certain to be imitated, and "civilized" society will gradually disappear and be replaced by numerous social cells existing side by side. Externally, the phalanx is a corporation whose members possess all the skills necessary for complete self-sufficiency. It embraces different *series,* each containing several *groups.* A series includes all those engaged in the same occupation, such as agriculture; a group within a series includes all those involved in a particular phase of the occupation, such as plowing, raising grain, or preparing fodder. Every worker is a member of a group, and all workers live together in a phalanstery, which consists of a complex of separate dwellings. Fourier's vision is obviously colored by elements drawn from the medieval guilds and idealized by the Romanticists, who extolled their merry fellowship, their *esprit de corps* and concern for each other, and their attempts to compete with each other. The French Revolution and industrialization had caused the medieval guilds to disappear; the division of work isolated the worker, who, in the routine performance of his solitary task, lost interest in everything he was helping to produce. Cooperative work, in which the operation as a whole is never lost from sight, provides incentives that make it attractive; the worker tries to do his best because he sees how his own efforts play a part in the operation as a whole; the group, in turn, competes with other groups; finally each worker understands the whole system of production and is not riveted to one task but may, depending on his tastes and changes in his tastes, pass from one task to another. Thus cooperative labor satisfies man's three main passions: the *composite* passion, which is the passion for contributing to the perfection of the whole on which he works; the *cabalistic* passion, which is rivalry between groups—not jealousy, which degenerates into hatred, but the desire to serve the group to which he belongs in the best possible way; and finally the *butterfly* passion, which is the desire for change originating in his satiety and the multiplicity of his tastes. All of this resembles the description of a game and the exuberant feelings that animate different partners and their teams. Indeed, "attractive labor" hardly differs from a game, and it involves many childish features.

In a phalanx, the family continues to exist, but all the restraints and the alleged duties that this word evokes have disappeared. The education of children is accomplished by observation of the occupations in which they are allowed gradually to participate; apprenticeship in all the occupations gradually brings out their dominant aptitudes and tastes. Conjugal fidelity is not obligatory, however, and either spouse may freely satisfy the butterfly passion; a woman in a phalanstery is even freer than one who espouses Saint-Simonianism.

Utopias such as these always presuppose (as with Plato) a harmony between man's desires and nature. If the desired effect is to be achieved, the natural tastes of the members of a phalanx must be as varied as their occupations. That is why Fourier, in choosing members for his experimental phalanx, considered a desirable number to be 1,620, each with a different taste, for he thought that every possible combination of the primary passions would result in this number of temperaments. But how could the permanence of such a variety of combinations be assured? In general, Fourier thought that the radical transformation of humanity resulting from the transition of civilization to a state of *harmony* would be accompanied by a radical revolution similar to those described in Cuvier's account of the history of the earth, in nature and living organisms. Fourier's imagination projects into the future the fables of the past: domestication of marine animals or formation of new organs—for instance, a thirty-two foot tail, which delighted the caricaturists of the period. Thus nature would always lend itself more and more, by a providential combination of circumstances, to the satisfaction of man's desires.

Such were the principles of this societal system, suggested by the Gospel as a desirable goal, and analogous, according to Newton's research, to the material world. It was the strange product of an age in which religious and scientific beliefs were allied to the search for a system that would eliminate all political and moral problems and, without subjecting humanity to painful toil, result in maximum efficiency of economic production.

II *Fourierism*

Fourierism spread rapidly, particularly after 1832, thanks to the teaching of a converted Saint-Simonian, Jules Lechevalier. Apart from Fourier's books, the doctrine was expounded in several works by Just Muiron (*Survey of Industrial Procedures,* 1824), Amédée Paget (*Introduction to the Study of Social Science,* 1824), Abel Transon, another converted Saint-Simonian (*"The Societary Theory,"* in Pierre Leroux' *Revue encyclopédique,* 1832), H. Renaud (*Solidarity,* 1836), and Victor Considérant, who edited *La Phalanstère ou la Réforme industrielle,* which became *La Phalange* in 1835, and who published *Social Destiny* in 1836. In 1839 Pellarin, also a converted Saint-Simonian, published a biography of Fourier, who had died in 1837, without ever having obtained the subsidy he needed to launch his experimental phalanx. Experiments were undertaken after his death, including the well known phalanstery for families (*familistère*), which was founded by Godin, at Guise, and which still exists. Traits of the Fourierist tradition can also be found elsewhere.

In the program of *Pacific Democracy,* which Victor Considérant published on August 1, 1843, he makes the following profession of faith: "We believe that humanity, moved by the breath of God, is called upon to bring about an ever stronger association of individuals, families, classes, nations, and races, which constitute its elements . . . ; that this great association of the human family will reach a state of perfect unity—that is, a social state in which order will result naturally, freely, from the spontaneous accord of every human element." The Fourierist was convinced that competition and strife between classes was due to purely accidental circumstances, that the revolutionary transition of 1789 could have been a peaceful transition, and that the future would see the union of capital, talent, and labor. Considérant eventually formulated a system of political and religious eclecticism closely related to Cousin's philosophical eclecticism. This was after 1843, when he described the state of political parties and divided them into extreme conservatives (Guizot and financiers), progressive conservatives, retrograde democrats—advocates of universal suffrage, nomination of an elected president, and foreign wars—and socialist democrats. According to him, they sin through exclusivism or negation of other principles, even though "they are generally legitimate in the principle which they assert or defend." He says further that "Protestantism, the guardian of the principle of freedom, Catholocism, the guardian of the sacrosanct principle of hierarchy and unity, and philosophy, which is rooted in the ground of pure reason, are destined to be united one day." In 1844 V. Hennequin, another Fourierist, also manifested his sympathy for Cousin's method, although he judged the doctrine of eclecticism to be vague.

But there were also orthodox Catholics among the Fourierists. For example, Hippolyte de la Morvonnais, the poet from Saint-Malo, protested against the idea that Fourier had introduced elements of a new religion, different from Catholicism, and insisted that he simply wanted to lead religion from the half-belief of Lamennais to the full belief which had existed in the Church from the beginning. De la Morvonnais' article was directed against Eugène Pelletan, also a Fourierist, who believed in a "progressive religion" because "as humanity evolves, a greater amount of universal life— in other words, God—enters humanity." With such views, Fourierism was approaching the historical pantheism of Hegel.[1]

The Fourierists played a fairly active role in the revolution of 1848. Considérant asked the assembly for the means to put their plans for reform into practice. At that time there were 200,000 Fourierists in America. After 1849 Considérant tried to found a colony in Texas.

---

[1] See various articles on the subject in *Les Dogmes, le Clergé et l'État, études religieuses* (Paris: Librairie sociétaire, 1844): p. 85 (Hennequin), p. 36 (De la Morvonnais), and p. 19 (Pelletan).

BIBLIOGRAPHY

Texts

Fourier, Charles. *Œuvres complètes.* Paris, 1841–45.

———. *La Fausse Industrie morcelée, répugnante, mensongère, et l'antidote: l'industrie naturelle, combinée, attrayante, véridique, donnant quadruple produit,* 2 vols. Paris, 1835–36.

———. Archival Material in the *Archives Nationales* in Paris, including 98 notebooks in manuscript.

Studies

Alhaiza, A. *Historique de l'école sociétaire.* Paris, 1894.

Bourgin, Hubert. *Fourier.* Paris, 1905.

Friedberg, M. *L'influence de Ch. Fourier sur le mouvement social contemporain en France.* Paris, 1926.

Manuel, Frank E. *The Prophets of Paris.* Cambridge, Mass., 1962.

Pellarin, C. *Vie de Fourier.* 1871.

Poulat, Emil. *Les cahiers manuscrits de Fourier.* Paris, 1957.

Zilberfarb, I. I. *Sotsialnaia Filosofia Sharlia Fure i Ee Mesto v Istorii Sotsialisticheskoi Mysli Pervoi Poloviny XIX Veka.* Moscow, 1964.

SOCIAL PHILOSOPHY IN FRANCE:
SAINT-SIMON AND
THE SAINT-SIMONIANS

1 *Saint-Simon*

Claude Henri de Rouvroy, comte de Saint-Simon, was born in Paris in 1760 and served as an officer until the French Revolution. From 1789 to 1813 he engaged in speculation and lost his fortune. After 1803, taking advantage of friendships established during his conversations with mathematicians and physiologists of his time, he became a publicist. From 1814 to 1817, his books and brochures bear not only his own signature but also that of Augustin Thierry, his secretary. In 1819 he had as his collaborator Auguste Comte, whose name appeared alone on the third book of the *Catechism of Industrial Workers*. He died in 1825.

Two radically distinct themes appear in Saint-Simon's reflections on the sciences: the theme of the unity of science, which goes back to Diderot through D'Alembert, whose *Preliminary Discourse* he reprinted in his *Introduction to Scientific Works of the Eighteenth Century* (1807–08); and the theme of the necessary passage of the sciences from a conjectural state, in which knowledge is theology or metaphysics, to a positive state. The second theme is traceable to his talks with Dr. Burdin.

The two themes are ill-mated. The first guides him toward the

Cartesian ideal of a general science which seeks to embrace both the science of nature and the science of man, and to unite Newton and Locke, the astronomer and the physiologist. It tries to generalize Newtonian gravitation by applying it to human and moral affairs. The second theme leads him toward the sciences that have not yet reached "the positive state," more particularly the science of man. In 1812 he interpreted this science in the manner suggested by Cabanis, who made psychology a branch of physiology. Only after 1814 did he class this science a "positive polity" (in 1820 he invented the expression adopted later by Comte).

The first theme makes no truly essential distinction between the objects of the various sciences, whereas the second rigidly separates the mathematical and physical sciences from the physiological and human sciences. Saint-Simon gradually relinquished the first theme in favor of the second, for after 1813 he began to see a qualitative difference involving a social factor between the sciences of raw substances and the science of man. Here Saint-Simon, who does not seem to have been struck by the difference previously, was simply falling back on a medieval idea which had been discarded in modern times: that the dignity of a science varies with the dignity of its subject. Thus scientists who study man should be ranked above those who study lesser subjects; furthermore, those who seek to perfect instruments of war contradict the pacific ideal of humanity. The Napoleonic wars forced this ideal upon him, and he was among those who sought to establish peace in 1814, after Napoleon's fall.

In his *Reorganization of European Society* (October, 1814) he assumed that peace could be assured if Europe, as the independence of each nation was proclaimed, would at the same time become a single political body. There was an attempt to realize such unity through a congress of plenipotentiaries in 1815, but the result was only a somewhat precarious European equilibrium. Even if this congress had been permanent, according to Saint-Simon, it would not have been an effective means of insuring the combination of independence and unity required for establishing universal peace.

What distinguishes his plan from the plans for perpetual peace formulated by the Abbé de Saint-Pierre and by Kant is the fact that he substitutes industrialists for ambassadors. He assumes that the coalition of industrial interests will create the conditions under which peace can be realized and that industrialists will have a place in the political hierarchy corresponding to their social influence. The idea of a European political union was supplanted, after 1816, by a preliminary investigation of more general interest: an attempt to demonstrate the social preponderance of industry. Saint-Simon claims that industry is absolutely inseparable from science, being an application of science, and that science itself is a kind of industry (see, for example, the work entitled *Literary and Scientific Industry, Combined with Commercial and Manufacturing Industry,* December 1816–March 1817). The old social system, he says in *The Organizer* (*L'Organisateur,* 1819–1821), originated in the idea that the country is the patrimony of the members of the governing class, who administer it for themselves. Now, on the contrary, it is assumed that the political system should contribute to the happiness of the governed, and happiness means the satisfaction of physical and moral needs. But this satisfaction depends in turn on the development of arts and crafts—a goal so clear that it rules out any trace of arbitrariness and makes all questions relating to social organization absolutely "positive." The interest of industry coincides with the interest of all, and wealth is a factor in progress, since most wars are caused by the poverty of a nation which covets the wealth of its neighbors. In the new political system, savants would be in charge of the spiritual instruction previously entrusted to the clergy, and industrial leaders would be in charge of material interests. The capacity of each individual to fulfil a particular function is soon manifested, and definitions of social justice (recalling those of the *Nichomachean Ethics*)—"To each according to his capacity" and "To each capacity according to its works"—again acquire their true meaning.

But our era, according to Saint-Simon, is a transitional era between the destruction of the old system and the establishment of the new. The forces of feudalism and the clergy, though condemned to perish, struggle to continue their existence. "Metaphysicists" and "legists" (that is, revolutionaries) think that they are going far enough when they abolish the old organization without trying to replace it, and the government accepts the subordinate, negative role of carrying out its police functions by maintaining order. In *The Industrial System* (1821) Saint-Simon compares the social state of his time with that of Roman decadence and concludes that certain features—the end of the social unity created by thirteenth-century feudalism, the breach of unity of belief with the rise of Protestantism, and the subordination of the spiritual power to temporal leaders, who took it upon themselves to form the Holy Alliance—have their counterparts in the period of decadence which preceded the formation of Christian society during the first centuries A.D. By analogy, he imagines a social renovation similar to that brought about by Christianity, and one of which he is supposed to be the Messiah.

The "new Christianity" he envisions is basically identical with the old, for belief in a remunerative God and a future life is not the permanent basis of Christianity, nor is this faith bound in any way to certain clerical institutions. Christianity is based solely (Schopenhauer was saying the same thing at approximately the same time) on a moral precept, "Love ye one another." This precept is understood immediately and wholly, and it is not susceptible of progress. The perishable side of Christianity is the form an institution—that is, the Church—takes, in putting this precept into practice. The Church is infallible as long as it fulfils social needs, but whenever it no longer serves society and has ceased to act for the benefit of the poorest class, it should be replaced. According to Saint-Simon, the so-called Christian religions have lost sight of their mission. To begin with, religious instruction in the Catholic religion gives preference to a dogma and a form of worship which make laymen dependent on the clergy, whereas moral ideas are very thinly sown and do not constitute a body of doctrine. The clergy, schooled mainly in a theology that is nothing more than hairsplitting, loses sight of the essential object of Christianity and allows itself to be surpassed by scholars, artists, and industrialists. The institution of the Inquisition is contrary to the spirit of Christianity because it condemns only offenses against dogma and worship, as in the Jesuit Society, which wages open warfare against the new state of affairs. In short, Saint-Simon sees Catholicism as the abettor of reaction and the supporter of the forces of the past represented by the Restoration. In his view the Protestant religion or Lutheranism was essentially a retreat that carried Christianity back to its starting point, back to the Christianity of Jesus, which was not subject to any political or social organization. Its demands were exclusively moral, and it allowed the reign of slavery and the strict patriotism of the Roman citizen to subsist, just as Lutheranism allows religion to remain dependent on the political power. Saint-Simon also charges Lutheranism with a lack of artistic feeling—that is, of a means of uniting men.

He claims that "new Christianity" will reorganize society solely by the new force given to the evangelical precept. The initiative will not come, however, from those whom it benefits—the poor. At the outset the diffusion of Christianity was due less to a popular movement than to a "Roman" like St. Paul or a patrician like Polyeucte. By the same token, Saint-Simon believes that "philanthropists," by their teaching and preaching, will show the princes that their true interests conform to those of the savants and industrialists and run counter to those of the nobility and clergy. He is too much an aristocrat to believe that the people for whom he labors can do anything to bring about their own regeneration. The Revolution of 1789 itself issued less from a popular movement than from the efforts of metaphysicists and legists. In the new restoration, everything is supposed to be under the direction of the king and of "philanthropists," who represent the savants and industrialists. The goal is not so much to change the form of the state as to substitute men of science for the clergy, industrial chiefs and bankers for the nobility. That there may be a conflict between these new powers and the interests of the poor does not cross his mind, and to him there is no social question, strictly speaking. Addresses to the king, a draft proclamation, a letter to the keeper of the seals, letters to bankers—these are his means of action; a national catechism, drawn up by the Institute of France, to teach the people the basics of the new organization, a budget voted by the industrialists, abolition of titles of nobility, reorganization of the national guard, with soldiers electing their officers, dissolution of the *Parlement,* proclamation of a dictatorship to impose his reforms—these are his proposals. If he rejects government by popular consent, he retains from Rousseau the idea of the necessity of a single legislator: "The conception of the new system must be unitary, that is, fashioned by a single head; an assembly cannot produce a system." But politics to him is only a means, and the most viable part of his ideas is revealed in this aphorism: "Civil power is the sole basis of political power." The civil power, according to his famous plan, is actually in the hands of three thousand savants, artists, and industrialists, whose disappearance would supposedly mean the end of French society, whereas it would hardly be affected by the sudden death of the thirty thousand persons who govern and administer the nation, and who constitute the anomaly of a political power independent of the civil power. Is not Saint-Simonian justice—expressed in the two aphorisms, "To each according to his capacities" and "To each capacity according to its works"— the basis for an ideal civil code to take the place of politics and to substitute the principle of distributive justice for the revolutionary principle of equality?

II Saint-Simonianism

The history of Saint-Simonianism is closely linked to the political and social history of France from 1825 to 1851. Preaching and propaganda, journalistic campaigns, famous trials—everything culminated in the creation of a state of mind which fitted in with several general tendencies of the period and exerted considerable influence on practical affairs.

The first years (1825–32) saw the great doctrinal productions of Saint-Simonianism: articles in *Le Producteur,* written by Auguste Comte, Olinde Rodrigues, Bazard, and Enfantin; lectures for a course given at the home of Enfantin beginning on December 17, 1828, then on the Rue Tavanne, and published under the title *Exposition of the Doctrine,* after they had been edited by Hippolyte Carnot; and articles published in *L'Organisateur.* A new period began on December 31, 1829, the day when Saint-Simonianism took the form of a hierarchy, with Bazard and Enfantin as the "supreme fathers," and adepts who called each other brothers; then and after the Revolution of 1830, the movement attracted many adherents, particularly among former students of the École Polytechnique. Barthélemy Enfantin aroused such enthusiasm that officers like Bruneau, engineers like Jean Reynaud, and industrialists like Fournel, manager of the foundries of Le Creusot, gave up their positions in order to follow him. *Le Globe,* a liberal newspaper, went over to the side of the Saint-Simonians in November, 1830. The doctrine was preached in four centers in Paris, in six churches in the rest of France, and in other churches founded in Brussels and Liége. A schism occurred in the school at the end of 1831. That was the time when George Sand was writing *Indiana,* and Romanticism, then in full sway, was calling attention to the oppression of women in society. This was a problem Enfantin resolved in a way that aroused the indignation of Carnot, Bazard, and Olinde Rodrigues; these men left the school.

After their defection, Enfantin became the sole leader of the school. He still had ninety disciples, but he stressed popular propaganda and action rather than doctrine. In April, 1832, the *Globe* concerned itself exclusively with projects of material interest: the sanitation of Paris, the creation of a railway system linking large cities, and last but not least, the introduction of European civilization into Africa, beginning with Egypt and Algeria. The church he had formed abandoned itself to ridiculous practices. "To rehabilitate the proletariat," he and his disciples engaged in manual labor, extending to the people "a hand which bears the mark of noble calluses." They devised a habit with a waistcoat which buttoned behind and which could be donned only with the help of a brother —a great symbol of fraternity. They had special rites for marriage, for adoption of children, and for funerals. Prosecuted for violating the law governing public meetings, they were judged and found guilty in August of 1832, then acquitted on the same charge in April of 1833. The second judgment recognized Saint-Simonianism as a religion and held that meetings of the members were beyond the jurisdiction of the court.

After spending several months at Sainte-Pélagie, Enfantin went back into action: from 1833 to 1838 he was in Egypt, where he intended to cut through the isthmus of Suez before constructing a canal across Panama. He worked with his companions to dam the Nile, then, in 1839, went to Algeria to spread European civilization. Upon his return to France, he turned first to the king, then to the king's sons, the Duc d'Orleans and the Duc d'Aumale, for help in carrying out his projects. After 1848 he called on Napoleon to set up a system of professional education, savings accounts, credit institutions, and help for the aged. In his view these social questions were completely separated from revolutionary liberalism; just as the Saint-Simonians were barely interested in the July Revolution of 1830, he was but little concerned in 1849 with freedom of the press, freedom of speech, and freedom of assembly, provided that there was action; and he looked indulgently (like Auguste Comte at the same time) upon the man who carried out the coup d'état of 1815. "What we need," he wrote in 1861, "is not freedom but intelligent authority." To him freedom is but a means to an end, and he accepts even the forced labor of the fellahs, whom he saw in Egypt, during the reign of Mohammed Ali. In 1830 he called for freedom of trade as well as for freedom of worship, of the press, and of assembly, but only in order to provide his own doctrine with a means of spreading. For the most part, the Saint-Simonians favored the intervention of the state in public issues. In 1848, for example, Laurent de l'Ardèche urged the state to repurchase every railroad company.

In this strange mixture of blustering publicity, naturalist morality, social doctrine, and practical undertakings, which constitute Saint-Simonianism, it is possible for us to discern the essential elements of every doctrine of the period: the tendency to organize and synthesize, and the urge to act.

What is a Saint-Simonian's definition of philosophy? "One can apply this designation only to a system of thought which embraces every mode of human activity and provides the solution of every social and individual problem. Suffice it to say that there have not been more doctrines worthy of this designation than general states of humanity, and that the phenomena associated with a regular social order occur only twice in the sequence of civilization to which we belong—in antiquity and in the Middle Ages. The new general state that we are announcing for the future will form the third link in this chain." [1]

The notion of philosophy depends, then, on the distinction between an organic epoch and a critical epoch. According to the Saint-Simonians, "philosophy" ceases the very moment when, from the point of view commonly held in the eighteenth century, it is just beginning. This definition is a complete inversion of the traditional one. To the Saint-Simonians the Milesian school in Greece and the Renaissance and Reformation in Europe mark the beginning of the decline of philosophy; free, individual investigation and sporadic approaches to isolated, mutually exclusive sciences replace the spiritual unity and collective thought which guides all men toward a single goal, as in the age of Greek polytheism or in the Middle Ages and feudalism.

"What is man's destination in relation to his fellow man? What is his destination in relation to the universe? These are the general terms of the double problem humanity has always faced. All organic epochs have been solutions, at least tentative ones, of this problem. But soon progress, accomplished with the help of these solutions— that is, within the protective frame of the social institutions established after them—made them insufficient and called for new solu-

[1] *Doctrine de Saint-Simon,* ed. Bouglé and Halévy, 1924, p. 126.

tions. Then critical epochs—phases of discussion, of *protestation*, of waiting, of transition—came to fill the gap with doubt, indifference toward these great problems, or *selfishness*, the necessary consequence of this doubt or indifference." [2]

Both the spiritualistic doctrine and the utilitarian doctrine are the fruits of selfishness, which Saint-Simonians confuse with individualism. Neither the direct impulsion of consciousness nor selfish motives can lead the individual to a state of organization, of course, for organization always assumes the sacrifice of self-interest to the interests of the majority. Saint-Simon's philosophy is not one of these vain, arbitrary constructions; it is the revelation awaited by the world. Here the Saint-Simonians rediscover De Maistre, Ballanche with his idea of palingenesis, and all the illuminists; supporters of Romanticism, they believe in inspirations which cannot be verified by science, are hostile to classical inspiration, and see salvation only in religion, in the predominance of sentiment over reason.

Thus Saint-Simonianism is a hierarchical social organization, which requires its members to practice the sacrifice of a monk and the obedience of a soldier. Such practices can be taught only by a reformed system of education, which establishes the necessary inner dispositions in each member. There are two forms of education, both narrow and inadequate: classical education, which seeks to develop human qualities in general; and technical education, which is limited to vocational training. As understood by a Saint-Simonian, education is social, for it adapts the child to the form of the society in which he is to live. To be sure, such a system of education exists only in an organic age: the civic system of antiquity and the religious system of the Middle Ages. The sign of a critical age like ours is precisely that of restricting ourselves to the first two kinds of education.

The Saint-Simonian ideal is to substitute association and rivalry for the exploitation of man by man. Education can reveal the capacities of a child, and once his capacities are manifested, he will find

[2] *Ibid.*, p. 195.

his place in the association where, working for all, he will work for himself. Thus each occupation truly becomes a public function in a system that assumes a kind of providential balance between the natural capacities of men and the needs of society. Unlike Fourier, the Saint-Simonians did not believe strongly in the spontaneity of such a correspondence, which probably explains why they assign the state a disciplinary role in the management of labor and even the compulsion to labor, just as Mohammed Ali forced his fellahs to work.

But the disciplinary role of the state is based on the principle that property does not retain the absolute character which confers on its possessors a right not to participate in social labor. Still, the Saint-Simonians are not communists, as they have often been accused of being, and we have already noted that they are not utopians, for they search for effective measures here and now rather than an image of the future. Seeking to make property a social function rather than a mark of selfishness, they attack the laws of inheritance and propose on one hand that the state be the principal heir in every collateral succession and, on the other, that each individual be allowed to adopt an heir if his own children are incapable of managing the estate. Furthermore, the state should establish banks to provide credit and supply the tools of labor to all those capable of using them.

Labor is the human utilization of natural forces. The faith that the Saint-Simonians manifest in labor and industry implies optimism —belief in the goodness of nature, which man uses for his own purposes. This optimism is the heart of the Saint-Simonian religion, which does not sacrifice the flesh to the spirit, like Christian mysticism, or the spirit to the flesh, like paganism. Every reality is divine:

> God is the all in all
> All is in him, all is through him,
> None of us is outside him
> But none of us is God.

This canticle, which caused the Saint-Simonians to be accused of pantheism (notwithstanding the reservation expressed in the last verse), is an expression of the optimism that caused Enfantin to rehabilitate, along with work, no longer a curse to man, the association of the sexes, which was supposed to eliminate the subjugation of women. This purely affirmative religion, without negations or ascetic practices, reflects the firm conviction that a perfect social organization would do no violence to natural human instincts.

Bibliography

Texts

Saint-Simon. *Œuvres complètes de Saint-Simon et Enfantin,* 47 vols. Paris, 1865–76.

——. *Lettres d'un habitant de Genève à ses contemporains,* ed. A. Pereire. Paris, 1925; written in 1803.

——. *Textes choisis,* ed. J. Dautry. Paris, 1951.

——. *Selected Writings,* trans. F. M. H. Markham. Oxford, 1952.

Studies

Dondo, M. M. *The French Faust, Henri de Saint-Simon.* New York, 1955.

Durkheim, Émile. *Le Socialisme,* ed. Marcel Mauss. Paris, 1928. Trans. Charlotte Sattler: *Socialism and Saint-Simon.* Yellow Springs, Ohio, 1958.

Manuel, F. E. *The New World of Henri de Saint-Simon.* Cambridge, Mass., 1956.

Plamenatz, J. P. *Man and Society.* London, 1963. Vol. 2, chap. 2.

SOCIAL PHILOSOPHY IN FRANCE: AUGUSTE COMTE

AUGUSTE COMTE, born in Montpellier in 1798, studied at the École Polytechnique in 1814 and 1815, during the Hundred Days. He served as Saint-Simon's secretary from 1817 until a breach between the two men occurred in 1824. During this period he outlined a system of positive polity, and published *General Separation between Opinions and Desires* (1819), *Summary Evaluation of the Recent Past in Its Entirety* (1820), and *A Plan for the Scientific Works Necessary to Reorganize Society* (1822). In 1826 he began to deliver a series of lectures on positive philosophy to an audience of scientists including the physiologist Blainville and the mathematician Poinsot. His course was interrupted by a severe nervous breakdown, followed by a lengthy period of melancholic depression. He resumed his teaching in 1829 and published the first volume of his Course in Positive Philosophy in July of 1830; the other volumes appeared in 1835, 1838, 1839, and 1842. Supplementing this work were his *Discourse on the Positive Spirit* (1844) and *Discourse on the Positivist Outlook* (1848). Living on his meager earnings as a tutor at the École Polytechnique, he was unable to find support for his nomination as professor there or at the Collège de France, where he tried in vain, in 1833, to persuade Guizot to found a chair for teaching the history of the sciences. The preface to the sixth volume of the *Course* contains an account of all his disappointments, which he attributes to the narrow specialization of scholars. Thereafter Comte lived mainly from the voluntary contributions of the friends of positivism. It was in 1844 that he met Clotilde de Vaux, who died in April of 1846, and it was at the same time that he began to dream of a religion of humanity. He proclaimed himself the first high priest of the new religion, inspired by Clotilde, whose memory presided over many of its rites. The main writings of this period are his *System of Positive Polity* (1851–54), *Positivist Catechism* (1852), and *Subjective Synthesis or Universal System of Conceptions Characteristic of the Normal State of Humanity* (1856). His death in 1857 cut short his projected series of works on ethics, on a system of positive industry, and on first philosophy, which was to be completed in 1867.

1 Comte's Point of Departure

What is the principal motive underlying Comte's thought? Does he seek to reform the sciences or, like Descartes, to bring about an intellectual reform? Certainly not. He aims to reorganize society and, in order to do so, to bring about an intellectual reform. He accuses the Fourierists and Saint-Simonians of trying to remake society through direct practical action, and he claims that their approach is wrong. The intellect must first be given new habits, conforming to the state of advancement of human knowledge. In a broad sense, the notion of making political progress depend on the general advancement of knowledge is common to much of political philosophy. Here we need only recall the name of Plato and all the philosophers of the eighteenth century. Still, this dependence has been interpreted in two distinct ways: when we speak of progress in knowledge, we may be thinking of the scientific spirit in general or the method of science, or we may be thinking of the creation of a particular science which studies society. Plato's *Republic* unites both points of view, since it deals at once with the social structure and the general method of the sciences, whereas a work like Aristotle's *Politics* is concerned exclusively with social science as a separate entity, and his *Ethics* explicitly considers the scientific life to be isolated from the social bond. This antithesis dominates the whole history of political philosophy: thinkers like Hobbes tend to subordinate politics to a scientific philosophy; but others, such as Montesquieu, adopt Aristotle's approach. The two currents are clearly seen, in the eighteenth century, in the *Encyclopedia*: the happiness of society is associated sometimes with the general development of reason, illuminated by the sciences, and sometimes with the sciences that bear directly on social facts—political economy, for example. Auguste Comte can be said to unite these two currents, for he believes that the scientific spirit is powerless to organize society by itself but must call on a science of social facts for support. He criticizes his contemporaries severely and claims that they can emerge from the state of dispersive specialization for which they are to blame only if such a science is founded. Nor does he believe that sociology can be founded in any way except by extending the scientific method to the study of social phenomena. This can be accomplished only after the encyclopedic scale of the sciences has been surveyed. Comte strongly opposes political economy and all other doctrines which claim to deal with social facts without any prior preparation; such sciences, like all "moral philosophy" traceable to Descartes, make the mistake of studying the most complicated facts without basing their study on the study of the simplest facts (*Course,* 4th edition, VI, 253). These disciplines fall into the hands of men of letters who are "incomplete philosophers" and degrade philosophy by reducing it to a speciality. The futility (and even harmfulness) of the scientific spirit without social science, the impossibility of social science without the complete hierarchy of the sciences—these are Comte's two constant themes.

But to these two themes he adds a third, completely independent of the first two: the antithesis between critical or revolutionary epochs and organic or stable epochs. The theme derives from the antirevolutionary philosophies of De Maistre and De Bonald, and from Saint-Simonianism. According to these philosophies, revolution and anarchy are one, for they involve an attempt to destroy legitimate powers—the temporal power and the spiritual power. This destruction extends even to the family and property, and the task of the regimes that came after the French Revolution was to restore the powers destroyed by the crisis. The substratum of this antithesis is in turn the antithesis between two theories of nature and society: one which reduces society to a throng of individuals bound together by a contract resulting from their own initiative, another which assumes the existence of social realities transcending individuals.

This antithesis is clearly related to the historical circumstances of the period, but Comte combines it with a third theme, borrowed from eighteenth-century philosophy—the theory of progress. Consequently his evaluation of history is strikingly different. Among the reactionaries, the antithesis had the practical consequence of bringing about the restoration of lost powers, and this fact became the driving force of French politics during the time of Napoleon and, to an even greater degree, with the Holy Alliance. According to Comte, on the contrary, the past must not return; the revolution was a necessary crisis. In an organic epoch, two elements which De Bonald confused should be kept distinct. De Bonald rightly conceded that there is no social power without a belief to support it, no temporal or spiritual power without belief in divine right; but it was wrong for him to assume that theological belief is the only belief on which society can be founded. If this were true, any form of reorganization would be hopeless. By abolishing theological beliefs, eighteenth-century philosophy and the revolution which issued from it accomplished a legitimate and necessary operation. Theological beliefs are grounded on an illusion which was dissipated by progress in the positive sciences. It follows that Comte's final goal is the same as De Bonald's: to restore the temporal power and the spiritual power. But these powers should be grounded on beliefs which are as efficacious as theological beliefs and can stand victoriously against philosophical criticism. Comte favors a social structure roughly identical to the traditional structure of the West since the Middle Ages, with the two powers—

the temporal and the spiritual—with the family, and with property; but to insure its solidity and legitimacy, he insists that beliefs have all the positivity required by the scientific spirit. We shall see that Comte makes few changes in the structure of society. To him this structure is an immovable entity and, consequently, incapable of progress. That is why he calls his study *static;* progress is entirely in the beliefs which constitute its basis; they pass from the theological state, now obsolete, to the positive state.

From this point of view the third theme tends to reunite with the first two themes, for Comte assumes that social science, grafted on all the other sciences, has the mission of providing the fabric of beliefs indispensable to social organization. At the same time we see the reason for linking the first two themes, frequently separated before Comte: without sociology the scientific spirit would be purely critical and negative, and without the support of the other sciences the study of social facts would consist of arbitrary affirmations. Thus the union of the two themes makes possible the solution of the problem of social reorganization, which the traditionalist schools tried in vain to solve. Comte also takes a different point of view when he bases social progress on progress in the sciences; for in the eighteenth century this expression meant promoting the happiness of the greatest number by diffusing knowledge, and with Comte it means using the sociological content of the sciences to strengthen social institutions. In the first instance, progress means giving man more power over nature; in the second, it means a change giving him more security with respect to social institutions.

Hence Comte's judgments concerning historical events since the French Revolution. The problem constantly confronting governments, in this period when theological beliefs had fallen and positivist beliefs had not yet arisen, was to maintain social unity by means of a doctrine contrary to any form of unity. The only practical solution of the problem was a dictatorship based on naked authority, and the assembly which had the best understanding of these conditions was the Convention. Danton, in particular, had

Comte's full sympathy because he saw clearly that a transitional regime required a provisional dictatorship. On the other hand, Comte criticizes the Constituent Assembly with its parliamentary system, borrowed from England, and its vain attempt "to convert critical conceptions into organic conceptions" (which means the attempt to make the negation of divine right the positive principle of popular self-government). He blames the Girondins for trying to obstruct Jacobin efforts to contain the divisive trend, and he accuses Robespierre, the "ambitious sophist," of "moving backwards," because he instituted the worship of reason in accordance with the teaching of Rousseau and wanted to restore the democracy of antiquity. He condemned Babeuf's stand against property, also predicated on the teachings of Rousseau, for the opposite reason: socialism attacks the very structure of society, and this structure is a permanent element (*Course,* IV, 289–320).

Only a naked dictatorship, without any doctrine, finds favor in his eyes. What he criticizes in Napoleon is not his dictatorship but his backwardness—his origin in a retrograde civilization. In pages written during the period when Louis Philippe was restoring the memory of Napoleon, Comte speaks of the "strange aberration" by which he was proclaimed the principal representative of the French Revolution. After Napoleon came the Restoration, a vain attempt, in the face of criticism, to restore superannuated doctrines in the government of Louis Philippe, who flatly refused to establish an intellectual and moral order; the July Monarchy, which was completely subservient to material interests, purely repressive, and incapable of providing leadership since it pointedly refrained from establishing an intellectual and moral order, is the epitome of a negative philosophy which recognizes no type of spiritual domination except that of journalism (*Course,* IV, 324–31).

After the coup d'état of 1852, when Comte believed the institution of the positivist regime to be imminent, the same considerations made him very favorably disposed toward Napoleon III, whose action represents the passage from a "vain parliamentary beginning typical of the English transition" to "the dictatorial phase which is truly and uniquely French." This "empirical dictatorship," lacking any doctrine and existing solely to combat anarchy, has its natural ally in the "organic doctrine" of positivism. Comte ends his career by making an appeal to the conservatives, telling them that positivism is the only means of disciplining the revolutionaries. Nor is there a contradiction between this last attitude and the advances he had made to the proletariat during the Revolution of 1848. He thought for a moment that he could convert the proletariat, who had then assumed the dictatorship, to his doctrine. The liberal or constitutional trends, which he criticizes at every turn, seem to him to have been abolished forever in 1852. "If the present dictatorship miscarries through retrogression," he predicts in a letter to Célestin de Blignères, "another will arise; but the reign of assemblies is irrevocably ended, except for possible brief interludes, which will make dictatorial needs even more obvious."

Comte's political theory is clear: social unity at any price through unity of doctrine when it exists, and when it does not exist, through a temporary dictatorship; but the positivist doctrine definitively insures the unity that the theological doctrine failed to establish.

II Intellectual Reform and the Positive Sciences

Intellectual reform is primary in Comte's thinking, yet its definition is elusive. As their history shows, the positive sciences, which are the substantive basis of intellectual doctrines, are subject to immanent conditions of development and the search for truth is their sole aim. This pattern of development, freed from all subjugation to an external goal, made possible the mathematics of Archimedes, the physics of Galileo and Newton, and the chemistry of Lavoisier. Subsequently this knowledge can be applied to material or social life, and in the mind of the scholar these applications can even be the driving force behind research, without in any way altering his freedom. Furthermore, according to Comte, the positive sciences are a means to social reform; directly or indirectly, they are all designed to achieve this end; and if this end does not prevent observation and reasoning from being the sole criteria of their certainty, or if it has no bearing on the objectivity of the results, it can and in fact does profoundly affect the direction and limits of research. Throughout the *Course of Positive Philosophy* there is a subjacent conflict between the radical freedom of science and the demands made on science as a means to an end. Because of this conflict, a doctrine apparently designed solely to introduce the positive spirit into every domain, either ignores or criticizes some definite trends in the sciences and sometimes narrows their fields of investigation.

In mathematics, for example, Comte opposes the calculus of probabilities, created by Laplace; in astronomy, he criticizes any attempt to determine the physical constitution of the stars, and he rejects any cosmogony outside the limits of the solar system; in physics, he rules out any attempt to determine the constitution of matter, and he considers systems typified by Cartesian mechanism to be semimetaphysical; in biology, he condemns all theories of the evolution of species, just as, in sociology, he condemns all investigations of the historical origin of societies.

All these exclusions, of which several contradicted actual trends in science, proceed from the same spirit. Each science is assigned a precise function and limited by the characteristic nature of its subject matter: when mathematics is applied directly to social phenomena, the calculus of probabilities is found to be outside the limits of science; astrophysics is incompatible with astronomy, which studies matter only insofar as it is subject to central forces; when physicochemical mechanics or atomism reduce the objects of physics and chemistry to raw matter, they make the object of science disappear; and the same applies to genetic doctrines in biology or sociology.

It is in the overall conception of science that this spirit is manifested most clearly. Scientists investigate laws or constant relations between phenomena, without knowing anything about the inner nature and causes of realities or essences. Newton's physics, as it was understood in the eighteenth century, really substituted the determination of laws for the futile search for causes; the aim of this substitution was to find a law to unify phenomena which seemed to be different; thus the corollary of the Newtonian movement was an attempt to discover the unity of law. Auguste Comte's legalism, on the other hand, is characterized by its inclusion of a multiplicity of essences and, with it, a multiplicity of laws; consequently the theme of a hierarchy of essences contradicts or at least radically modifies the basic idea of legalism. Here we detect the same influence that manifests itself in the philosophy of nature. After Newton, new sciences came into being, concerned with forces irreducible to gravitation: electricity, magnetism, chemistry, not to mention biology. Scientists no longer claim to know the essence of these forces any more than they claim to know the essence of gravitation; they simply look for the laws governing their actions —the law of the distribution of the positive and negative factors in magnetism and electricity, the law of definite proportions in chemistry, etc. From the diversity of laws they infer the diversity of the forces whose activities they calculate. Thus they remain faithful to the spirit of the Newtonians' legalism, and what seems to be an Aristotelian hierarchy of essences is in truth only an empirical hierarchy of laws, arranged in a graduated series from the lowest to the highest.

With his conception of science as the search for laws, Comte was continuing a tradition which had not been altered by the discovery of new sciences. In his writings it nevertheless assumes a distinctive character, linking it with certain scientific currents of his time. Comte was struck by Fourier's mathematical theory of heat.[1] Fourier discovered and expressed the mathematical laws of the propagation of heat without formulating any hypothesis, mechanical or otherwise, concerning the nature of heat (*Analytical Theory of Heat,* 1822), whereas physical mathematics—as understood by Laplace, for example—is always linked with mechanical hypotheses concerning molecules. To Comte, following the path of Fourier,

[1] Bachelard, *Étude sur l'évolution d'un problème de physique* (Paris, 1927), chap. v., pp. 55 ff., "Auguste Comte et Fourier."

the mechanical hypothesis, which he calls semimetaphysical, is no more justifiable in the sciences than any Aristotelian hypothesis whatsoever concerning qualitative essences. In the same spirit, Cuvier was investigating the structural laws of living beings without using any hypothesis concerning nature and life, and Chevreul, in organic chemistry, was engaged primarily in classification. Here we see clearly the general tendencies represented by Comte, who writes: "Today all good minds realize that our real studies are strictly limited to analyzing phenomena in order to discover their positive laws" (*Course*, III).

On the other hand, this conception of science is linked with Comte's attitude toward intellectual reform. Here the object is to substitute purely objective conceptions of the productive realities of phenomena for the subjective conceptions which prevailed during the theological age and the metaphysical ages. "The human brain" must be "transformed into an exact mirror of the external order" (*System of Positive Polity*, II). This statement must be interpreted in the broad context of the sciences, including both sociology and astronomy. To Comte, the word "order" refers to the fixity of the structure of reality; human intelligence discovers no principle of order within itself, and he never tires of calling attention to its weakness (*Course*, VI, 193–94; 278); its organization is supposed constantly to reflect an external order, whether fictive as in the theological state or real as in the positive state. Explicitly and repeatedly, he refutes the theory of Cousinian spiritualism, which claims to arrive at the principles of intelligence by introspection and self-reflection. His criticism is directed less toward psychology as the science of the phenomena of consciousness than toward a theory of knowledge based on psychological observation; intelligence can discover its own principles only by taking the external world as its model, not by self-examination. This conception of intelligence is an integral part of his legalistic conception of science, for its claim can be justified only if the order it reflects is not imaginary, and this order is imaginary if it is not verified or at least verifiable by experience. He condemns outright any hypothesis which is not directly verifiable, even though it may square with all the facts—as the hypotheses of luminous ether and electrical fluids did at the time of Comte—and admits only one type of hypothesis: the anticipation of a law. The only remedy for the congenital weakness of intelligence is faithfulness to reality, which is itself possible only if the sciences are restricted to defining laws.

Comte does not pretend to define the essences that separate the objects of the different sciences. He offers no definition of life, quantity, or society. He retains only the logical characteristics of distinct essences—those which today are called "extension" and "comprehension," and which he calls "generality" and "complexity." Essences, according to him, are arranged according to their decreasing generality and increasing complexity. This new formulation of an old idea means that their comprehensibility increases as their extension decreases, and it allows him to classify realities while disregarding their profound nature. Hence the six basic sciences, each dominating the arts or techniques to which it gives birth: mathematics studies quantity, the simplest and most indeterminate of all realities; astronomy adds force to quantity and studies masses endowed with forces of attraction; physics adds quality to force and studies such qualitatively different forces as heat and light; chemistry rises to qualitatively distinct objects; biology investigates life, which adds organization to raw matter; finally, sociology studies society, which connects all living beings by a bond independent of their organisms. This hierarchy of the six basic sciences also indicates the necessary historical order in which they originated, since the mind could have passed on to the most complicated object only after reaching the simplest. Mathematics and astronomy had existed since antiquity, but physics originated in the seventeenth century, chemistry began with Lavoisier, biology with Bichat, and Comte considers himself to be the creator of sociology. This historical and logical order is at the same time the pedagogical order: mathematics constitutes the necessary introduction, and sociology the consummation of education.

The *Course in Positive Philosophy,* which takes up each of the six basic sciences in succession, is not a treatise on method, for "method can be studied with true, fertile efficiency only in its most extended and perfect applications" (III, 68); general logic, isolated from any definite system, should be replaced by mathematics (III, 290). Nor is the *Course* a simple summary of the actual state of the sciences, for in the name of positivism, Comte passes judgment on the scientists of his time and shows them the path to take. It is an attempt to coordinate scientific work by studying methodically the mutual relations between the sciences, which are already using each other's procedures spontaneously (III, 69): the essential procedure of physics is observation, that of chemistry is experimentation, and that of biology is comparison; yet chemistry, for example, uses the biological method of classification. "On seeing these great spontaneous harmonies and sensing these vast mutual applications among sciences commonly treated as isolated and independent, scientists in different fields will doubtless come to understand the reality and utility of the basic conception of this work: the rational and nevertheless special cultivation of the different branches of natural philosophy under the prior impulsion and preponderant direction of a general system of positive philosophy, the common basis and uniform link between all truly scientific works."

Each science will then be understood in terms of its role in the system. "To understand clearly the true general character of any science whatsoever, one must first assume that it is perfect, then take into consideration the basic difficulties which always interfere to some extent with the actual achievement of this ideal perfection" (II, 276).

Let us pursue, according to this method, Comte's own conception of the first five basic sciences.

To begin with, mathematics developed historically by going from the concrete to the abstract. Descartes reduced geometry to numbers; his successors did the same thing in mechanics, and Fourier had just reduced thermology to numbers; thus natural phenomena of increasing complexity are represented by functions. But to Comte the abstract is always independent of the concrete. The most abstract part of mathematics, analysis, deals with the study of functions themselves, independently of their concrete signification. The history of analysis in modern times shows that it tends toward unity and perfect logical precision. This tendency is most apparent in the history of transcendent analysis, created by Leibniz and Newton. For a long time it appeared an alien import, all too imperfect as a logical tool. For example, the method of Leibniz consists in eliminating from the results the infinitely small auxiliaries used in his calculations. But by what right is this elimination accomplished? Leibniz himself compared his infinitely small quantities to grains of sand, and this makes his method a calculus of approximation unless one can demonstrate, as Carnot did, that the errors committed offset each other. Transcendent analysis reached its perfection the day Joseph Louis Lagrange used derivative functions to reduce it to ordinary analysis. In a general way, the practice of substituting related functions for magnitudes—logarithmic, exponential, and circular functions (Euler and Bernoulli)—promotes the unity of mathematics, and progress here is made possible by the invention of new expedients of this kind. By contrast, Comte does not believe in an indefinite extension of mathematics; and he draws support from Lagrange in trying to prove the fanciful nature of a general solution of all indeterminate equations.

Geometry is the first of the natural sciences. Any attempt at analytical demonstration of some of the propositions contained in geometry is futile. Descartes indicated the goal this science should move toward: the reduction of a situation to magnitude, using the expedient of coordinates, in order to express forms analytically. Ideally, for Descartes, every possible form would be expressed, so that the real forms presented by nature could never catch us by surprise. Thus Kepler's discovery would have been impossible without the Greek geometers' works on the ellipse; but by virtue of a happy coincidence and the fact that the planetary orbit is elliptical, this discovery was accomplished. Analytical geometry, if it achieved its goal, would not have to wait for such coincidences; in fact, it is brought closer to its goal by the investigations of geometers who have used Monge's classsification of surface families to extend Descartes' method to curved surfaces or S-shaped curves (Clairaut) and to discontinuous lines or surfaces (Fourier).

To try to demonstrate basic propositions in mechanics—propositions which depend solely on observation, such as the law of the composition of forces—is a great mistake. Lagrange showed the inadequacy of the demonstrations attempted by Bernoulli, D'Alembert, and Laplace. The irreducible element in analysis, already present in geometry, increases in mechanics. The three great principles—equality of action and reaction, inertia, independence of movements—are derived from observation. On the other hand, by means of these principles many properties of movement which have first been observed directly can be transformed into demonstrated theorems. One of many examples is the conservation of energy, which Comte refuses to acknowledge as a primary law of nature. Curiously, he thinks that the principle which today manifests most clearly the necessity of a direct recourse to experience—Carnot's principle—simply expresses losses of energy due to friction in the transformation of heat into motion.

Positive astronomy, based on the Newtonian law of gravitation, which reduces to unity Kepler's three laws concerning the orbits of the planets, is assumed by Comte to be the model of positivity, provided that it remains inside its domain, which is the solar system. Nothing tells us that gravitation, known by observation of the planets, extends beyond the solar system. Thanks to positive astronomy, the notion of the world, limited to the solar system, is positive; but the notion of the universe is not. Celestial dynamics tends to demonstrate the permanence and independence of our system: its permanence, since all perturbations, occurring periodically and over very long periods, tend to restore the primitive state of the system; its independence, since its distance from other stars makes perturbations originating in other worlds imperceptible. Opposing Descartes' metaphysical cosmogony, which issues from an arbitrary hypothesis concerning the mode of production of phenomena, is Laplace's cosmogony, which begins with the assumption that the sun has a uniform rotary motion and does not go back beyond the state immediately preceding our own. It is obvious that astronomy, to be positive, must have bounds of time and space. Neither stellar astronomy nor astrophysics can come within these bounds.

Physics, on the other hand, is typical of a science whose positivity is still incomplete. One of the rules given by Comte for detecting positivity is as follows: when a physical investigation cannot be reduced to analytical conditions except by means of a hypothesis concerning the structure of matter, we are still stranded in metaphysics. From this point of view the divisions of physics can be arranged in the following order, in which the role of structural considerations in establishing the equations of phenomena—and consequently the absence of positivity—becomes increasingly important: barology, thermology, acoustics, optics, electrology. For example, there is a perfect contrast between the use of analysis in thermology by Fourier, who identified a numerical law concerning the propagation of heat in the immediate knowledge of the phenomenon, and its use in acoustics or optics, where the phenomenon is first reduced to a geometric or mechanical phenomenon.

Positivity may also be recognized by the following two characteristics: our ability to predict phenomena and our influence over them. But across the hierarchy of the positive sciences, one of these two characteristics increases when the other decreases. For instance, in astronomy our predictions are perfect and our influence is nil; in biology our predictions are uncertain or imprecise, but our means of influencing the outcome increase significantly. On this point, physics occupies an intermediate position.

Another mark of positivity is the relative character of laws. According to Comte, there are no truly universal laws because extrapolation beyond the limits of observation is never allowed. As we have just noted, gravitational attraction cannot be extended beyond the solar system. But Comte goes further. It was at this time that Regnault, the physicist, again took up the experiments on which Mariotte's law was based, and showed that the law was no longer valid for very high and very low pressures. Comte charges that these investigations are contrary to true positivity, which here designates our needs and usage; Mariotte's law is a simple law, which satisfies our needs; investigations that might be accomplished outside the limits of ordinary experience are useless, and endless besides. Excessive precision is incompatible with the existence of laws (VI, 638). But in refusing to search for the absolute, Comte does not realize that he is rejecting the precise investigations on which the great advances in physics were based.

Finally, one of the marks of the positivity of a science is the way in which relationships between distinct phenomena are established. Mathematical analysis, applied to structures directly and without hypotheses, can reveal these relationships. Thus Fourier's equations for the propagation of heat correspond to the progression of the ordinates of a straight line and to the equation of uniform movement. This positive analogy differs sharply from the analogy which was attempted between light and sound, for example, by reducing both to the movement of a fluid.

Chemistry is the science in which any use of mathematical analysis ceases definitively. Moreover, it still has far to go before achieving its rightful perfection, for its predictive power is weak and its explanations are incoherent. It must first purge itself of the metaphysical hypotheses that encumber it: the unity of matter, founded on an unreflective desire for unity of understanding raised to the status of a law; affinities, shown by Berthollet to be wholly relative since there is no invariable affinity; the difference between inorganic chemistry and organic chemistry, which is attributed solely to the origin of the substance studied, and which Chevreul sets aside; the reduction of chemical affinity to electrical force, which would place chemistry back in the realm of physics. At this time chemistry, particularly quantitative chemistry, was turning toward the atomic hypothesis, thanks to the law of definite proportions. Comte vehemently censures this tendency; he attacks the law itself, which does not allow us to foresee results; it tells us what the proportions of the components will be if a compound is produced, but it does not tell us that a compound will be produced. Furthermore, Comte accepts the criticisms of Berthollet, who saw this law as the exception and not the rule; solutions and alloys involve different proportions and are related to chemical facts, and so-called organic compounds lack definite proportions. Comte's full sympathy goes to classificatory and qualitative chemistry, which is the positive part of chemistry: Berthollet's discovery of ammonia, which made possible the generalization of the notion of acid, Berzelius' electrochemical investigations, and Wöhler's synthesis of urea.

The Comtian conception of positive biology is based mainly on Blainville's *Course in Physiology* (1829–32). The biological problem is to discover a function when an organ is known or an organ when a function is known. The study of organs is statics or anatomy; the study of functions, dynamics or physiology; and biology is the fusion of statics and dynamics. Life itself is defined as a double movement of composition and decomposition, or, better, of absorption and exhalation. Comte considers the method of experimentation impossible in biology, where one organ cannot be studied in isolation because of its consensus with the others; but pathology, which studies alterations of organs and functions, is a kind of spontaneous experimentation since, as Broussais expressed it, the pathological does not differ from the physiological. Comte criticizes quantitative investigations in biology; vital phenomena, because of their complication, are not calculable, and numerical chemistry is inapplicable to substances which constantly vary in their molecular composition. The sole research tool is comparison—the comparative study of organs throughout the whole range of the animal kingdom, beginning at the top with man. Positive anatomy began with the comparative anatomy of Daubenton and Cuvier. Here again, comparison of one organ with another (for example, the analogy, discovered by Bichat, between the cutaneous system and the mucous system) is the principal procedure.

Biotaxy or classification plays a primary role, not as an end but as a methodical means, provided only that it is accomplished with comparison in view—that is, the position of an organism in a classification should reveal its nature. Consequently classification is not a mnemonical device but a natural method, which acquaints us with the "true organic hierarchy"—a linear series in which, starting from the lower organisms, we see a gradual increase in the diversity of organs and the activity and number of functions. Comte supports Cuvier against Lamarck: the theory of descent would deprive biology of every methodical means, for "the precise realization of the series with definable species is possible only if species are fixed"; between an organism and its environment there is a stable equilibrium, and organisms that fail to adapt, disappear; the principle of conditions necessary for existence supplants the old principle of finality, yet Lamarck denied this equilibrium at the expense of environment.

The same stress on positivity that leads him to criticize experimentation, calculation, and the theory of descent, persuades him, in statics or anatomy, to limit investigations to tissues and organs, almost excluding microscopic investigations, which give rise to the notion "of a chimerical assemblage of a kind of organic monads that are supposed to be the true primary elements of all living bodies." Beyond tissue there is nothing, for there is no longer any organization. This view contradicts the cellular theory, which was to revitalize biology; to Comte such a theory is indistinguishable from metaphysical theories which see life diffused everywhere and confuse vitality with spontaneity.

In dynamics or biology, Comte, like Bichat, makes a distinction between the study of organic life and the study of animal life; but contrary to Bichat and in agreement with Blainville, he assigns the two properties of animal life, irritability and sensibility, to muscular tissue and nervous tissue, exclusively and in that order; and he insists that every distinct property must have a distinct anatomical seat. That no function lacks an organ is the principle which causes him enthusiastically to accept Gall's phrenology, for it ascribes to intellectual and moral functions a precise organic seat—to each function a distinct region of the cerebral cortex, according to the true spirit of positivism. He even considers this biological treatment of the intellectual faculties to be the greatest service biology has rendered to universal positivism. Limited to consciousness, psychology had to be the study of a function without an organ—something that contradicts sound philosophical sense; ideology, by giving primacy to intelligence and selfish motives while subordinating feelings and instinct to them, culminated in Helvétius' doctrine of self-interest and the quality of intellects. Gall begins with the innatism of the basic dispositions of each individual and the plurality of irreducible faculties; in this way he provides an escape from belief in an arbitrary, indefinite modification of reality by education, as education was interpreted by Helvétius. The unity of the self, which might be used as an argument against the dispersion of juxtaposed faculties, is simply a reflection of the theological theory of the unity of the soul. Besides, Comte rejects Gall's whimsical localizations; he even deems it necessary to eliminate provisionally any anatomical investigation of the physiological analysis of the faculties, and he sees a means of analysis in monographs on eminent scientists and artists and in studies of mental pathology. Consequently, if he is remote from Cousin and Condillac, he remains, in spite of his phrenology, very close to psychology, in the modern sense of the word.

All in all, Comte's conception of physiology, based on the simple principle of assigning distinct functions to distinct organs in a fixed, invariable order, clearly reflects the spirit which later asserted itself in his sociology. Here, moving from mathematics to biology, we see the scientific ideal shift gradually; perfection in science depends less on the precision of our determinations than on the harmony of our conceptions, and from this angle physicochemistry, condemned to proceed from parts to the whole, is inferior to biosociology, which goes from the whole to parts. Now the positive sciences as a whole, beginning with sociology, form a system whose unity depends on sociology: they study the physical environment of society (astronomy, physics, and chemistry), then the social agent (biology), and finally society itself. The rationality of mathematics, with its disastrous indifference to moral issues, has proved impotent.

Sociology is the most rational of all the sciences, for it establishes the superiority of the systematic view over the particular.

III *Sociology*

Comte's sociology (the term is introduced in the *Course*, VI, 185) in its final form exhibits the following traits: the social structure exists independently and has permanent characteristics or organs, which persist in the midst of progress; social statics determines these organs and is completely independent of social dynamics, which embraces the laws of progress. It is futile, therefore, for us to go back to the beginning of societies or to try to construct and reconstruct them on a rational plan, as the philosophers of the eighteenth century did. To them there was no social philosophy except dynamics, which boasts of explaining the very origin of societies; to Comte, however, dynamics is subordinated to statics. Progress springs from order and can only improve the permanent elements of any society: religion, property, family, language, and the relation between the spiritual power and the temporal power.

The subordination of dynamics to statics brings to an end the critical and revolutionary period during which, inversely, the reason for the structure of society was sought in the genesis and progress of society. One circumstance may prevent us from grasping the meaning and import of this transformation. Comte was concerned almost exclusively with dynamics in his first work, the *Course in Positive Philosophy*, and it was in his *System of Positive Polity* that he gave a full explanation of statics. Dynamics seems to be self-sufficient—that is, it seems that the law of the three states, which is the basic law of his dynamics, makes each of these states, and notably the positive state, generate a distinct social structure. Comte's doctrine then would seem to be completely indistinguishable from a revolutionary doctrine. But the situation is entirely different if the social structure remains essentially identical as it passes through the three states (just as the solar system and the stellar system remain unchanged in Comte's astronomy, and species remain fixed in his chemistry and biology); no theory is less affected by the idea of evolution than Comte's; the "three states" are those through which humanity has passed in its attempt to organize better and better a social structure which remains a final, fixed datum. Thus positivism succeeds where theology and revolution failed: it institutes a religion of humanity, which unites men better than any other religion, a system of property that develops altruistic instincts, a family structure that confers on women a truly spiritual power, a political organization that clearly defines the role of the spiritual power and the temporal power; but it originates neither religion, nor the family, nor property, nor the separation of powers, which are like social constants. To him, all doctrines that deny these constants or seek to destroy them—socialism, for example—are aberrations that he does not even refute.

Dynamics is reduced to the law of the three states, and this law is a law of intellectual evolution, which has no direct application in the domain of affections and actions; statics studies a social structure rooted in human affections, in egotism and altruism. It follows that if positivism is defined solely as the doctrine of the law of the three states, this doctrine will seem in every instance to be an attempt to exempt no domain of reality from the employment of scientific methods; and this is what is ordinarily called Comte's first philosophy, the philosophy Littré wanted to accept as definitive. But if we remember that the law of the three states is only his dynamics, inseparable from his statics, then we can see that this first philosophy would make no sense apart from what is ordinarily called his second philosophy—that is, statics or Positive Religion, which is presented fully in his *System;* doctrinal unity is perfect, regardless of the importance of modifications in his religious views, which may have been brought about by Clotilde's death. In preparing the *Course,* Comte himself seems to have sensed the insufficiency of his treatment of statics, and in the sixth volume he announces his intention of devoting a special treatise to political philosophy (published as his *System of Positive Polity*), which would resolve the question of social statics—that of the convergence of the intellectual, political, social, and moral evolutions, which are presented separately in the *Course*. The *Course* offers us a philosophy of history rather than a sociology in the sense this word acquired in Durkheim's school (Durkheim is concerned primarily with statics rather than dynamics), and perhaps those who tend to see Comte as the doctrinaire of organic unity will be unsympathetic to the *Course;* but it is certain that Comte does not intend to separate progress from order.

His philosophy of history dates from his earliest treatises and is perhaps the oldest part of his doctrine. His *Plan for the Scientific Works Necessary to Reorganize Society* (1822; *System of Positive Polity,* IV, Appendix) consists of three parts: the first deals with historical data relating to the progress of the human mind, which constitute the positive basis of polity; the second deals with positive education, and the third with man's domination of nature. Here social statics has no part. His philosophy of history, like all others of his period, originates in his awareness of the danger to which society was exposed by the revolutionary crisis. Following many others, Comte sees its origin in the spontaneous disorganization of the spiritual power which began in the fourteenth century and culminated in the emergence of Protestantism in the sixteenth. Hobbes' philosophy engendered all the negative philosophy of the eighteenth century, with its destructive criticism of the temporal and spiritual powers; the success of a philosophy as "weak" as that of the eighteenth century would have been a miracle, apart from the general trend toward fragmentation, which it brought to an end. It led to the revolution with its dogma of popular sovereignty, which is a covert acknowledgment of the absence of any positive principle; political economy with its principle of free competition; and the legists' belief in their power to modify society at will through political institutions; all these consequences betray the same negative spirit.

These statements lack the dramatic character they acquired with De Maistre and Lamennais, for Comte (this is the postulate of his whole philosophy of history) is convinced that this destruction extends only to one form of society and not to society itself, which is as indestructible as the solar system or the species which make up the animal kingdom. A purely negative state never exists alone in history; society continues to be supported by the old system of ideas, which criticism seeks to destroy, until this system is replaced by another, which is gradually elaborated as the first is destroyed. Comte's philosophy of history, inspired by Saint-Simon, is not the same as that of the Saint-Simonians; in a strict sense, he does not discuss a critical epoch but an organic one which dies away as a new epoch emerges. Thus he presents the history of disorganization mentioned above as the history of a reorganization which also began in the fourteenth century and for which the basis was laid earlier by industrial capacity initiated by the emancipation of the communes and scientific capacity resulting from the introduction of the positive sciences in Europe by the Arabs; these same capacities were antagonistic, one to the military power and the other to the theological power, and gradually dispossessed them of temporal and spiritual domination.

History embraces three states: a past state or theological system, in which the spiritual power belongs to a pope who represents God on earth and the temporal power to emperors and kings who are God's elect; a future state, in which the spiritual power will be exercised by savants, and the temporal power by captains of industry; finally a transitional state, our own, which does away with the past and prepares the way for the future. Hence the peculiarities of the politics of Comte's time: a reactionary party, which rightly feels that it must organize but wrongly tries to revive a moribund past and contradicts itself by demanding for itself the freedom it denies to all in the name of its principles; a revolutionary party, which rightly feels that a complete change is in order but understands the necessity of an organization and contradicts itself by converting its critical principles, such as freedom of conscience, into positive principles. But the revolutionary party succeeds only in instituting the arbitrariness of an unprincipled administrative despotism; in this situation, only positivism is coherent.

But to Comte this philosophy of history rests on something more than induction, for he believes that political development is governed by a law of intellectual development. His demonstration is based on the following argument: the political state of an age depends on its intellectual state and its belief; there is no political progress apart from intellectual progress; the best illustration of this principle is the brilliant period of the Middle Ages, that of the Crusades and the thirteenth century, which Comte cites frequently, when all political relations were dominated by the Catholic faith. The elementary law of intellectual development, originated by Dr. Burdin and passed on to Comte by Saint-Simon, is well known. In acquiring knowledge of things, the mind passes through three successive states: the theological state, in which it explains phenomena in terms of divine powers; the metaphysical state, in which it substitutes abstract, impersonal forces for gods; and the positive state, in which it abandons the search for causes and simply determines the laws or constant relations between phenomena. This law can be supported by innumerable observations drawn from the history of the sciences. At first physics was a mythology, in which phenomena depended on the whims of the gods; then, particularly in Scholasticism, it became a metaphysics, which reduced each class of phenomena to a constant force; still semimetaphysical with Descartes, who tried to discover imaginary mechanical constructions underneath phenomena, it became positive with Newton. The passage from alchemy to chemistry, from metaphysical vitalism to positive biology, from astrology to astronomy would supply additional proofs. But Comte goes beyond observation and connects this law with the new characteristics of the mind itself. As we have already noted, the extreme weakness of the human mind is one of Comte's constant themes; the order found in it can only be the reflection of the external order, as the mind conceives it; naturally, it begins to conceive this order in the easiest possible way, by imagining outside itself beings similar to itself, which produce phenomena just as it produces its own movements and which are equally capricious. Progress is accomplished by abstraction and generalization; from its starting point, fetishism, in which the world is peopled by innumerable ill-defined wills, man passes to polytheism, in which each class of phenomena—the sea, the air, etc.—is assigned a distinct god, who has precise attributes and stands apart from the facts under his control, and then to monotheism, in which the multiplicity of gods is replaced by one omnipotent God outside the world. This brings the theological state to an end; the personality of God is then erased. Since he acts only through general laws, he can be replaced by impersonal forces, which, by the necessity of their action, enable facts to be foreseen; by a new, definitive effort based on abstraction, the mind searches for means of prediction in laws or constant relations. It is in this state and this state alone that the mind grasps the external order as it is; in the two preceding states the imagination was more or less dominant and peopled nature with its fictions; in the positive state, every fiction is abolished, and the mental order conceived by science represents the real order; thus the mind has reached its definitive equilibrium. The law of the three states expresses the necessary interplay of the faculties, passage from the absolute to the relative, from imagination to reason.

Furthermore, the swiftness of the transition from one state to another in mankind depends on the science currently in question. If we consider the six basic sciences, we shall find that their passage to the positive state occurred according to their hierarchical order and that its relative ease depended on whether the subject matter of a particular science was more general or less complex. The latest of the sciences, sociology, is still at the metaphysical state with the legists and revolutionaries, and Comte takes upon himself the task of making it pass to the positive state.

If we return now to the philosophy of history, we shall see that in Comte's view (and this is why he is so certain of it) it can be considered to be an application to sociology of the law of the three states: the monotheistic Middle Ages, preceded by polytheistic antiquity, are based on the theological belief; the transitional age or negative crisis is based on metaphysical ideas; finally, the future and definitive state of humanity is based on positivism. There is an affinity between the theological state and military polity, both of which rely on a kind of violence and on centralized authority to establish social unity; slavery and forced labor are associated with this state. There is an affinity between the metaphysical state and the theory of popular sovereignty and human rights; here men are considered in the abstract, like metaphysical forces. There is an affinity between the positive state and industrial and peaceful development. Comte foresees, in 1841, the final advent of a completely peaceful era, the decay of the colonial regime, and the limitation of the army's role repressing internal disorders (*Course,* VI, 350).

There is some ambiguity in this application of the law of the three states to political evolution. To begin with, the metaphysical state is at variance with the revolutionary transition; intellectually, it is continuous with the theological state, for the forces of nature are gods conceived more abstractly; politically, it is a negative force, which destroys the anterior state. More important still, as the science of societies passes to the positive state, how can it discover an organization that will put an end to the revolutionary crisis? Comte is not thinking of anything like the practical application of science that Condorcet and others hoped to make. He is concerned only with a change of mentality analogous to that produced by Catholicism in the Middle Ages; he wants to create a new spiritual power, to be the head of a new church. But is there a direct correspondence between a positive study of social facts and a change that is supposed to renovate the world? Moreover, to what extent has Comte actually studied social facts? Even if he has demonstrated the social fact that the mind must pass from the metaphysical to the positive state in the study of social facts, he has only revealed a procedure.

IV *The Religion of Humanity*

We need only pass from the *Course* to the *System* to learn the unexpected way in which Comte resolves these questions. The new order is produced, not by positive sociology, but by a will to order inherent in society, which is consummated by positive sociology; progress derives from order, movement from existence, the dynamic from the static. This order is possible only if the intellectual superiority of the savant can be united with the social aptitude of the theologian to discover a system that is best suited to intellectual needs and can satisfy moral needs, and that will put an end to the scandalous "insurrection of the mind against the heart" or the characteristic conflict between critical intelligence, which says "No" in the name of reason, and theology, which says "Yes" in the name of the heart. Only on this condition can society be consolidated.

But the formal exigency of positivity in sociology leads us to a reality that satisfies all these conditions—Humanity. A positive sociology is a sociology which retraces the necessary continuity of all human works and thoughts; it shows each individual that he exists only by virtue of the past, that he draws from Humanity everything that makes possible his material, intellectual, and moral life, that the dead are more alive than the living. Humanity, a thoroughly positive notion, which can be analyzed and known through history, is like the Providence of the individual who, as the embodiment of great men and inventions, should be the object of a cult. No longer is there anything fictive in this object; sociology makes the human mind the mirror of the world, not only of the external world but also of the human order.

Religion is the power to guide and unite individual wills. This power can only belong to a religion that replaces the fictive concept of God by the positive concept of Humanity. The religion of Humanity brings together the intellectual unity of Greek polytheism, the political unity of Roman polytheism, and the moral unity of Christianity; it terminates the "regency of God," indispensable during Humanity's minority; it puts an end to the "insurrection of the mind against the heart," characteristic of the conflict between critical intelligence and theology in the eighteenth century, for here faith is grounded on the positive notion of Humanity and joins with love in regulating actions.

Comte prides himself on preserving everything that constituted the unifying and organizing force of Catholicism, and even increasing it, due to the objectivity of the notion of Humanity. His religion attempts to reproduce every form of the Catholic religion, including even its rites, sacraments, and calendar, and to replace God by Humanity or the Great Being, and the saints by great men. He institutes a spiritual power or priesthood charged with the teaching of dogma. This priesthood, which constitutes the intellectual aspect of society, must not be permitted to indulge in the divagations that characterize existing science; its work is less research and analysis than synthesis—synthesis accomplished with a view to positivist doctrine. For the most part this "subjective" synthesis involves the preparation of "philosophical treatises in which each science is reduced to its normal extension and properly incorporated into the religion of humanity." Here normal extension is defined not in terms of the internal exigencies of scientific work but in terms of its social usage.

Intelligence cannot discover these limits in itself; the spiritual power does not have absolute domination, according to Comte; intelligence can think only to act, and it acts only from motives which originate in the heart and character. Consequently, outside the spiritual power, which proclaims dogma, there is a temporal power with the essential function of regulating industry—that is, rationally exploiting nature for the satisfaction of man's needs. In Comte's view, the foundation of industrial activity is property, a permanent element of society, and its motives are egotistical; contrary to the economists, however, he thinks that in spite of these motives it is useful in developing altruistic inclinations by making everyone used to working for others.

Still, neither intelligence nor action, by themselves, can achieve the incorporation of the individual into humanity. Alongside the temporal and spiritual powers, which alone were identified in the *Course,* the *System* shows the necessity of an independent source of altruistic affections, which is the ultimate origin of the whole cult of the Great Being—the heart, distinct from intelligence and will. Altruism is wrongly thought to be alien to our nature. But altruistic inclinations are truly developed only within the family, which positivism treats as an essential institution. Comte defends it against utopias of Greek origin and tries to strengthen it by prohibiting divorce and instituting the birthright. In the family, the emotional impulse originates in the wife, and positivism will owe its final success to the spiritual influence she exerts in the home. Comte's love for Clotilde de Vaux made him intensely aware of the importance of sentiment; in his imagination, woman, the ultimate support of the cult of Humanity, becomes the object of a cult; and the utopia of the Virgin Mother becomes "the synthetic summation of positive religion, every aspect of which she combines." By means of this virginal maternity he hopes "to produce a caste lineage, better adapted than the vulgar population to the recruitment of spiritual and temporal leaders" (*System of Positive Polity,* IV).

Recognition of the power of sentiment leads him, in the *System,* to the conception of a seventh science, higher than sociology. This is ethics, which, in the *Course,* he did not separate from sociology. The necessity for the new science is linked to the role of sentiment as the ultimate source of the cult of Humanity. "After profane science has properly supplied knowledge of the environment [astronomy, physics, and chemistry] and the body [biology], the sacred science [sociology] undertakes the systematic study of the soul, examining its collective existence. . . . But this necessary examination constitutes a final preparation, the incomplete character of which remains unexceptionable. Here one feels that the special study of intelligence and activity are separated from the study of sentiment, and therefore permit an appreciation only of those results whose source and destination belong to the next science [ethics]" (*System of Positive Polity,* IV). "In ethics, religion is apprehended, no longer in its object, but in its subjective origin, so that the different sciences are no longer anything but "branches of ethics."

Comte's thought tends finally toward a form less linear than circular. The religion of humanity is so close to fetishism that Comte believes that it will be possible to avoid all the intermediary stages traversed by Western civilization, when the West is committed to instructing savage tribes who have remained fetishistic. Rational reflection regresses toward myth and the immediacy of sentiment. Religion is the beginning and end of humanity; spontaneously, man is nothing but a religious creature, and it is only the resistance of an unfavorable environment that spurs him on to egotistical action and the study of the outer world; but positivism regulates intelligence and activity in such a way that they again become subordinate to sentiment, and the role of education is to eliminate the bad effects which might result from unlimited progress in theory and practice.

BIBLIOGRAPHY

Texts

Comte, A. *Opuscules de philosophie sociale 1819–1828,* including the 1822 "Plan des travaux scientifiques nécessaires pour réorganiser la société." 1883.
———. *Cours de philosophie positive,* 6 vols. 1830–42.
———. *Discours sur l'esprit positif,* prefixed to the *Traité philosophique d'astronomie populaire.* 1844.
———. *Discours sur l'ensemble du positivisme.* 1848.
———. *Calendrier positiviste.* 1849.
———. *Système de politique positive,* 4 vols. 1851–54. Trans. J. H. Bridges, Frederic Harrison, and others: *The System of Positive Polity,* 4 vols. London, 1875–77.
———. *Catéchisme positiviste.* 1852. Trans. Richard Congreve: *The Catechism of Positive Religion.* London, 1858.
———. *Appel aux conservateurs.* 1855.
———. *La Synthèse subjective.* 1856.
———. *The Positive Philosophy of Auguste Comte,* 2 vols., trans. Harriet Martineau. London, 1875–90. (A condensation of the *Cours.*)
———. *Lettres à Valat.* 1870.
———. *Lettres à divers,* 2 vols. Paris, 1902–05.
———. *Lettres inédites de J. S. Mill avec les réponses de Comte,* ed. Lévy-Bruhl. 1899.
———. *Correspondance inédite,* 4 vols. Paris, 1903–04.
———. *Testament d'Auguste Comte.* 1884.
———. *Lettres à des positivistes anglais.* London, 1889.

Studies

Devolvé, J. *Réflexions sur la pensée Comtienne.* Paris, 1908.
Ducasse, Pierre. *Méthode et intuition chez Auguste Comte.* Paris, 1939.
Dumas, George. *Psychologie de deux Messies positivistes: Saint-Simon et Auguste Comte.* Paris, 1956.
Gouhier, Henri. *La jeunesse d'Auguste Comte et la formation du positivisme,* 3 vols. Paris, 1933–41.
Lacroix, Jean. *La sociologie d'Auguste Comte.* Paris, 1956.
Lévy-Bruhl, Lucien. *La philosophie d'Auguste Comte.* Paris, 1900. Trans. Kathleen de Beaumont: *The Philosophy of Auguste Comte,* New York, 1903.
Littré, Émile. *Auguste Comte et la philosophie positive,* 2d ed. Paris, 1864.

309

Mill, J. S. *Auguste Comte and Positivism.* London, 1865.

Manuel, Frank. *The Prophets of Paris.* Cambridge, Mass., 1962.

de Rouvre, C. *L'amoureuse histoire d'Auguste Comte et de Clotilde de Vaux.* Paris, 1917.

———. *Auguste Comte et le Catholicisme.* Paris, 1920.

Whittaker, Thomas. *Comte and Mill.* London, 1908.

SOCIAL PHILOSOPHY IN FRANCE: PROUDHON

PIERRE JOSEPH PROUDHON (1809–65), the son of an artisan in Besançon, and a printer in his early career, was a self-taught man whose works and deeds initiated many important social movements: syndicalism, mutualism, and pacifism all draw their inspiration from him. His publications include the following: *What Is Property?* (1840), *On the Creation of Order in Humanity* (1843), *System of Economic Contradictions* (1846), *Justice in the Revolution and the Church* (1858; 2d edition, 1865), *War and Peace* (1861), and *On the Principle of Art.*

Is Proudhon a philosopher? This is the question raised by M. Guy-Grand in the Introduction to the new edition of *Justice in the Revolution and the Church.* Proudhon is harsh in his judgment of professional philosophers. "By what flight of fancy can a man say that he is exclusively a metaphysician?" he writes. "How is it possible, in a scientific, positive century, to have professors of pure philosophy, men who teach the young to philosophize outside the bounds of science, literature, and industry—in a word, men who, with utmost conscientiousness, ply their trade of selling the absolute? To philosophize for the sake of philosophizing is an idea which will never enter a sane mind." Pure speculation is the fruit of Romanticism, the "literature of decadence," which claims inspired intuitions, revelations of another world, which are restricted to a few initiates. In truth there is one human certainty that belongs equally to all, for its quality remains the same no matter what the extent of knowledge; the most learned arithmetician has no more certainty than the person who sees that $2 + 2 = 4$. On the other hand, philosophy is present in every human activity, for its unique role is to search for a principle to guarantee our ideas and a standard to guide our actions; furthermore, "in practicing his craft, no artisan fails to use one or more means of justification. . . . To guide him in his labor, the worker has a measure, a scale, etc. Similarly, no worker is ignorant of the destination of his work or the complex of needs and ideas to which it relates. . . . What the artisan does in his speciality, the philosopher seeks to discover for the universality of things."

Philosophy must cease to be speculative and become "practical and popular"; it belongs to primary instruction. But does Proudhon go beyond mere aspiration? To think, he needed the stimulus of polemics, which he pursued freely, seeking adversaries everywhere; he had neither the time nor the taste for digesting ideas and fitting them into a coherent system. His flashes of brilliance are deposited in summaries of undigested readings. "This Proteus is not easy to grasp," as Guy-Grand says. He is hostile to both private property and communism, to despotism and universal suffrage, and to any form of popular, revolutionary, or anti-Jacobin sovereignty, yet no man is less disposed to advocate a middle course or more hostile to eclecticism. The essential mysticism of *War and Peace,* in which war appears to be a kind of judgment of God, and his conservative theory of the family, one that treats marriage not as a breakable contract but as a kind of fusion of persons—are these attitudes thoroughly consonant with the rationalism of his treatise on *Justice?* The Hegelianism which enabled him to reconcile contradictories in *Creation of Order* (the Hegelianism which he learned from Marx, but without ever fully accepting it) is abandoned in *Justice.*

Proudhon's mysticism, however, has limits. Like Comte, he feels that war belongs to the past and that a new era of peace is dawning; on the other hand, subordination and hierarchical arrangements exist only within the family, which is the constitutive part but not the model of society. Finally, his Hegelianism is momentary and superficial. There remains the doctrine of his *Justice,* which is most in keeping with his ideas of social reform. In 1849 Proudhon defended his system of "mutualism" or free credit against Bastiat. He does not seek, like Marx, to eliminate capital but to eliminate interest charges on capital, because of its injustice; capital, unproductive by nature, should not yield a profit to permit the capitalist to live without working, for this would be a "contradiction." His reform is inspired by an idealism opposed to the spirit of Marxist materialism; the same idealism is found in Proudhon's philosophy as this is expressed in *Justice.* In this book, truly remarkable in spite of all its confusion, Proudhon spontaneously arrives at a conception of the universe which recalls that of Heraclitus and the Stoics, with whom "right reason" is at once the physical force that guides matter, the criterion of knowledge, and the principle governing the moral conduct of society. Similarly, with Proudhon, justice designates, not an ideal of conduct which man constructs for himself (he opposes the genetic and utilitarian explanation of moral ideas as vehemently as innatism), but rather a universal reality, which manifests itself in nature by a law of equilibrium and in society by a reciprocity based on the equality of persons. Thus it corresponds to the two problems posed by philosophy: "To a reasonable being, it is at once the principle and form of thought, the guarantee of judgment, the standard of conduct, the goal of knowledge, and the end of existence. It is sentiment and notion, manifestation and law, idea and fact; it is life, spirit, universal reason" (*Justice,* ed. Guy-Grand, p. 223). In its moral form it is respect, spontaneously felt and reciprocally guaranteed, for human dignity, regardless of the person or circumstance involved." Its discovery is the work not of an individual but of "collective spontaneity," for philosophy is the creation of the people rather than of an individual. It is a kind of "group metaphysics."

According to Proudhon, there is at bottom no other philosophy, and everyone is in agreement on this point. There is a division of opinion only with respect to its basis, and here again there are only two contrasting systems. "One, that of transcendence, places the subject or author of right outside man, either in a God or in an established authority such as the church or state." This is the system exemplified by the Catholic Church, but only by virtue of greater clarity does it differ from the doctrines of Rousseau, Kant, Spinoza, the spiritualists, the socialists, and Auguste Comte himself, "who, in denying God, seizes upon the great humanitarian being." The other system, that of immanence, typified by the French Revolution, "places the juridical subject in consciousness and makes it identical with man." It is only by abstraction that man is considered to be in a state of isolation and untouched by any other law but egotism. Immanence is the application to man of a principle which is itself probably only a form of justice—relativism. According to Comte's teaching, investigation of the absolute must be eliminated from science; by the same token, it must be eliminated from the moral sciences, where the absolute could only be the individual freed from all bonds. Individual absolutes must come into conflict in order to bring about the equilibrium in which all that remains of them is what they have in common—"public reason" or "collective reason." By virtue of these views, as C. Bouglé has shown, Proudhon is a sociologist in the current sense of the word; he goes so far as to say that justice is both the "essence of society" and "the characteristic form of the human soul." It is in this sense that Proudhon fights for the revolution from inside the Church; he is not an iconoclast like Voltaire; he attributes the evil of contemporary society to the absence of belief and the arbitrariness in which this absence results, and he calls upon Napoleon III to say "what spiritual force he intends to substitute for the spiritual force of Catholicism" (*Justice*, p. 239). He is against those who believe only in matter and force.

Proudhon's philosophy is less a system than a radical transformation in the statement and classification of problems. His attempt to put an end to the schism between nature and man by means of his concept of justice, and the equivalence he establishes between all "transcendent" systems, whether theism or pantheism—then the object of much controversy because of their mutual hostility—are indicative of the great value of his philosophical speculation, still rich in suggestion

BIBLIOGRAPHY

Texts

Proudhon, P.-J. *Œuvres complètes de P.-J. Proudhon,* 26 vols. Paris, 1867–70.
———. *Œuvres complètes de P.-J. Proudhon,* ed. C. C. A. Bouglé and Henri Moysset, 11 vols. Paris, 1920–39. Not complete.
———. *Correspondance,* 14 vols. Paris, 1874–75.
———. *What Is Property?* trans. Benjamin Tucker. Princeton, 1876.
———. *System of Economic Contradictions,* trans. Benjamin Tucker. Boston, 1888.
———. *General Idea of the Revolution in the Nineteenth Century,* trans. John Beverley Robinson. London, 1923.

Studies

Brogan, D. W. *Proudhon.* London, 1936.
Dolléans, Edouard. Proudhon. Paris, 1948.
Lubac, Henri de. *Proudhon et le christianisme.* Paris, 1945. Trans. R. E. Scantlebury: *The Un-Marxian Socialist: A Study of Proudhon.* London, 1948.
Prion, Gaëtan. *Proudhon et le syndicalisme révolutionnaire.* Paris, 1910.
Sainte-Beuve, Charles A. *P.-J. Proudhon.* Paris, 1872.
Woodcock, George. *Pierre-Joseph Proudhon.* London, 1956.

ITALIAN IDEALISM

1 *Rosmini-Serbati*

From 1800 to 1850 Italian philosophy followed a curve similar to that of French philosophy. It abandoned ideology at the beginning of the century and turned toward a form of spiritualism suffused to some extent with Kantian ideas. Just like Cousin and Royer-Collard, Pasquale Galluppi (1770–1846) sought in introspection not only the certitude of the self but also that of the constitutive relations which are the principles of knowledge. With the self, and indissolubly linked to it, we are given the existence of the external world.

Antonio Rosmini-Serbati (1797–1855), ordained a priest in 1821, only abandoned the solitude of Stresa on Lago Maggiore, where he had settled in 1840, to serve the king of Sardinia as envoy to the pope in 1848; Gioberti, then minister to the king, had chosen him for this role.

Both Rosmini and Gioberti were anxious to provide Italy with a system of philosophical speculation more suited to its genius than sensualist ideology; intellectual reform and political innovations permeate the thinking of both. Logical rectitude and Christian sentiment, writes Rosmini, in *Psychology* (1846–50) are the two characteristics of the Italians; this is why the nation has always liked logical writers and religious writers; this is the true reason for the success of Galileo in Italy, whereas the response to the appeal

317

of the powerful sixteenth-century geniuses who professed philosophy (Bruno, Campanella) was marked by the indolence and slowness of old age. But Galileo was not a philosopher, and the philosophers of that time who were even remotely linked with the heresy of the North, Protestantism, were repudiated by Italy. "Thus, he concludes, this country remained without a philosophy, and this is what prevented it from forming a nation."

Rosmini's task, therefore, is to create a national philosophy. He is acutely aware of the hostility of the Italian mind toward all doctrines which ground knowledge of truth on the nature of the human faculties—Cartesian speculation, Kantian forms, sentiment, Scottish instinct. With equal force he condemns traditionalist doctrines and doctrines of common sense, and he holds that there is truth only where a mind has intuitive knowledge of a "first truth" which precedes it, which is the standard for other truths; thus his doctrine has an affinity with those of Malebranche and Plato, who stressed the priority of being over knowledge. But this being is not a datum which the soul comes upon accidentally; it is an intelligible, linked so closely to intelligence that there would be no intelligence at all without this link. For to think that an object is real is to think that it cannot be other than what it is, and this implies that being has first been conceived as such—external, uncreated, immutable, simple, and completely indeterminate. Being is divine without being God; it is to the reality of God as the abstract is to the concrete (Rosmini insists that he is not an ontologist and denies any connection with a vision of God); it follows that the first object of intelligence is ideal being. Rosmini considers truth, not the correspondence between an idea and an object, but an eternal type, like the Platonic idea.

We also know finite things, of course, but how can a limited being, sensed by an animal sensation, be the object of an intellectual perception? It is because we apply the idea of indeterminate being to it. "Being is attributed to finite things as a result of the necessity we feel for knowing them and the impossibility of knowing them unless they first become beings—that is, unless they are united to being by thought. Thus the essence of being does not become confused with sensible realities; it unites with them alone, and makes them intelligible." This kind of union, which, like Platonic participation, is responsible for the real obscurity of the system, should be sufficient to avoid pantheism; for "the essence that is manifested in the Idea always remains distinct from reality insofar as it involves finite things."

The idea of being serves as the norm for knowledge, and by the same token it is the standard of conduct. "Beings are good in proportion as they exist . . . ; ethics is only a corollary of the theory of being . . . ; each object possesses in itself, in its essence, an intrinsic order, which determines the necessity of its parts and qualities . . . ; knowledge of being leads us to knowledge of its goodness and worth." [1] Morality consists in love of being, and the imperative can be stated in this way: Love being as you know it and in the order it presents to your understanding. Rosmini therefore contradicts the Kantian thesis of the autonomy of will; he finds in it the same subjectivism that he exposed in the theory of knowledge; obligation can come only from a principle outside the agent; and moral evil is painfully experienced as a kind of denaturing of our being.

Clearly discernible in Rosmini's philosophy is the spirit of Malebranchism, which continues, in Italy, the spirit of Cardinal Gerdil.

II *Vincenzo Gioberti*

To a much greater extent than Rosmini, Vincenzo Gioberti (1802–52) participated in the political life of his country. Ordained a priest in 1825, he was exiled in 1833 for his republican ideas and went to Paris, where he established relations with several publicists and philosophers. At first inspired by Lamennais' *Words of a Believer,* and friendly toward Mazzini, he gradually accepted the idea of a constitutional monarchy, and rejected the *Outline of a Philosophy;* he thought that the Piedmont should be the nucleus of the

[1] As quoted by Palhoriès, *Rosmini,* p. 274.

future Italian confederation. He returned to Italy in 1847; at the end of the following year, during the war between Piedmont and Austria, he served as Charles Albert's prime minister. He spent his last years in Paris.

"Only ontological nations," according to Gioberti, "are capable of heroism, for they alone cling to the great truths, know how to live by them, and when necessary make sublime sacrifices for them." [2] From the ontological point of view, being is primary; it is imposed as a datum, independently of any positing by mind. The enemies of this tendency include most of those associated with modern philosophy, which has its roots in Lutheran freethinkers. For example, Descartes, the great skeptic, the ludicrous and childish dreamer, set philosophy back for several centuries by grounding it on the *Cogito,* which suggests that the mind can posit itself and posit God. It leads to psychologism, the incredible madness of looking upon the very author of the universe as a product of the mind's activity.

Gioberti goes farther in this direction than Rosmini, for he claims that the mind first knows intuitively, not ideal being, but the real Being, who alone can be immense, absolute, and immutable—in other words, God. To him, being is not, as with Rosmini, a simple standard or model; its activity is creative causality; knowledge involves grasping this creation in the process. We would never conclude that a sensible thing exists without adding to our subjective impression the idea of a creative cause, which alone can support the impression; pure psychologism, which curtails this idea, finally reaches a state of skeptical subjectivism. Knowledge collides with an incomprehensible element, which is grasped by neither sense nor intelligence: it is a superintelligible or unknowable element, whose existence is nevertheless certain. According to Gioberti (who seems not to be acquainted with Plotinus and Damascius), no philosopher has speculated on it; the superintelligible is the difference that exists between the human intelligible, which is limited, and the divine intelligible; it is the mysterious heart of reality,

[2] As quoted by Palhoriès, *Gioberti,* p. 181.

comprehensible to God alone; it is the Kantian noumenon, except that it is an object not of reason but of a suprarational faculty.

This notion of the superintelligible is linked to Gioberti's criticism of theological rationalism, many examples of which we have already seen during this period. His aim is to defend the notion of the supernatural, of mystery, and of revelation against the threat of naturalism. Chateaubriand and Montalembert were wrong, according to him, in trying to make religious truth acceptable to reason. Nor does Gioberti accept dogmas which express the supernatural as complete, definitive truths. He insists that there must be a continuous development of theology, constantly establishing an equilibrium between dogma and the state of civilization: "Tradition is life; if it ceases to live, it becomes useless." [3]

III *Giuseppe Mazzini*

The intellectual tremor which spread through Italy in the first half of the century had its impact on Giuseppe Mazzini (1805-72), known as one of the members of the triumvirate who governed Rome from 1849, when it was proclaimed a republic, until a French expedition restored the authority of the pope a few months later. In Mazzini we find, along with much more mysticism and much less activity, a spirit analogous to that of Polish Messianism: to him Italian political unity is not the satisfaction of national egotism; a nation is only the indispensable intermediary between the individual and humanity; national independence should serve the world. He is equally hostile to individualism and traditionalism: "Individualism or appeal to the individual conscience by itself leads to anarchy. The social idea, the appeal to tradition alone, without a constant attempt to interpret it by intuition of the individual conscience and in this way impel man toward the future, leads to despotism and stagnation." Mazzini therefore defends the idea of progress which preserves all the steps of the past, just as the French

[3] As quoted by Palhoriès, *Gioberti*, p. 378. The information contained in the above paragraph was taken from this book.

Revolution recapitulated the three steps of history: freedom, which Greco-Roman antiquity introduced into history; equality of men, the idea of which originated in connection with a universal religion such as Christianity; and fraternity, which France tried to put into practice in 1789. But the individualism of the Rights of Man is now insufficient, for Mazzini thinks that right depends on duty, and that duty can be known by the individual conscience only in its negative aspect of defense: "Conscience needs a standard to verify its instincts—reason and humanity" (*Duties of Man*, 1860). The difficulty is in uniting these two forces: "The conscience of the individual is sacred; the common consent of humanity is sacred. Whoever fails to consult both deprives himself of an essential means of knowing truth. . . . One substantiates the other." Without individual activity, without the needs and inclinations of man, there are only abstract, inert principles; individuals and nationalities (they, too, are persons) give life to humanity.

Mazzini's doctrine has the same tone as Rosmini's and Gioberti's. The Italian mind, as it is manifested in these three thinkers, rejects doctrines based on immanence alone, and clings to the idea of a reality higher than the individual

Bibliography

I

Leetham, Claude. *Rosmini*. London and New York, 1957.
Pagani, G. B. *Vita di Antonio Rosmini*, 2 vols. Turin, 1897. Trans.: *The Life of Antonio-Rosmini-Serbati*. London, 1902.
Palhoriès, F. *La théorie idéologique de Galluppi*. 1909.
Rosmini-Serbati, A. *Sistema filosofico*. 1845.
——. *Teodicea*. 1845.
——. *Psicologia*. 1846–50.
——. *La Teosofia,* 5 vols. 1859–75 (posthumous).

II

Gioberti, V. *Introduzione allo studio della filosofia*. Brussels, 1840.
——. *Considérations sur les doctrines religieuses de V. Cousin,* trans. Tourneur. 1847.
——. *Lettre sur les doctrines philosophiques et religieuses de M. de Lamennais*. Brussels, 1843.
——. *Protologia*. 1861 (posthumous).
Palhoriès, F. *Gioberti*. 1929.

III

Mazzini, G. *Opere,* 18 vols. 1861–91.
Vaughan, C. E. *Studies in the History of Political Philosophy,* 2:250–323. Manchester, 1925.

INDEX